STEEL MY
SOLDIERS' HEARTS

Neil J. Stewart

*With all best wishes to another
Grenadier Guardsman*

Neil Stewart

Printed in Canada

Canadian Cataloguing in Publication Data

Stewart, N. J. (Neil John), 1923-
    Steel my soldiers' hearts

    ISBN 1-55212-439-8

    1. Stewart, N. J. (Neil John), 1923- 2. Tank crews--Biography. 3.
World War, 1939-45--Personal narratives, Canadian. I. Title.
D811.S78 2000   940.54'8171   C00-910905-6

TRAFFORD

This book was published *on-demand* in cooperation with Trafford Publishing.
On-demand publishing is a unique process and service of making a book available for retail sale to the public taking advantage of on-demand manufacturing and Internet marketing.
On-demand publishing includes promotions, retail sales, manufacturing, order fulfilment, accounting and collecting royalties on behalf of the author.

Suite 6E, 2333 Government St., Victoria, B.C. V8T 4P4, CANADA

Phone	250-383-6864	Toll-free	1-888-232-4444 (Canada & US)
Fax	250-383-6804	E-mail	sales@trafford.com
Web site	www.trafford.com	TRAFFORD PUBLISHING IS A DIVISION OF TRAFFORD HOLDINGS LTD.
Trafford Catalogue #00-0104		www.trafford.com/robots/00-0104.html

10   9   8   7   6   5   4   3   2

CONTENTS

A POIGNANT RETURN

The sun dappled the wavelets edging steadily, inexorably toward the sand and pebble beach, marking the French coastline of the English Channel, "La Manche," at Berniéres sur Mer. A flight of seagulls wheeled lazily in a soft onshore breeze, their plaintive cries heard only faintly above the sounds of three small children playing on a sand dune nearby. Wisps of cirrus clouds hung in stationary suspension, high above the long sand and gravel beach that ran for seemingly endless miles to east and west.

Another peaceful summer day unfolded for the few tourists and the local idlers, taking their ease on bright colored picnic blankets spread upon the sand. Others lounged around the beach houses clustered close to the low seawall at the top of the beach.

Two couples, all approaching late middle age, to use the current euphemism, walked slowly and carefully forward across the beach from the road behind them. Sporting summer tans, with cameras slung around their necks, the two men advanced into the loose sand a few paces ahead of their wives, who stepped gingerly behind. That they were tourists was unmistakable, unacquainted with this beach or the small village snuggled into its edge. They said little to one another as they approached a tall masonry pillar erected on a height of land which paralleled the water's edge of the Channel sweeping away to the horizon ahead of them. They peered closely at the text, carved first in French and then in English, in block capital letters on two plates mounted high on the facade of the pillars facing away from the sea:

ICI LE 6 JUIN 1944   HERE ON THE 6TH JUNE 1944
L'HEROISME DES   EUROPE WAS LIBERATED
FORCES ALLIES   BY THE HEROISM
LIBERÉ L'EUROPE   OF THE ALLIED FORCES

Talk was unnecessary, as they stared fixedly at the spare, forceful message, its simple words dredging up a hundred haunting memories. Finally, the dark haired, thick set man broke the silence, turning with raised eyebrows to his silver-haired friend.

"If this is the place Ken, does it look familiar to you after fifty years?" he asked softly.

The other man remained silent as he peered intently about him, his eyes squinting narrowly in the rising morning sun. He was a tall, rather lean man, with an upright stance. Deep-set eyes stared out penetratingly beneath thick, dark eyebrows which had not whitened to match the thatch of hair that crowned his head. The face was firm and browned from exposure to the warm, summer sun that he and his wife had enjoyed with their friends during their vacation in France.

He looked critically around him, gazing closely at the concrete wall, recently painted a Kelly green, which bordered the sandy road they had followed to the beach. Then his eyes shifted slowly along the beach toward a smallish, square red brick building jutting out into the beach from the village behind it. For some reason, it was eye-catching, although not ostentatious. Just a very simple two-storey structure with traditional Norman timbering and the two-sloped faces of the Mansard roof that characterized so many buildings in northern France. Certainty replaced doubt in his expression, as he turned toward his friends.

"This is the place. There's no doubt about it now. The look of the place deceived me for a few minutes. You see, we never really saw this part of the coast from this vantage point. Now you look over neat, red-tiled, roofs of houses, painted walls and fences, with healthy trees in between. A clean, tidy beach slopes gradually down to a calm sea. There's no wind and we have a cloudless sky. But, the greatest differences of all is; it's quiet here now, quiet like it should be at a little coastal town. The first time, the noise, the unbelievable sound level –," and he shook his head for lack of words.

The thick-set, dark-haired man, his curiosity aroused, pursued his interest further. "What is it that distinguishes this place from the rest of the places along the coast, Ken? Why are you so certain about where we are now?"

"It's the inn there; the brick building with the Mansard roof. That was our left marker and as soon as I saw it again, a bit battered over the years but still standing here, I knew this was the place. I would never mistake that, after studying pictures of it for weeks in England, and finding it just where we expected to see it when we came ashore."

The smaller of the two women asked rather hesitantly, "Was it very different when you first saw it?"

"More than you might imagine. We were looking at a beach rising from the water that we had to occupy quickly. All the buildings were burning or destroyed from the bombing and shelling that preceded us. The sea was rough and the weather was foul, with a sharp wind blowing the smoke across our front. All along the beach, and extending down into the water were every kind of beach barrier you could imagine. There were steel pylons and tetrahedrons scattered everywhere, most of them wired with mines to prevent their removal. And that cement wall there that someone just painted green, was part of a pill-box built at the edge of the sand. There was lots of artillery firing from locations further back from the beach. It was all designed to prevent anyone coming ashore along this coastline."

The taller man paused for reflection, and then continued quietly, "But over and above all, the most memorable feature had to be the noise; the unbelievable, raging, crashing noise all around us, that never came to an end. The awesome booms when shells landed in here from the naval vessels offshore; the continuing crashes of bombs dropped further inland by the medium bombers flying over us; the sharp crack of tank and anti-tank guns firing close at hand; and the constant chatter of machineguns all around us; the hammering of the Canadian weapons and the tearing bursts of the high-speed German guns. I'm sure no one there had ever heard a volume of sound that even approached what we heard when we landed."

After taking a number of photographs of the scene facing out to sea, past the beach monument, the two men walked down to the water's edge to take more pictures facing toward the village, particularly featuring views of the old Norman Inn which had figured so prominently in identifying their location.

"When I last saw that building," the white haired man stated, "the west wall had some holes in it from shell bursts, but they've all been patched up. It doesn't look bad there on the old building now."

Next there were requests that he pose next to the beach monument, and then in front of the Norman Inn. He patiently strode about to the various locations requested by the dark-haired man. There were going to be a lot of photos: they were assured of that.

Then the four of them walked solemnly back toward the highway through the village, where they had parked their car, talking quietly among themselves. They paused now and then for a further glance or a gesture back toward the beach they had just left, which still fully occupied their interests.

Just before re-entering their car, the foursome stopped to look one more time at the placid seascape behind them. They all thought for an instant of a time many years earlier when the attention of the world had been focused on this tranquil coastline. The dark haired man broke the lengthening silence by saying, "I think we will always remember today Ken, but for different reasons. You, because you were here, immersed in it and participating in it. We, because we were in other parts of the world, doing other things, but hearing about it and knowing that so much of our futures turned on the outcome of it. Everyone knows where he or she was when the news of it was announced. I am very pleased that you took us here to show us a place that none of us will every forget now: you least of all, Ken."

"Perhaps that's true," came the considered reply. "You know, we came into this campaign because we had to; because our regiments taught us what had to be done when we got here. And when we arrived, the rest of the regiment began doing what they had been trained to do. And you did your part too. You couldn't do anything less. For most of us it was that simple. You joined the unit of your choice and went with it, wherever it sent you. The language on that monument on the beach is rather exaggerated. Europe was not liberated on June 6, 1944. That was just the beginning of it, and there was a lot of heavy fighting still ahead before it was liberated, as you know. We sometimes forget that a lot of guys had been fighting our war for years before June 6, 1944 in other parts of the world. It's just that what became the main act in liberating Europe began here on that day. And some of us are still around to talk about it."

Then they climbed slowly and gingerly into their automobile and headed out along the coastal highway, past the chintzy tourist souvenir shops and the tastelessly named eating places that local entrepreneurs had erected along the route, designed to capitalize on their unique location. They never slackened their speed, as they passed the "Café Liberation," the "Place de Montgomerie," the "Restaurant Eisenhower," and other establishments with equally offensive titles, which offered no attraction to anyone in the car. But the subject of lunch and where it should be had was raised and given active consideration. The white haired man who was driving the car, was pleased with the change of subject. Old memories conjured up by the sight of the old Norman Inn, the beach line slanting away from it and the rest of the half-forgotten images that returned unbidden and inescapable with them, had to be put aside. It was good to be an old man now and then. The reason - old men forget.

CHAPTER I

THE TROOPSHIP

The great, grey bulk of the troopship, "Ile de France," ploughed a steady, ruler-straight furrow in the blue Atlantic, heading eastward from Halifax. It was mid war, and she had been loaded with what some estimated to be a full division of troops; perhaps fifteen thousand passengers. Rated as one of the four or five largest troopships in the world, she traveled alone, at high speeds far in excess of the pace of any convoy, and indeed well above the speed of most naval vessels. It was assumed that big liners like the Ile de France availed themselves of the best protection possible, through traveling fast and alone, away from the attention that groups of merchant vessels attracted as they moved along at the pace of the slowest of them, in convoys guarded by circling naval vessels. And in truth, the Ile de France looked safe and independent, as she surged forward through the slow, even rollers under a bright, cloudless day, a splendid day to sail out onto the North Atlantic.

She bore little resemblance to the ship she once had been. After a distinguished career as one of the most luxurious ships afloat, and indeed at one time the pride of the fleet of the French Line, she had been seriously damaged in a fire in harbor while undergoing a refit. A few brochures could still be found in the officers' quarters, testifying to the former elegance of her staterooms, her dining rooms and stair cases set in expensive, dark wood paneling with costly paintings hanging about, for the pleasure of the discriminating passengers. But that was all gone in 1943.

Stripped of her finery, she resembled any other large troop-carrier. Painted a dull gray throughout, her decks had been cleared of almost all partitions, leaving immense cavities in which rows of steel posts had been installed from floor to ceiling. Bunks had been bolted to the posts, usually at three levels, one above another, to accommodate the thousands of troops brought aboard.

The top deck, still containing many of the appointments installed in the ship in her ocean liner days, was reserved for officers and members of the ship's crew. The remaining decks, from "A" to "E," served the needs of the hoi polloi, which included the widest imaginable assortment of men from all of the services, with all sorts of non-commissioned ranks within a multitude of backgrounds and experiences.

A young westerner, born and raised in Edmonton, Alberta, found himself in a draft of armored corps soldiers traveling as part of the many army passengers on their voyage. He was Ken MacLean, currently assigned to bunk 151C, along with all of his spare clothes and equipment, on "D" deck.

Surrounding him were other members of his draft, all of whom had trained together at Camp Borden for the past many months. MacLean had developed many friendships among this group of men all with similar interests, who had lived and worked with him, day and night, throughout their army training. They all unslung their web equipment and packs at the bunks assigned them, chattering and teasing in suppressed excitement, in anticipation of a brand new experience for all of them. They looked forward to their voyage overseas as a fulfilment of a most important ambition in their military careers, a trip abroad to other countries where new sights, new people and the real action for soldiers awaited them.

"Come on MacLean," shouted Henry Condon from nearby. "We're going up on the main deck to look around this ship. We don't want to stay down here any more than we have to." Condon, a blond-haired, Torontonian, open faced and an adventurous young man, was joined by three or four other friends as they grabbed MacLean by the tunic and headed for the stairway.

"Did you see Jack and Andrews there?" asked Bill Forsythe, another of the group. "They found a crap game already started as soon as they arrived on "D" deck. That'll keep them occupied for the next few hours, whatever happens around them."

"And look at Mellish there in the can, sick and barfing, and we've just left the dockside," jeered Condon in a voice directed at the unfortunate Jim Mellish, on his knees before the toilet.

"Go boil your head, Condon. Your turn may be coming soon," came the reply, between heaves and groans.

MacLean and his friends hurried up the stairs, well aware that the smell below decks was indeed somewhat less than salubrious, and that it was probably part of the reason for Mellish's malaise. Although electric fans attempted to change and circulate the air inside the ship, the task plainly exceeded the capacity of the air circulation system when a full load of troops was aboard. A broad array of smells could be identified; the odors of cooking cabbage, engine oil, sweat and stale tobacco smoke moved through the lower decks, and the lower the deck, the more pungent the smells. Most of the passengers, with the exception of the dedicated crap shooters, wanted to escape the atmosphere of the insides of the ship as much as possible, and see the sights around them on the top deck. That's where MacLean and his friends were headed.

The sunshine and brisk breeze that greeted them when they emerged from below was a marvelous change from the thick fug that permeated the lower decks. They spread their arms and gulped in the refreshing air around them.

"Now that's more like it," said Forsythe, smiling with satisfaction, as they strode to the ship's rail, already crowded with other troops. That was the place for kibitzers; the place to study the passing throng, satisfy their curiosity about the other passengers and perhaps spot long-missing friends among them.

A small contingent of navy personnel drifted past, staying close together for moral support as they wandered through the crowd. They were a youngish group, probably traveling overseas to join a ship's crew in Britain, with only one or two of the "old salt" type of long-experienced seamen among their number.

The air force was quite heavily represented. The largest number seemed to be aircraftsmen and junior non-commissioned officers, but a substantial fraction were clearly newly-commissioned officers and sergeants with brand new wings sewn on their tunics, fresh from graduation from one of the many air training fields scattered across Canada.

The officers among them appeared ill at ease with the sudden defer-ence paid them by the hundreds of lower rank troops who acted on their instructions to "salute all officers." Whether out of trained re-spect, or a bit of sheer perversity, the other ranks kept the officers busy returning salutes wherever they went.

By far the largest contingent on the ship were army personnel, representing a wide range of corps. The soldiers' headgear was the best guide to their employment. Infantrymen wore khaki berets, as did engineers, artillerymen and representatives of all the supply serv-ices. Here and there, a soldier with a regimental hat could be spotted; a Glengarry or a Tam-O-Shanter from a highland regiment; a black wedge from a rifle unit. And, of course, the armored corps people wore their distinctive black berets. A handful of maroon berets iden-tified paratroop recruits mixed in among the rest.

The mass of humanity aboard the Ile de France posed a large feed-ing problem which was partly resolved through limiting meals to two per day. The time required to prepare meals, and serve them to the seemingly endless lines waiting to be served made this decision man-datory. Each passenger was given two color-coded cards when he boarded the ship: one told him where and when he would be served his meals, and the other stated the precise location of his bunk on the deck to which he was assigned and the hours when he could sleep on the bunk. Some of the bunks had to serve more than one passenger when there were so many troops aboard.

The departure of the mighty, grey liner from Halifax had been sudden and unmarked by any ceremony, notice or announcement. The subdued hum from the engine room suddenly increased in vol-ume and a slight vibration could be sensed throughout the ship. Without blasts of sound from the whistles or pulls from fussy harbor tugs, the Ile de France had dropped her shorelines and gangways, re-versed slowly into the middle of the harbor, and then picked up head-way as she passed McNab's Island and headed out to sea. All fanfare and ritual was eliminated from a sailing such as hers for the remain-der of the war. They quickly passed the eastern-most headland of Portugal Cove, and the last sight of Canada disappeared astern of them in the restless rollers that crossed the wake that followed them.

"Did you see the 'great uprising' in the can this morning when Atkinson went in there?" asked Henry Condon. "That was the best sight aboard this ship."

"No. What do you mean by 'the great uprising'?" queried Ken expectantly.

"Well, you know that long metal trough that they have for a toilet on each deck, with a stream of sea water running through at the bottom. You drop your pants, sit on the metal bar above it, and do your business into the trough. You've used it, haven't you?"

"Yeah, but what about it?"

"Well, Atkinson can't leave anything alone. He got some newspapers and waited until they had a long row of guys all sitting on the bar. Then he lit the newspapers on fire and sailed them down under all those bare asses. They had a great uprising! And you should have heard the language," laughed Condon.

The sunshine was warm on their backs, as they strolled forward on the broad deck, dodging this way and that among the hundreds of passengers going the opposite way. Many of the passengers stood dumbly, gaping out to sea, a sea that virtually none of them had ever seen before and not a few wondered whether they would live to cross again. Seagulls glided astern of the ship, but there were few pickings for them because everyone aboard, crew as well as passengers, had been warned against throwing anything overboard at any time, lest the enemy take advantage of a trail of debris that could lead back to the Ile de France. To many it seemed unreal that in this peaceful seascape, a deadly war was being fought somewhere on this very ocean, over the horizon ahead of them.

The walk on the deck concluded sometime later as the supper hour approached. MacLean and his colleagues descended to "D" deck to retrieve their mess tins, utensils and cups from their packs beneath their bunks, and then joined the long lineups on "B" deck leading back from the serving table.

Food on board the ship varied widely, depending upon where one was served. Wieners and beans or sauerkraut, with plenty of bread and tea formed an alternate to the frequently served stews for the lower ranks. Of course there were many complaints about the diet being served, as there would have been even if everyone was offered pheasant-under-glass. Bitching about the food was part of serving in the armed forces. On the whole, it had to be admitted that the meals were hot, nourishing and adequate; no small accomplishment in light of the gigantic administrative problems presented in feeding such a hungry multitude repeatedly throughout the voyage.

Condon, the rather artful dodger of his group, inveigled his way into a waiter's job in the Officers' mess, located up on Deck "A". This presented an opportunity to gorge himself surreptitiously on a much more varied and upscale level of food served there. He was even able to smuggle some dessert goodies down to his friends on "D" deck on occasion, much to their enjoyment. The special food privileges for officers came in for severe condemnation from the lower rank troops as one might anticipate, but this was routine as well.

The first evening at sea was a memorable one for Ken MacLean. Everyone had returned from dinner to their "home deck," to while away the time reading, arguing or shooting craps with the gamblers among them. As a non-smoker, MacLean found the mixed odors and the stale air below deck more than he wanted to put up with. He wandered idly up the stairs and out onto a partially deserted deck, as the first shadows of night began to darken the eastern horizon. To the west, the sun was disappearing behind them in a magnificent show of gold and orange in a cloudless sky. The seagulls still glided in the eddying air, silent and peaceful now, like the small flocks of "Mother-Carey's Chickens," the sea birds that traveled the lonely wastes of the oceans at wave-top level, heading to God knew where, and coming from the same places, without any care or interest in mankind and his objectives.

MacLean leaned against the ship's railing, enjoying the fresh, easy breeze in his face and the isolation, however temporary, from the throngs of jabbering people that pervaded every room, every space, every minute of the day below decks. Like many, many others aboard that ship, he wondered if and when he would ever return to the country he had just left so willingly. Thoughts crowded in of what he was leaving and why he had decided many months ago to take the steps which led to his present voyage.

He thought of his early days as a student in Edmonton during the Depression years, when his parents, like those of many of his young friends had not found it easy to make all the ends meet. But he was certain that his had been a happy childhood, in circumstances which had always permitted him to do the things that he had considered important. Sports had always been high on his list of priorities, particularly hockey and football. His interest in school studies had been high as well, but never quite high enough to induce him to strive for really good grades. Having fun, and horseplay had occupied his attention to an important degree too. He could remember his mother reading the oft-reported comment in his report cards from his teachers, "Ken will always pass his subjects comfortably, but having fun interferes with his reaching his capabilities as a student". She would sigh over this diagnosis, knowing it was accurate. Her disappointment never brought forth anger or resentment, but it showed in her face sometimes. And for Ken himself, school days had been grand days and he had wonderful recollections of them.

When the Second World War began, he remembered the almost haunted look that came into his parents' eyes. They, like the parents of many other boys and young men, still harbored memories of the consequences of the First World War. They had looked at their sons with a new and deep apprehension, wondering whether the generation that they had raised would be consumed in the new conflict, like many of their own generation had been only two decades earlier in "the war to end all wars". He could remember the almost tangible gloom and foreboding that September 3rd, when Britain declared war. His mother had been crying, and his father morose. His own feelings at the time were that it was ridiculous to worry about such an eventuality, when he was only 15 years old.

Now he was on his way overseas in fulfilment of their worst dreads. He felt a deep sympathy for the restrained anguish of his parents, caught up in forces far beyond their abilities to influence, or even completely understand. For himself, he felt no concern for his own future. His was to be the role of the participant, who saw and experienced the new things before him firsthand, while they would be restricted to the bystander's position, told only what the nation wanted to tell them, hoping for the best but fearing the worst, every time they received mail or news.

For some unknown reason, MacLean's thoughts drifted back to Corporal "Mac" McDonald, a man he hadn't thought about for a long time. "Mac" was one of those men who, in the depression years with a great deal of time on his hands, willingly spent many hours helping Boy Scout troops and other youth organizations throughout the city. He was a corporal in the Royal Canadian Corps. of Signals, and in his plentiful spare time, he dedicated himself to teaching and coaching the signaling teams in the 6th Troop of Boy Scouts, where Ken MacLean fell under his spell.

As all the details of the scout training swept through his mind once more, MacLean smiled quietly to himself: the long Saturday afternoons signaling in quasi-military fashion with flags in the large, grassy field near Mac's house; the hot cocoa prepared and served by Mac's wife in their humble living room after each practice; the pads and pencils passed out to each team member along with the cocoa, so they could practice their code reading by taking down the morse code stuttering in from a short-wave transmitter in Australia at 4:00 p.m. every Saturday. With this kind of practice, winning the trophies at the annual signaling competitions among all of the Edmonton scout troops was a foregone conclusion. Certainly 6th Troop would win. The tough part was satisfying Corporal McDonald. After feeling so put upon by the unyielding demands he made upon them, they all came to bless his name in later years when their competence in handling Morse code was demanded.

Then, for some unknown reason, MacLean's thoughts drifted onward to the long, open fall of 1940, as he sorted the factors that had contributed to his current circumstances. That was the time when he and a somewhat older friend of whom he thought a great deal, had joined Canada's militia force as boy soldiers, in a unit known as the 19th Alberta Dragoons. This reserve regiment had been a cavalry unit in World War I, and carried on a syllabus of training at the old Connaught Armories in South Edmonton. But the big attraction to young MacLean and his friend was the unit's annual military camp at Sarcee, near Calgary, where they spent two solid weeks. There the rudiments of army training and drill were hammered into the heads of part-time soldiers, living under canvas in the wide-open expanses of the foothills countryside. The instructors were exasperated full-time soldiers whose guidance was supplied to the accompaniment of a most imaginative variety of foul and abusive curses. MacLean and his friend had never heard anything that even approached it, as they struggled through long days of drill and ill-fitting boots and fatigue uniforms, just to get a few hours of practice on the rifle range with live .303 ammunition.

MacLean recalled his fairly lengthy association with the reserve army in Edmonton with considerable pleasure. He had felt at the time that he was learning from the lectures and the practice, something of what made armies of men function together effectively, albeit on a very elementary level and he made friends with a few other members of the militia, who, like himself, planned to enlist in the Active Service as soon as their ages permitted. Without any doubt, there were drones in the Reserve Forces who maintained their membership strictly as a screen, to permit them to postpone, or possibly avoid altogether, any active service in the armed forces. But MacLean regarded this as a failing in the defence policy of the Government, rather than a failing of the reserve regiments. His training in the reserve forces had been a considerable help in his adapting and accommodating himself to the demands made on him when he later enlisted in the active forces.

Immediately after graduating from high school, MacLean made use of the railway ticket provided at the Army branch office in Edmonton. He rode the "Chinook" train to Calgary to enlist at No. 13 Military District Depot at Mewata Armory. He wanted very much to be able to exercise a choice of service, before all choices were filled or withdrawn. He realized that he would not be able to choose a regiment for himself, because all the regiments had departed for destinations overseas long ago. As a new reinforcement, he would have to go wherever he was sent, but his hopes lay strongly in the direction of the tank corps.

There was really no cause for lingering about in Edmonton when school ended. A number of Ken's friends were already enrolled in the armed services, and his parents were reconciled to his "joining up" in whatever branch of the services he preferred, just as his friends had done. There would be no "maids a'mourning" at his departure, either. Ken's greater current interest had been sports, either as a participant or as a spectator. Awkward and shy with girls anyway, he was certain that the few he knew would never miss him, as they pursued their latest interests of the moment. He had decided that female companionship, pleasant though it might be, was much too costly for a young man without a salary, so it would have to await other things in his life which, for the moment at least, he rated much more pressing.

When he began his interview with an avuncular-looking lieutenant in charge of personnel selection in Calgary, he was greatly pleased to hear that he would make a good candidate for the armored corps., and that he would be sent to a basic training centre for armored units.

"Why would anyone want to fight in a tank unit?" was the question he remembered having to answer many times from his friends and relatives. MacLean reviewed once again in his mind the answers that he had given, as he stared out over the restless ocean he was crossing to do just what he had talked about.

Ever since entering high school some years earlier, Ken MacLean had been greatly impressed with the power of tanks charging forward through fences, walls, ditches and streams at the head of army advances anywhere in the world. The then current newspapers and newsreels portrayed armored forces at the leading edge of most military events in the war up to that point. For a young man who wanted to see action, he was sure that the armored corps was the place to be. Now, after months of training, he was still of the same view.

He had no over-romanticized notion that tanks were omnipotent on the battlefield, for he had seen enough pictures of them knocked out and destroyed to disabuse him of any such thoughts. He fully realized that, like other weapons, they could meet counter-weapons too. But he reasoned that if the sight of crashed aircraft did not prevent men from enlisting in the air force to fly combat planes, the sight of destroyed tanks should not be a deterrent to fighting in armored forces either. He was convinced that a combination of skill and good luck was necessary for success in combat in any fighting force, and given an average amount of good luck, the rest was up to his own skills as a tank man.

In the early 1940's, the belief was widely held by people in very elevated positions in government and even in the armed forces, that the war could be won by bombing the Axis forces into submission, and that there would be no necessity for the fearful carnage of massive land engagements which had characterized World War I. In one of the lectures which young Ken MacLean had heard during his reserve army training, he had heard a very persuasive speaker outline the reasons why, in his opinion, World War II could only be won by men on the ground; by the Allies attacking and occupying Europe, and he was totally convinced that this was the correct prediction. This became a part of the decision he had made concerning his own future. He recognized the fact that the other services were important and necessary to the Allied cause, but he was convinced that the vital role of actually defeating the Axis forces had to be performed by the army, and particularly by his chosen branch of it.

MacLean had never held a passion for killing German soldiers, nor anyone else for that matter, but he was certain he would not shrink from taking enemy lives, if and when the time came. He had never had any dreams or delusions of becoming a decorated hero, nor of obtaining rapid promotion. His youth and lack of experience rendered such possibilities clearly absurd. His ambition was limited to his becoming an accepted member of a good armored regiment, where his presence would be acknowledged and respected as a soldier who could be depended upon. Secretly he feared that all the real action might be over before he got there. He kept these thoughts to himself, for he did not want to be roasted or teased by his comrades if he uttered sentiments that sounded unduly lofty, or sacrificial. He had noticed that, whereas many men were proud to be in the armored corps, very seldom indeed did they ever expatiate upon just why they had made the choice they did.

The possibility of being killed in the fighting had entered the thoughts of most members of the armed services, particularly those who planned to enter units training for active combat. But this was a consideration which, at MacLean's age and level of experience, was lightly passed over, frequently with a joke or a jibe that "no one lives forever, you know". Partly hollow bravado, no doubt, but partly also a recognition of the general awareness that young soldiers should not be overly preoccupied with the risks ahead. That would be very bad form. Anyway, bad prophesies had a way of becoming self-fulfilling, so why waste time worrying in advance about something that might never happen?

He turned solemnly away from the rail, as the darkened ship sliced through the green-black waves. Walking with slow steps toward the stairs to his bunk below, he said to himself that, whether his parents understood his decision to join the tank troops or not, they would have to accept it. They would understand that.

There had not been much time to see his parents since he enlisted in the services. Directly after his short stint at the district Depot at Calgary, Ken had been sent to Brampton, Ontario, for basic armored training. Then, after two enjoyable summer months, he joined a large draft of men who were sent to Camp Borden, the immense armored training camp located north of Toronto.

Happy recollections of the months spent training at Borden persisted, notwithstanding the hard work and sometimes unpleasant duties of repairing a broken tank track while out on a training exercise at 25° below zero. Bare fingers working on cold steel in a northern Ontario winter produced long-lasting memories. And there had been a few winter bivouacs which the instructors had insisted upon, to toughen the troops under their supervision. All of the participants would rather forget them.

Balanced against the hard days however, were the many happy experiences in his class of students. Regular weekend passes every fortnight allowed the soldiers to visit Toronto and other nearby communities of their choice where hostels were plentiful and inexpensive. They had all the panoply of sporting events, servicemen's clubs, dances and other entertainments for small-town boys in the big city. Hundreds of romances bloomed, as young men met young women in highly suitable circumstances, where fun and enjoyment were the dominant themes. Life might be short, so everyone set out to enjoy it while they could.

One of the members of MacLean's class in radio and gunnery, Jack Mosher, an exceedingly bright, university-trained, American citizen who had come to Canada to enlist in the army before the United States entered the war, made a name for himself among his many girlfriends. Jack was not blessed with good looks, but he more than made up for it with his eloquence in his vast exchange of correspondence. He had organized his own "lonely hearts club," exchanging romantic letters with a host of anxious females, both in Ontario and in Michigan, where he had attended university before deciding to come to Canada. Many a quiet evening in the barrack room was rendered boisterous with laughter as Mosher read aloud from some of the letters he exchanged with his love-sick correspondents.

"For God's sake Mo," Bill Forsyth would shout. "You mean to say you actually send out that overblown tripe to live women? I can't believe anyone would really fall for it. You're having us on again, Jack."

"Think so, do you?" Mosher would laugh. "How many letters do you get per week? I get six or seven, so beat that, if you can. They think I'm a downtrodden, free-spirited intellectual that craves rescue from the hands of the rough, coarse brutes that inhabit all army barracks, and they are quite correct about that."

"Instead of the lecherous old bastard that we all know you to be," Forsyth would interrupt. "What would these adoring, clinging vines of yours think if they knew you were just playing games with them, and reading out the juiciest parts to all of those savages, just for laughs? Look at the beginning of this letter you wrote to some dame named Joan Evans in Detroit. 'My dearest Joan. My sweet, demure enchantress.' Great Christ, that sort of turns my stomach, and it's a conflict in terms anyway."

"To hell with you and your stomach, Forsyth. I don't know what the girls think when they read my letters. But it's good for their souls to believe that they really understand and help some poor, downtrodden, poetic soul lost in the toils of the faceless military. Besides, who knows what they are doing with my letters? Maybe they're reading them out to their friends for laughs, just like we are here. It's a good catharsis for both sides and I make no apologies."

"What's catharsis?" Bill Fox would ask, and be told, for the umpteenth time, that it was Mosher's word for a clean-out, or a physic, either physical or mental, which Fox probably failed to understand any better than "catharsis".

By the time Mosher's training at Borden was almost complete, the United States had entered the war. Jack applied for and later received a transfer to the armed forces of his own country. The farewell gathering to say "goodbye" to Jack Mosher was "a stem winder" as they used to call it, an hilarious, bibulous gathering of most of Mosher's friends, as they said farewell to a comrade in arms they would never forget. At least MacLean would never forget him.

The training at Camp Borden finally ended and Ken and his colleagues were transferred to what was called the "Trained Soldier Regiment," or "T.S.R.," although they still had a great deal of training to absorb, as MacLean had suspected. Within a week at T.S.R., his class was placed on a draft which took them eastward to Windsor, Nova Scotia, where a large holding camp had been constructed. MacLean remembered their two or three week sojourn at Windsor, while their numbers built up to fill an ocean liner, docked at nearby Halifax. The meals had been wonderful, unforgettable for army messes. He wondered if he would ever see their equal again.

Bringing his thoughts back to the present, MacLean glanced solemnly about him. The Ile de France sailed steadily onward, headed sometimes southeasterly into noticeably warmer temperatures, and at other times decidedly northeastward toward the colder stretches of the north Atlantic. But always they sailed eastward for five more days without a mishap, a storm or even an eventful sighting of another vessel. Sunshine blessed their days and stygian darkness did the same for their nights, while the huge, restless throng of passengers idled their time with whatever diversions they could find. The daily drills for abandoning ship were rehearsed every morning, to the annoyance of the entire complement aboard, but fortunately they never got beyond the rehearsal steps.

Toward evening of the sixth day of the voyage, another large ship, traveling in the opposite direction, could be seen at a considerable distance to the south. No identification was passed to the passengers, although the crew undoubtedly were in communication with the other vessel. Then it swung off westward into the misty distance and disappeared. Almost immediately afterward, a faint smudge appeared on the horizon beyond the starboard bow and the address system carried an announcement that the coast of Ireland had been sighted. Since none of the passengers knew the destination for which the ship was headed, in the interests of security at the time, it became a matter of wide and wild speculation as to where they were headed. The betting favored Liverpool, although some held strongly for Belfast, after hearing that they were in sight of the Irish coast.

In the lengthy evening light that followed, other land appeared ahead on the port and the starboard bows. A sparkling, white lighthouse emerged on the starboard side, marking the point at which they began to enter the outer reaches of the Firth of Clyde, as the address system confirmed. The ship had reduced speed noticeably. A pilot's boat headed out from a building near the lighthouse to intercept it and place a harbor pilot on board.

The lush, green hills of Ayrshire slanted gently downward to tidy, white houses along the margins of the broad Firth. Sheep dotted the slopes stretching away to the Highlands beyond. The fading daylight touched the uppermost tips of the highest hills with a rose and purple glow. An awed hush fell over the men crowding the decks, seeing the pastoral loveliness of the outer Scottish shores for the first time. They found it difficult to believe that this was a country engaged in a bitter and devastating war that had continued for over three years. But they felt deep within their bones that they too would fight to protect homes such as they saw before them.

The opening of the anti-submarine net to admit the ship to the inner anchorages brought everyone back to reality again. Two large Sunderland flying boats bobbed at anchor in the placid waters of the Firth near the southern shores, their purpose belied by the machineguns poking from the front turrets. Some small motor craft buzzed about on errands of their own, staying well clear of the great, gray hulk easing into the river mouth at dead slow speed.

Henry Condon was the first to spot a grey man o'war ahead, riding at anchor off the starboard bow. Clearly she had been involved in heavy action somewhere at sea, for her stern had been torn apart above the water line by bombs or shells.

"Look at her decks there. Wherever she has been, she was lucky to get back here at all," Cordon observed.

"There's a war on somewhere over here all right," said Sergeant Major Waters at the back of the crowded deck. "We're gonna see a lot like that before we get back."

Anchors clanked downward soon afterward, signaling the completion of the voyage from Halifax, safe and sound for everyone. To the mild surprise of many aboard, the Ile de France had anchored in mid-harbor, directly off the snug Scottish town of Dunoon, as darkness closed in around them. The voice of the captain was heard on the public address system, speaking slowly and deliberately:

"Now we have come to the end of our journey. Let us all give thanks to Almighty God for preserving us as we traveled safely through the perils that await those that sail across uncertain seas in the presence of their enemies. We have much for which to be thankful."

After these words, the lights were covered or extinguished, and the great throng slept.

CHAPTER II

SOJOURN IN BRITAIN

Early in the morning after arrival in the Firth of Clyde, lighters appeared at the side of the Ile de France and began ferrying the troops from ship to shore at Greenoch, a large town on the south bank. Across the Firth, the small town of Dunoon clutched the lower levels; clean white buildings with red roofs and a church steeple overlooking the town from the waterfront. Stretching away above Dunoon to the point where they touched a sparkling blue sky above; were the lush, green Ayrshire hills, dotted here and there with small flocks of sheep steadily cropping the verdant fields around them. Grey stone walls divided the farms from one another, often bordering narrow roads that climbed up to the headlands, overlooking the countryside spread for many miles. To all the new arrivals from Canada that had seen nothing but an unrelieved waste of waves during the past week, the scene surrounding them was stunningly beautiful and universally appealing.

As the various drafts of men reached the docks at Greenoch following the short lighter ride from the troopship, they were marched aboard waiting train coaches at the railway station, after enjoying cups of hot tea served by a group of elderly Scottish ladies. Within a surprizingly short time, all the waiting trains departed with their carefully organized loads of troops to a variety of destinations in the Aldershot command in Southern England.

After first scoffing at the diminutive British locomotives they spotted, while boarding their coaches, the Canadian troops were forced to change their impressions when they saw what the trains could do. Even the toots of the locomotive whistles brought derisory smiles. But when the trains gained full speed beyond Glasgow, streaking through towns and some cities on their way south, the passengers shook their heads in astonishment; almost disbelief.

"You know, this has been the best organized troop movement that I have ever seen in all my time in this man's army," said Doug Jack, a huge blond-haired hulk of a man in MacLean's draft. "Two hours ago we were still on that bloody troopship, and here we are going like hell toward England, with all our draft together, our kit all loaded, and a breakfast eaten en route. Unbelievable!"

"If the Canadian Army had arranged it, we'd still be trying to find the right stairway to get off that ship," added Henry Condon.

This was a bit much for old Sergeant Major Waters, ("old," in that he had been a soldier for ten years or more.) He took these jibes as ridicule of the sacred organization to which he had given his best years. He just had to come to its defence.

"Now just hold on there about the Canadian Army and how it performs. If you guys had seen as much of what the Canadian Army can do as I have, you wouldn't be so quick to criticize. This move ran well I admit, and the British were responsible for it. But they don't have a perfect record either. They have some tremendous organizational foul-ups to answer for too. Think back to 1939-40 when they made their advance into Belgium so the Germans could cut them off. But for a bloody miracle at Dunkirk, they'd have lost everything wouldn't they? Who organized that schmozzle? Who was the originator of the Dieppe raid? You answer those questions for me, and you won't get hung up in your underwear praising the British Army efficiency. They have their days, and we do in our army too."

MacLean and his colleagues decided to leave the subject as it stood. Staring out of the coach windows at the lush English countryside whizzing past, they wondered where they were going at such speed. No one had ever told them their destination, as a matter of army policy. In the interests of "maintaining security," rank and file soldiers, and indeed many at higher levels, were only given information they had to know. Up to a point, this policy was fully justified, but like most policies, it could be, and often was, carried to stupid and ridiculous extremes by zealots with a great deal more enthusiasm then sense. The removal of all road signs at intersections and all railway station signs, ordered in 1940, purportedly to confuse the German invaders at the time that a cross-channel invasion threatened, was a prime example. Long after the menace of a German invasion had become unrealistic, most of these signs were still missing. Meanwhile the confusing of civilians as well as the military using the road and rail systems was compounded and re-compounded every day the policy continued.

The troop train carrying MacLean and his draft passed through Clapham Junction in London, whether or not they were aware of it, where it was switched to a westward track that would take them on to Woking, a handsome, clean and neat town in Surrey within the large Aldershot military command. There, everyone was transferred along with their kit, onto a fleet of trucks which headed out along a winding road. They traveled among stately oak and beech trees through a beautiful countryside. Before long they arrived at an enclave of two-storey red brick buildings, known as Blackdown Barracks. This would be their new army home. This was No. 3 C.A.C.R.U. (Canadian Armored Corps Reinforcement Unit.)

As they soon found out, the neatly paved roads, the shapely trees and hedges, and the trim, brick buildings fronting on the huge parade squares, belied the interior conditions of the buildings.

A single staircase had to serve all the troops quartered on the upper floors. Only one bathroom, with four ancient toilet bowls fitted with massive water tanks halfway up the wall, had to accommodate over 100 men in each building block. No great imagination was necessary to see trouble arising from these inadequate facilities at Blackdown, and it certainly developed.

All the pipes for plumbing the buildings were installed on the outside of the walls, to the bemusement of the Canadian newcomers.

"They have a winter here too, although not like ours back home," commented Henry Condon. "How do they keep the pipes from freezing?"

"They don't, stupid," said a small, officious English corporal standing nearby, who was part of the barrack maintenance establishment.

"That's why they put the pipes on the outside of the buildings - so they can get at 'em without opening up the bloody walls."

'And it never occurred to anyone to shelter the pipes so they wouldn't freeze?" asked Condon, smiling wryly toward the rest of the group standing around them.

"You don't understand the problem at all," persisted the English corporal. "There's no sense in arguing with you."

The beds attracted their attention too. Each of the units consisted of a wooden frame with legs standing about 4 feet tall. Wooden slats were installed in rectangular frames about 6 feet long and possibly half as wide. The uppermost frame was nailed in place at the top of the legs of the bed, and the lower frame about eight inches above the floor. No mattresses were provided; each man assigned to a two-man unit was expected to stuff straw into a large cotton-covered bag and use this expedient as a mattress. It was known as a "palliasse" among quartermasters. The palliasse had its practical advantages too, occupying little space until it was filled from a straw-pile, thus avoiding the problem of dealing with the bulk of an ordinary mattress. But it suffered from the disadvantage that straw was sometimes inhabited by straw lice, making life miserable for anyone unfortunate enough to become acquainted with what was termed "mechanized dandruff". Barrack room conditions had changed little if at all since the days of the Duke of Wellington, and the British soldiers in charge seemed proud of it.

The mess hall at Blackdown was also a disappointment to the newly arrived draft. Pleasant enough from the outside, the building was medieval inside, containing nothing but a collection of wooden tables and benches. Everyone was obliged to use his own mess tins and the cutlery issued to him upon enlistment in the army. Most soldiers also had a metal mug for tea, but not everyone, by any means.

This meant that, for example, if the meal consisted of mutton stew and brussel sprouts, (and it often did) the mix of stew and sprouts was plopped into the larger of the two mess tins by a bored and indifferent staff cook, while bread and butter, with or without biscuits, and the rice pudding dessert were dropped in the other. If the soldier had a mug for tea, that is where he got the strong, sweet tea available. If his mug had disappeared, the tea was poured into one of the two mess tins on top of whatever was already in it. Although the diet and methods of serving were handled entirely by Canadian Army cooking staff, they closely resembled the British practices in the same barracks over the years. It harked back to the days when the officers feared the lower ranks as though they were close to animals, and treated them as if they were.

Nevertheless, all in all, the soldiers found the food nourishing, if somewhat strange to palates accustomed to beef and potatoes as staples in their diet. The switch to mutton with brussel sprouts, and large amounts of fish, bread and cheese, whether cheddar or Stilton, (commonly called "tight arse" for well-known reasons, around the mess halls) was accomplished without difficulties. In general, the Canadian soldiers ate virtually everything that was made available to them, complaining of course about what they were receiving, which was normal at all times, but usually without much foundation. Hungry men will eat first and complain later.

One weekend, the cooks in No. 3 C.A.C.R.U. surprised their ungrateful diners with a large and tasty meat stew, followed by ample helpings of steamed pudding, with a tasty lemon sauce. They even went the hither-to unheard of lengths of offering second helpings of the dessert to the ravenous troops, who had worked hard all week and greatly relished an unusually heavy meal to conclude it.

Many were the expressions of satisfaction and pleasure after the Saturday dinner, as the troops wandered idly about, gossiping or preparing and cleaning kit and uniform for the next week. A few began getting ready for bed. The blackout covers were put in place over the windows and the camp settled itself for what it hoped would be another quiet night, free of air-raids or other disruptions.

MacLean was one of the very lucky ones that night. He had been in bed only about an hour when a sudden, violent griping pain seized his abdomen. Recognizing the first warnings of an impending purge, he leapt out of bed, sprinted to the toilet, vacant of all occupants at the time, and made full use of the facilities there. After experiencing an absolute "clean-out," as he called it, Ken quietly made his way through the barrack room darkness to his bed, crept into it and prepared to resume his sleep, meanwhile wondering what had so upset his digestive system. But sleep eluded him, and everyone else, for the first half of the night.

First there were only one or two other men who hurriedly climbed from their beds and sprinted single-mindedly toward the toilet. Then a rising murmur of voices could be heard as the numbers of men rapidly increased. The sounds of men running in the halls upstairs and on the staircases swelled as night advanced. Chaos developed in the toilet room, as men pounded on the doors of the cubicles, desperately anxious to get inside and use one of the "thrones," while those already inside refused to leave because their gripes were still continuing. Wild curses and threats were issued in the swarming darkness, as men milled about like cattle, frantically seeking a place where they could relieve themselves.

Quickly discovering that the hopelessly inadequate toilet on the main floor was not going to provide relief in time, a desperate host of men poured out the doorways of the barrack rooms in search of "any port in a storm." Neighbouring barrack blocks seemed to have the same trouble. Everyone could hear their doors banging, shouted curses and the sound of many feet running. Even underground air raid shelters were resorted to in desperation. The night guard, attracted by the sounds and shouting hurried over from the Guard House.

"Turn off those bloody lights! What the hell's going on here anyway?" demanded some loud and angry voices as the din increased.

It was about midnight when the uproar subsided, and people crept back to their bunks to try to gain some rest. As far as Ken could see, everyone in his block had been struck by diarrhea. Suspicions for the cause of it soon focused on the latest dinner served by the cooking staff. It was roundly recognized that some of the cooks had shown mounting resentment concerning recent criticisms to the Orderly Officers of their culinary accomplishments. Their suspicions were confirmed for them when they recalled the offers of second helpings of the steamed pudding with lemon sauce and the very solicitous inquiries on Sunday morning by the cooks as to whether the men had enjoyed a good night's sleep. That removed all possible doubts. Although nothing could be proven, of course, it appeared that the cooks had "got even." There should be no further groundless complaints about the quality of the food at No. 3 C.A.C.R.U.

The average day's training was spent in sharpening up the drill of the men at the Camp, along with a fair emphasis on physical training. There were also advanced courses in wireless (ie. radio) repair and usage, motor mechanics and some of the technical aspects of tank gunnery. Unfortunately, no arrangements existed for practical weapon usage or practice at this stage of the training. No men were sent to the firing ranges from No. 3 C.A.C.R.U., on the theory that it was merely a holding unit, assembling partially trained reinforcements for the armored regiments. Practical gunnery was postponed until they were dispatched to a regiment for further development.

MacLean and his cohorts wondered aloud about the lack of training upon real tank weapons, in their course at Blackdown Camp. "Do you suppose the German tank crews that we are going to face have had as little gunnery training as we are getting?" asked Red McKenna, in talking to MacLean one day. "We are strangers to the guns we're supposed to use. I hope we get some real practice and experience when we get to the regiments, because we're sure as hell not getting it here."

"Amen to that," replied MacLean. "I thought that would be the central theme here, but it's just put off time and again. We'll just have to wait and see. There's nothing we can do about it, but it bugs me too."

Training on the drill square, usually known as "square bashing," still proceeded anon, along with the advanced armored training. MacLean and his fellow soldiers made the acquaintance of drill Sergeant-Major Mills, a martinet of a man boasting almost 30 years in the British Army, much of it marching up and down a drill square. Mills, along with several of his fellow drill instructors, openly yearned for the return of peace, not for the reasons espoused by most civilized people, but rather to get back to "real sojering," as he called it. He meant the formalities of full dress parades, with pomp and pageantry, inspections by distinguished visitors, bands playing and crowds of spectators watching admiringly. That was the world of Sergeant-Major Mills, who had gloried in the foot drill he had learned and later taught at Caterham and Pirbright. His life had been spent with the Coldstream Guards, whose shoulder flashes and hat badge he still wore proudly.

With his pacing stick revolving, to assure that everyone was taking a pace of exactly 30 inches he marched in line with the front rank of any body of soldiers under his command in supreme happiness, ramrod straight, forage hat pulled low over his forehead and eyes glinting forward. He had no interest in, nor much knowledge of what mechanized war required of its participants. He deeply regretted the introduction of noisy, smelly tanks into the army's order of battle. Though an anachronism, he was still useful in the training process he taught, firmly believing that discipline had to be instilled in all soldiers, whatever they were going to do. He insisted that their abject submission to discipline began with teaching them how to dress themselves, how to stand and how to march together and in absolute conformity with the model described in official army instructions. And in all truth, the basic standard set by Mills was indeed the foundation for developing an army that would work together obediently, and effectively. The great Clausewitz might have agreed with Mills and his fellow drill instructors on that.

It has been said that Kaiser Wilhelm II adored uniforms, military parades, pomp and circumstance, and deeply regretted the actual fighting which he helped cause because of what it did to the ranks of the soldier's he so much admired. True or otherwise, this was very much the attitude of Sergeant-Major Mills, as he shouted and raged at the troops on "his" parade squares. It was the drill he loved, the moving pageant of marching men, precisely in step and in line. He really just wanted to "sojer," but all who came in contact with him and his discipline went away better men as a result, whether they appreciated it or not. Regularly damned publicly by the troops, he was privately admired as a personification of what the army stood for. Hundreds and hundreds of troops had passed through a term of training at Blackdown Camp, without retaining strong impressions of what they had done there. But none ever forgot their brushes with "Mr Mills," as he preferred to be addressed, and his week-end ceremonial drill parades, which he held to be an absolutely necessary part of "sojering." His superiors agreed with him.

The weeks of training at Blackdown for MacLean and his friends passed quickly, as one sun-drenched summer day followed another. Field schemes and exercises took them to Bagshot Heath, where they camped for a week under make-shift shelters constructed from army-issue ground sheets. To their surprise, their meals went through a marvelous transformation for the better, while they were in the hands of the Bagshot cooks. At the end of very full days, there was time for them to familiarize themselves with the pleasant villages and towns within easy walking distance of their barracks. Nearby they found and enjoyed the hospitality of Camberley, Frimley Green, Woking and Brookwood, where they made the acquaintance of English beer served at room temperatures. They also became friends with a number of English publicans and their staffs.

Just a few miles north of Blackdown was the neat and attractive town of Farnborough, known in Allied military circles for its airfield and the experimental aircraft that flew in and out of it. Soldiers training in any of the numerous army camps scattered throughout the Aldershot command, became accustomed to seeing all manner of aircraft buzzing about over their heads before landing at Farnborough. Not infrequently, MacLean saw captured German airplanes, with the enemy identification marking carefully painted over and replaced by R.A.F. roundels, flying above their heads, but always closely chaperoned by a busy Hurricane fighter flying beside them. On a few occasions, models of British planes that never got into mass production would pass over the training camps. Curiosity was whetted whenever a plane from Farnborough climbed above them.

On one occasion, MacLean watched a weird, Blohm and Voss seaplane, somehow captured intact from the Germans, as it limped heavily into the air and slowly circled the Farnborough airfield. On another, MacLean's class was just about to end their day's training when they heard the whine of a low-flying plane approaching Farnborough at great speed. Suddenly above their heads, a Mosquito aircraft, still a curiosity to Allied troops, tore past, just above tree-top level. Only one engine was working; the other had been badly damaged by gunfire. Holes in the wing foil allowed the men on the ground to look through the wing to the sky above. Wherever the Mosquito had been, its pilot was making a daring flight to reach Farnborough airfield, a long way inland from the coastal airfields, for reasons known only to himself. But the flight served to remind everyone that saw the plane that, however peaceful it may appear along the quiet byways of Blackdown, only a few minutes away by fast aircraft, men were engaged in deadly conflict.

At the conclusion of two months at Blackdown, a variety of tests were given the men in MacLean's group. The tests were to determine their abilities to strip and reassemble Browning machineguns; operate and maintain a No. 19 wireless set; transmit and receive Morse code at a reasonable speed; navigate from one map reference to another in daylight and in darkness; strip and reassemble cut-down models of the breeches of the six-pounder and the .75 mm tank guns; and conduct discussions on the wireless set with other stations using proper procedure, with correctly encoded terms for map references. Having paid attention to the lectures and studied the text, MacLean's group passed these tests without great difficulty, and were rewarded by being promptly sent away for a ten-day stint on the channel coast at Lulworth.

Lulworth Cove proved to be one of the most beautiful places in the entirety of southern England. A tiny community of quaint houses with a ruined castle, it nestled among the towering oak, beech and chestnut trees that graced the south coast roads and farmsteads throughout the area. The entirety of Dorset county boasted many arresting landscapes, with quiet, winding country ways among the peaceful pastures, divided from one another by dry stone walls or well-trimmed hedges. But none had greater charm than Lulworth.

There, cattle grazed contentedly on the verdant slopes of gently undulating fields. Now and then, rustic farmers would appear, speaking some esoteric language, clad in rough wool trousers, thick leather leggings and huge heavy boots, as they wandered along the roads or rode their ancient horse-drawn carts, just as their ancestors had done centuries earlier. On occasion, the soldiers wandered into "The Old Wheatsheaf," the pub in Wool, a village of about two dozen souls, to partake of the local hospitality. There they attracted the friendly stares of the farmers of Lulworth Cove, and once the language barriers between the two groups were breached, they all took great pleasure in one another's company.

The flat twang of the Canadian visitors seemed to be readily understood by the local rustics; but the strange rural vocabulary of the Dorset men, most of whom had never been twenty-five miles from home, perplexed the soldiers for some time. But amity prevailed between the middle-aged and parochial yeomen and the far-from-home Canadian youth as the ale flowed. Within the Old Wheatsheaf, thoughts of war were pushed aside, as convivial conversation claimed their few hours together.

The pastoral image of Lulworth was really an illusion. Actually, the area swarmed with British and Canadian troops who had been sent there to practice live tank-gun firing at off-shore targets in the narrow bay. This target practice took place almost every day, as different regiments cycled gunners through the tests in the tanks permanently located there.

A few miles to the north of Lulworth was the huge Bovington Army Camp, where the British Army wireless school trained thousands of troops to become effective wireless operators on many different sizes and types of wireless equipment. In contrast with the bucolic setting at Lulworth Cove, where the presence of army troops was revealed only occasionally, when the tank guns were being fired, the establishment at Bovington was marked by extensive, wide-spread lecture halls and barracks in which a large staff was permanently accommodated. The many large buildings of Bovington had been the target of several bombing and strafing missions by the Luftwaffe but Lulworth, totally concealed in the leafy canopy above it, had been spared from any enemy air raids.

Extremely anxious to try their hands at firing live ammunition at the Lulworth tank ranges, MacLean and his colleagues were unable to wangle an opportunity to do so, because they were not attached to any regiment. Their presence in the Lulworth Camp was accounted for by the training course in gunnery theory and practice on models in the lecture hall, but there was no firing practice provided for them, much to their chagrin. After two weeks in this pleasant, sylvan hideaway, they returned to Blackdown, purportedly fully trained soldiers, ready for transfer to armored regiments. The last step was eagerly awaited by all of them.

One day, shortly after their return, MacLean and the other members of his class were drowsily sitting through yet another lecture on map reading, when it was interrupted by a corporal from the base staff.

"The following men are required at the Orderly Room right away: Campbell, Robinson, McKenna and MacLean. Just follow me," the corporal directed.

This turned out to be almost comic opera for the four men identified. It developed that all four of them had scored well on the "M Score" test given every soldier upon enlistment. They had also maintained relatively high grades in their courses and training ever since. They were told that they had been selected as candidates for officer training, and upon their acceptance, would be transferred to Pirbright, or another nearby locality, preparatory to commencing full scale officers' training probably at Sandhurst.

"A great time to hear this," exploded McKenna to the other members of the foursome sitting in the waiting room. "Just when we finally became eligible to join a regiment and put all this training into practice, they offer us a chance to become bloody officers. That would mean at least another year or more of steading training."

MacLean shared the feelings of big Red McKenna completely. He could feel his gorge rise as Red was speaking.

"The second front is supposed to be opening up in the near future. That's all we've heard and read lately. The whole war could be won and over within a year from now, and we'd still be taking courses and training to become officers. Everything we've taken so far would be just ignored. What the hell did we come overseas for? To take a bunch of courses and end up a 'one pip wonder' after the war ends? All the guys with any guts would have finished with all the action and gone home. I don't think I could face that. If we have any choice in this, my choice is not just 'no'. It's hell no!"

"That's for me too," stated Red McKenna emphatically. "We went through this nonsense when they were offering transfers to the Intelligence Corps, about a month after we landed in England. Big deal that was! Fiddle away your time sitting in an office somewhere looking at paper being shuffled from one desk to another, with a small promotion thrown in. And this, after we've been through all this tank training! It might have been interesting a year or two ago, but by Jesus, not now. We want to go to a regiment and see some action!"

Robinson and Campbell were much less outspoken about their choices when re-examined by the interviewing officers. They felt flattered that they had been offered candidature at officers' school, opportunities for which many in camp, both staff and trainees, would have given their eye teeth. Neither MacLean nor McKenna ever did hear what these men answered when called in for their interviews, because they never saw them again. They strongly suspected that they accepted the transfers offered.

The staff lieutenant with whom they talked was mightily surprised by the quick rejections from MacLean and McKenna. Wide-eyed, he began writing briskly in their respective personnel files.

"I would be greatly surprised if you don't regret the choices you have made," he said to them as he closed the interviews. "But I wish you luck when you go to whatever regiment takes you. You'll need it there."

"Thank you sir," replied MacLean for himself and McKenna. "We'll need some luck where we're going I know. But if I'd made the other choice, I know I'd always regret it."

'Me too," echoed Red McKenna.

Within days, McKenna and MacLean were again called to the orderly room to be told that they had been taken on strength of the Second Armored Brigade. Both men were slated to join B Squadron of the Fort Garry Horse Regiment. They would be the newest reinforcements necessary to bring the unit up to full strength for the special training in which it was to participate. They hurriedly left the group of men that had trained with them in Canada and sailed overseas with them without a chance of bidding them good luck, or fond farewell. With perhaps one or two exceptions, they never saw any of them again. It was so typical of the army; there was never time to say "goodbye" to friends and colleagues with whom soldiers had lived night and day for months or even years. Transfers were usually effective immediately, and there was never time for sentiment. Regrettably, this had to be the rule, certainly among the other ranks, and generally among the officers as well, for the forces could not await the pleasure of their members in winding up old associations.

From the reinforcement centres like 3 C.A.C.R.U., men who qualified for positions in the regiments of the armored corps were dispersed to a wide variety of units, representing any number of geographical locations in Canada. New attachments were expected to develop between the men and the units to which they would be assigned, bonds that would link them with the people and the units with which they would probably spend the rest of their days in the services. Their future interests would focus on their new regimental homes.

Army members, including Ken MacLean and his colleagues, were sometimes surprized at the speed and dispatch of the administration in transferring soldiers to combat units. They had all seen examples of the long and frustrating delays that frequently ensued when someone of their acquaintance made application for transfer to one of the service units. Sometimes the transfers never did materialize. But an application for transfer to an infantry or armored regiment seemed to receive prompt and effective treatment. Recognition of the need, either immediate or not long to be deferred, for reinforcements of the combat units certainly existed, and for those who chose a career in one of such regiments, his wishes would be soon gratified.

As the war wore on, the pace of moving new, and in some cases under-trained reinforcements from training units to combat regiments became not only brisk, but excessive in many instances. The needs for combat reinforcements finally became critical.

In any event, MacLean and McKenna soon journeyed south to a camp near Fawley in the Southhampton vicinity, where they found B and C Squadrons of the Fort Garry Horse, undergoing some very special training. The Regiment had been informed a short time earlier that it would come under the command of the 3rd Canadian Infantry Division, along with the rest of the 2nd Armored Brigade, for all training purposes.

The focus of the training was directed at amphibious operations; improving cooperation between the navy and the army in landing tanks on enemy-occupied shores. Tank drivers and crew commanders, the two crew members most directly involved, had to become expert at loading and unloading the tanks from landing ships and landing craft.

The affiliation of the Fort Garry's with the 8th Infantry Brigade was communicated to all members with the knowledge, brought to them through a visit by General Montgomery himself, that they would be in the assault division when the Allies attacked the French coast. This meant that soldiers of the North Shore Regiment, the Régiment de la Chaudiére, and the Queen's Own Rifles, would be fighting their way ashore with the Fort Garry Horse Regiment, a relationship that seemed to please everyone.

The reception of Ken and Red into the Regiment was quite informal and without difficulties. The Adjutant, Captain Fraser, explained to them that they were joining what he believed to be one of the outstanding tank regiments in the Canadian Army. He assured them that they would shortly become familiar with the role that they would play in the assault, for which special training was being given at that time. McKenna was told that he would be joining the crew of a tank in 2 Troop of B Squadron, and MacLean heard that he would become the new loader-operator of Sergeant Chapman's tank in 4 Troop. They were both informed that Major Meindl commanded B Squadron, and that both he and his 2 I.C., Captain Hall, were greatly respected as top leaders.

Glad to receive definite postings to specific crews, the two new recruits picked up their kit and headed out to meet their new comrades. There would be a plethora of new names to conjure with, all the way from Lieutenant Colonel R.E.A. (Ronnie) Morton, who commanded the Regiment, down to the other members of the crews of their own tanks.

For Ken MacLean, who was somewhat shy in his new surroundings, he resolved to keep a low profile until he became more familiar with the people and equipment around him. He was introduced to his crew commander, Sergeant Ed Chapman, a regimental veteran dating back to the days of mobilization.

Tall, broad shouldered and blond-haired, Chapman had farmed in the Brandon area of Manitoba. Not quite handsome, but very close to it, he looked good-natured and intelligent, as he strode about among the tanks. The fit of his uniform betrayed a powerful physique, developed during his years on the farm. With a strong set to his jaw, and a steady gaze to his gray eyes, he looked every inch the leader that he was in his Squadron. Ken was much impressed with him.

"And this is our gunner, Ron Osborne," said Chapman, taking over the task of introducing MacLean to the rest of the crew. "He's a good one, and I think you'll get along well with him. There's a lot he can show you," he concluded as MacLean and Osborne shook hands and sized one another up.

Osborne was a chunky, dark-haired, former grain company employee from Winnipeg, who appeared pleased with what he saw in Ken MacLean, as the new man in the turret. He too had been with the Regiment since its mobilization, through all its moves and training exercises.

MacLean heard later that Osborne had been offered a promotion to crew commander in another tank, in recognition of his solid, effective performance as a gunner, but had refused it in order to stay with Chapman's crew, where he felt well-placed for the fighting ahead. MacLean was certainly reassured to hear this anecdote about their gunner, who appeared to know everyone and everything that Ken asked him about. Apparently MacLean's predecessor as loader-operator had become sick and had been transferred out of the unit, to no one's regret among the crew members.

Next, Ken had to meet Allan Robinson, the tank driver and Jack Metcalfe, the co-driver and bow gunner, both Winnipeg men, where they had been employed for some years as truck drivers. Both drivers wore bushy, military moustaches then in fashion. They inspired Ken with confidence that, in their independent, laconic ways, they were men who could be depended upon in tight circumstances. They had both accumulated much experience in the exercises participated in by the regiment, and went about their duties with the quiet confidence of familiarity and talent. Reassuring as it was to MacLean to witness the professionalism of the crew he was joining, and upon whom his life would soon depend, he nevertheless felt himself a callow youth among them. But he was determined to hold up his end too, as they made ready for the new training ahead of them. MacLean felt fortunate to have joined the crew he did. They were professionals.

Confident of his ability to operate the radio equipment in the turret of their new Sherman tank, after his many months of practice with it, he was less sure of himself with the .75 mm master gun, the rapid loading of which would be his responsibility too. He had had plenty of practice with the somewhat smaller 6 pounder guns in the Ram tanks upon which they had practiced time and again in Canada, but the new .75 mm gun in this tank was much less familiar to him. The loader-operator was also obliged to feed belts of ammunition into the .30 calibre Browning machinegun coaxially mounted with the master gun in the mantlet of the turret, but this was a relatively simple duty.

The new training proceeded, and MacLean's Squadron moved, along with C Squadron, to a location near Gosport on the south coast. Ken noticed a rapid insurge of new equipment on all sides of him; vehicles and material meant to support an invasion, beyond any doubt. New Sherman tanks equipped with the powerful, long-barreled 17-pounder gun, and nicknamed the "Firefly," arrived for distribution among the various troops of the regiment. New light tanks for the Reconnaissance Troop and re-built Crusader tanks equipped with twin anti-aircraft cannons for the "ack-ack" troop were delivered, ready for familiarization training. Scout cars, armored half-tracks and transport trucks were plentiful. The R.C.E.M.E., (Royal Canadian Electrical and Mechanical Engineers), imported some new heavy tank-recovery vehicles. Jeeps swarmed about the area, as the build-up reached a fever pitch. There could be little doubt in anyone's mind, however many training exercises they had participated in, that the next exercise would be the real thing, the invasion.

Interesting as it was to watch the never-ending gathering of troops and material in the background, MacLean and his buddy, Red McKenna were even more fascinated by the special training being given to B and C Squadrons for the distinctive roles they were to play. Their training was carried on as secretly as possible, hived off from the remainder of the regiment, and hopefully unrecognized by the German reconnaissance planes that appeared above them almost every day, apart from and in addition to the bombers that droned overhead most nights on nuisance raids over Southern England.

The men of the Fort Garry Horse were told that two squadrons of the First Hussars Regiment, which would also accompany the assault infantry ashore, were also receiving the same special training. They too were to become familiar with "DD Tanks;" (duplex-drive vehicles) that were designed to swim ashore and deliver heavy fire on enemy fortresses and pill boxes that might survive the pre-invasion bombing and shelling along the coast. Previous experience had taught the army command that assaulting infantry were particularly vulnerable to enemy fire from the moment they emerged from their landing craft until they got across the beaches and worked their way inland. The DD tanks were conceived as a means to correct this exposure, by having armor arrive immediately ahead of, or with the assaulting waves of infantry on the beaches.

The DD tanks were a British development of the Sherman M4 tanks for amphibious operations. MacLean and his uninitiated friends at first scoffed at the idea of a steel monster weighing 32 tons being made to float, and even swim to shore, but they soon learned that this was precisely what they would be involved with. The staff instructor led them to the tank park where several DD tanks were parked.

"These vehicles can float and swim, whether you jokers believe it or not, and you'd better pay attention, because you'll be riding in them yourselves right away. The floatation gear has been fully tested and we know it works. The type developed for these tanks adds very little to the dimensions of the tank, so it doesn't really affect the number of tanks that can be loaded in a tank-landing craft, and that is important," added the instructor.

After pausing for emphasis, the instructor continued: "When the tanks are completely water-proofed, through the use of a very sticky gunk called 'Bostick' on every seem and joint on the hull, the DD equipment is utilized. This consists of the collapsible canvas screen that surrounds the tanks, tightly attached to the hull, and erected by rubber tubing that can be filled with compressed air in a matter of a few minutes. When the screens are erected, the tanks will float. It is propelled by the two propellers which you see at the rear of the vehicle, powered by the normal process of running the tank's engines, via the tracks and rear idler wheels. It is abundantly simple, and it can move through the water at about four knots, using the tracks and propellers to steer in much the same fashion as on land."

"You make it all sound so natural and normal to take one of these things into the water. Have you ever been in one when the water got rough?" asked Red McKenna, his interest in the instructor's words just as intense as MacLean's.

"You don't have a lot of freeboard," admitted the instructor, "and when the waves are high, say over four feet, you just don't take them in the water. But you don't want high freeboard sticking out of the water either, or you attract fire from shore emplacements. And remember, your outer shell is only canvas when you are at sea in these tanks, so if you get a burst that tears up your canvas screen, you're on your way to Davy Jones' locker."

"Who all uses these D.D. tanks, and how far from shore do they launch them from the LCT?," inquired MacLean.

"The British and Canadian assault units will be using DD tanks to get ashore. Some of the American formations will be using them too, but we hear that there are others that are not happy with them. The launching of the tanks will be settled between the naval and army commanders in your landing craft, but it will probably be from 3000 to 4000 yards off-shore. That's the safety margin the navy may insist upon."

"Can you shoot the tank guns while swimming shore?" inquired Red McKenna, clearly still skeptical.

"Not unless you want to blow the front of your canvas screen away and let the water in," came the instructor's sarcastic answer. "When you're swimming, the tank is well down below the surface, and the water is near the top of the screen. That's protection for you too. When you get ashore, you can immediately drop the screen and then fire at any targets you see."

"God! I never thought I'd see a Sherman tank swimming in the water, and I can still hardly believe it," concluded McKenna, his head shaking dubiously.

"Everyone else in your squadron has been trained on them, young man," responded the instructor in a tone of some annoyance. "And you soon will be too. If a 20 ton bomber can fly in the air, a 35 ton tank can float in the water. It's all a matter of weight in relation to displacement, as the engineers explain it."

"And luck," added McKenna. "Tanks are built with thick steel skins, so they can ignore small arms fire, and some shell fire. The DD tank takes that advantage away from us because it is vulnerable to small arms fire and flying shrapnel while swimming. Why not just stick with the ordinary tanks then and land as best you can? Why risk getting drowned just to get some tanks in earlier in the battle?"

The instructor was quick to reply to the novices on this question.

"We know the infantry want to have tanks arrive on the beach at the same time as they do, or even earlier. That will be a tremendous advantage for the entire landing assault. Also there are tradeoffs for coming ashore in a swimming tank that you haven't recognized. In the first place, you present a much less obvious target when you are mostly below water level, and you are much harder to hit by fire from shore guns. Secondly, you now know a lot more about these things than the Germans do. The DD tank should be a real surprise to Jerry when you land, and you only land once. After that you shed the canvas screen and fight your tank just like any other tanks. Besides, no one said it was going to be a holiday outing, getting to France."

The amphibious training continued day after day, and frequently at night to preserve secrecy, as McKenna and MacLean became more accustomed to the tanks and the crews they had joined. Both became more appreciative of the skills that they had learned and practised during the long months of training together. MacLean was particularly impressed with the expertise displayed by their driver and crew commander when the two combined their abilities to launch the tank into the water and manoeuver it about toward their practice objectives. The remainder of the crew had little or nothing to do, except sit in their respective places and keep their mouths shut (not always an easy task) while these exercises took place. Mastering the behaviour of the DD tanks in the calm waters close to the shore of the bay was awkward enough, and in more difficult waters the unseaworthy craft were even more unruly.

The launching practice from an LCT was really hair-raising. An LCT was itself an unpredictable vessel, with a flat bottom and its engine and bridge toward the stern. Its homely, blunt hull butted every wave it encountered, as it wallowed along at a top speed of 10 knots. In a "beam sea," it would swing about like a pendulum. Since the DD tanks full speed in the water was only 6 knots, the LCT had to sharply reduce its speed at the time of a launching, to the point where it had very little steerage itself. Its great flat, slab sides tended to catch the wind, making it tricky for the helmsman to position the vessel in the wind for the launching.

The LCT would then lower a large ramp which performed like a monstrous brake in the water, while the vessel slowed and almost seemed to go into reverse to permit the tank to run down its steep plunge into the water. When the tank entered the water, it would sink with the impact until the sea was less than six inches from the top of the canvas pocket around it. Every launching was indeed an adventure, for no two were the same and success was never guaranteed.

Gradually MacLean came to accept the sea-going role of his tank, with the equanimity of his crew mates but he never was able to take it completely for granted.

The practising produced some incidents from time to time too. The Canadian 2nd Armored Brigade published an order that all practice launches of DD tanks would be carried on with crews wearing uniforms only, without web equipment, so that in the event of a sinking, the crews could apply their lessons for "submarine escape," clambering out with minimum impediments and make for the inflated rafts nearby. The emergency drill had been valuable on a few occasions previously, when tanks had sunk in training, but without loss of any crew members.

They were told of a nearby British regiment practicing launchings with DD tanks, that insisted on the crews wearing full battle order and helmets during their training. When one of their tanks turned turtle for some unexplained reason, it quickly sank, taking all of the crew members with it. And furthermore, the British order remained.

The canvas boat structure around the tank and its supporting struts were fragile at the best of times and the craft had to be sailed with the seas rather than against them. If small amounts of water slopped inside the canvas, a bilge pump was available, but heavier seas would certainly swamp it.

CHAPTER III

THE WAR FROM A HIGHER PERSPECTIVE

The Officers' mess of the Fort Garry Horse Regiment was located near Gosport, on the Southampton Water. Though adequate for the time being, it was in no sense palatial. Two red oak and three chestnut trees graced the front lawn of an aging Tudor house, set well back from the road to Fort Gomer. The paint on the stucco panels of the upper two storeys was flaking off. The timbers that divided the panels needed a coat of stain. The clinker brick facing on the ground floor was still in excellent condition, like the steep, slate-covered roof that capped the building. It was a tall, handsome residence. Some maintenance was needed on the fence around the lot, and a good coat of paint would have improved everything, but all in all, it was completely serviceable, free of damage from any of the air raids that had pounded other similar structures nearby.

A bar had been set up on the second floor of the house, in what had been the master bedroom. A broad, carpeted stairway led upward from the front hall in a graceful curve, to a picture-lined hallway on the second floor. Someone had tacked a small sign on the wide door at the near end of the hallway, reading "Murphy's Bar," in honor of Joe Murphy, the irrepressible corporal who attended the officers there.

Slumped in a huge, leather-covered chair in the far corner of the bar sat a long, lank captain, with black hair slicked down like the movie actors of the '30's. He continually fingered the jet-black, dagger-type of moustache which adorned his upper lip. Like most wearers of "hairy martial garbage," as Evelyn Waugh called it, this officer took pride in his moustache, as he stared at his scotch and water on the side table before him. This gentleman was George W. Gibson, recently made second-in-command of B Squadron, behind Major Meindl, a regimental fixture from years past. Captain Gibson was alone in the bar and appeared to be at loose ends, searching for company while he drank.

44

The door opened to admit a serious-looking young lieutenant, who broke into a smile when he spied Gibson across the room.

"Just in time for a little prune juice, Sproule," cried the captain enthusiastically. "How goes the battle? Is your troop about ready to roll?"

"Yes sir. I'm satisfied with them," came the reply. "I don't know what more we can do at our level. I wish we had a few more people like you who have been in action before, to steady them down. Most of them are brimming with confidence, a damned good thing before their first exposure. But I've heard enough about the landing at Dieppe to be a little concerned about the reaction to over-confidence. When we start taking a lot of fire instead of just handing it out, as in practice, does their morale slump drastically? How high was the confidence level in the Calgary Tank Regiment when you went into Dieppe?"

Gibson motioned the younger man to join him at his table while he studied his youthful face. The captain's thick, black eyebrows pinched and the deep-set eyes took on a far-away look. His hand reached for the ever-present stubby, black pipe in his pocket, as he thought about his answer.

"Sproule, I'm glad to see you recognize the signs you mentioned. It's not every young shavetail troop officer that would. I don't want this to sound like another bloody lecture because it's not meant to be. But confidence is what you want to inspire in your men before any battle, offensive or defensive, and it's almost impossible to have too much of it nowadays. They'll know something about what the German .88 mm can do to a tank from lectures they've attended. Some of them will have already talked directly to men with experience in action in Italy, or North Africa, or like me, at Dieppe. They'll have heard an earful about the bloody German weapons. There is no sheltering them from that, and even if there was, when they have their first brush with real, high-powered anti-tank guns, aimed by some of the most experienced Teutonic gunners in the business, they'll gain a mighty respect for the enemy weapons in a real hurry. Whatever illusions they may have that almost all of the fire will be outgoing, they will be shocked to see how much will be incoming. Everyone goes through that shock in their first action, and there is no way of fully preparing people for it. Some never master that shock, and they have to be weeded out. Most get over it, and realize that they are in a hellish competition in which they are certainly going to have to smarten up if they wish to survive. They start out with a lot of confidence in themselves and in their commands and, however much it is dented by their first exposure to enemy fire, they'll remind themselves that other men have faced this sort of thing and still carried out their battle plans, so they can do it too."

"You don't think over-confidence can lead to a shattering disillusionment, with the troops unwilling to obey commanders whom they might feel have misled them?" queried Sproule.

A cloud of pipe smoke rose from Gibson's mouth before he replied.

"Sure, that can happen. But I think it will be rarer in light of what they have been told to expect. If they've had the idea that fighting the German army will be a cake-walk once they get at them, then they are just out of touch with reality, and they'll soon learn better. But much worse would be taking troops into action that lack any confidence in their ability to do what is expected of them. That's almost a certain recipe for disaster. Men won't run risks at all if they don't believe there is any chance of success. And the running of risks is the means by which any battle is won."

Several other officers had wandered into the bar to mark the end of another long day of fussing with details. Administrative trivia seemed particularly annoying at a time when they wanted to focus exclusively on completing the preparations for the tanks and crews in their own troops. Seeing their colleague Matt Sproule in deep and earnest conversation in the far corner with Captain Gibson, they quickly gathered around Captain Gibson's corner to hear more of what they felt they could never hear enough. Sproule was full of questions.

"When you people went to Dieppe, were you pretty optimistic about the outcome of the raid?"

46

"Yes, I think so. The whole idea behind the raid, as it was explained to us shortly before we sailed, was to establish our abilities to fight our way ashore against a defended coast, shoot up the place and the enemy troops in it, and then leave again. Not a particularly brilliant military manoeuver, when you think about it, as I often have. Months ago I heard from a staff officer I know, that it became extremely important at the very top of army command to have somebody on our side do something to indicate that we were serious about a 'second front.' He felt that Dieppe was the outcome."

Lieutenant Sproule's brow clouded. The thought that the planners who had badly miscalculated in connection with exercise "Jubilee," the code name for the Dieppe raid, could make it all happen again in "Overlord," upon which they would soon embark, was deeply troubling.

"I have been reading a few articles about the Dieppe raid in the military journals and they quote some of the top brass, including even Mountbatten, saying that many lessons were learned from the assault on Dieppe which were of great value in planning for the opening of the second front. Maybe Dieppe wasn't just a bloody waste after all," Sproule added.

"I tend to agree with my friend the staff officer, who says 'Balls to all that.' He said that Mountbatten was determined to conduct a series of raids, of ever increasing size, on the French Channel coast to gain amphibious experience with their tactics and equipment for the opening of the second front. Nothing wrong with that. But Jubilee was a scheme that was just a retread of an earlier plan developed by Montgomery and his staff to capture a continental port and use it as a base for expansion into a full scale invasion. My friend tells me that Monty developed the original plan and that the top Canadian command, including Crerar and McNaughton, approved the original and the revised versions of it without change, just as you might expect from a couple of generals who were anxious to be on the right side of the British chiefs at all times. I don't think they gave a damn about what Major-General Roberts said. He was only the Division Commander, directly in command of the raid, and people like Crerar and McNaughton wouldn't be influenced by whatever he might say."

"You're not a Monty fan then," said Sproule.

"Absolutely right there, although he had his moments, I must admit. He won more than he lost. But on this one, it's interesting to read his comments in the press, where he was desperately trying to distance himself from Jubilee after seeing it was a bloody disaster. He had planned its predecessor, "Rutter", which never came off, due to inclement weather. When it was revived a short time later by Mountbatten under the name "Jubilee", it was still almost the same basic plan that Monty had developed. Montgomery then moved on to other things and disavowed the whole damned thing. But it really was essentially his. Once again the old adage: 'Success has many fathers, but failure is always an orphan'."

"But there must have been a lot of redeeming features to "Jubilee" if everyone at the very top supported it. Do you think the whole plan was betrayed to the Germans in advance? Some say it was."

"I can't say, Matt. I'm only a captain, one of the two officers of the Calgary Tanks who landed at Dieppe and then got off again. All the rest were made prisoners or were killed in the fighting. I, like you, serve at a relatively low level in this man's army. But I try to keep my eyes open and my mind alive to what happens. If you forget for a moment all the approvals that the guys with the red tabs on their collars may have offered, advisedly or otherwise, how does the grand plan for the Calgary Tanks strike you? Here was a regiment with utterly no training for close quarter fighting with infantry in a fortified town, and with no intelligence about the surface of the shore on which they were going to land. All of our practices had been on sandy beaches. But Dieppe was covered by hard, chert rocks and boulders that our tank tracks could not grip, so they just spun their tracks. The landing was made in broad daylight, without the benefit of heavy naval and air bombardment, not even to the level set for Rutter, the exercise that was later scratched. Only the light guns of some destroyers were available to help us shoot our way into Dieppe. Without a heavy bombardment, all the defences were intact. The attack was just cut to pieces by the German artillery. Most of the tanks and a fair number of the infantry never got off the beach. Whatever redeeming features of Jubilee commended it to the top army brass, none of us recognized them."

"Do you think the Germans were surprised by the raid? Surprise was supposed to be the central theme of "Jubilee," wasn't it?" asked Lieutenant Sproule.

"I suppose there was some surprise for the Germans, in the sense that I do not believe the whole raid had been betrayed to them in advance," answered Gibson. "But they were reasonably alert to our approach, and responded very strongly. If there was any real surprise for the Germans, it was probably that the assault was attempted at all without a heavy bombardment to soften up the defenses. It defied all the basic principles of assault landings against a defended coast, and so it failed. I don't think we gained a scrap of knowledge or understanding from the Dieppe raid that we didn't already have or should have had. It was just a god-damned foul-up in planning as well as in execution, and now those responsible for it are trying to make allowances for the wastage of men and material that resulted. 'Excuses for the inexcusable', I would call it."

"I hope we're not heading for another Dieppe when we go ashore," said Lieutenant Art Reynolds, a solid-looking lieutenant who led 1 Troop in C Squadron.

Gibson eyed him through the pungent blue cloud of pipe smoke hanging around them. He tapped ashes from his pipe into the ash tray, glanced again at his listeners, and said very carefully to them, "I share your hopes. I firmly believe that if Dieppe taught anybody anything, it was that it's great to surprise the enemy, but if the surprise part of it fails, you must have all the help you can get from any supporting arms within the army, as well as the navy and the air force. From all the signs that we have around here, I am sure they got that message."

Then dinner was announced in the dining room downstairs. Gibson, with Sproule and the rest of the officers in the bar rose and slowly filed out.

"Not a word of all this to Colonel Morton please," cautioned Gibson. "Commanding this regiment leaves him with more than enough on his plate already."

"Not a word of it," assured Lieutenant Sproule, as he rose and joined his fellow officers wandering down to the dining room. Sproule had an enormous respect for Captain Gibson, along with a certain amount of restrained fear. He shared these feelings with the other officers, both above and below Gibson in rank. The troop commanders, being lieutenants in every case, were in awe of Captain Gibson, not simply because he outranked them, but more particularly because of his broad and comprehensive knowledge of military activities, a knowledge which he kept expanding through his own reading of any army publication available, and through his contacts with certain well-placed officers in Army Intelligence who knew him and seemed to confide in him. Furthermore, Gibson was the only officer in the Regiment who had been in action in the current conflict, albeit very shortly.

Other regimental officers of equal or senior rank to Gibson also held him in respect, if not in admiration, for his ability to eloquently articulate a problem or a solution within a minimum of words. His sarcasm could be biting and devastating at meetings or at meal time, which made him a crowd of one in the mess, not infrequently. That he should have been promoted at least one rank, was beyond any question, if he could just show greater deference and willing obedience to the commanders above him, both within and beyond the unit. But that was not in Gibson's nature. Quite indiscriminate in his criticisms, and certainly more inclined towards silence than loquacity when his opinion or comment was invited, he gave it, frankly and sometimes mercilessly. Much as the senior officers appreciated the benefit of the thoughts he would express, they sometimes shuddered at the ill-concealed scorn and ridicule that he, a mere captain, poured on some policy or plan developed by senior army command. They had decided that, at least for now, Captain Gibson was a good man to have along, but that he should remain a captain for the time being.

CHAPTER IV

THE PRELUDE

The arrival of brand new Sherman tanks in May of 1944 for the regiment was greeted with a mixed reception. Considerable mileage had been built up on a lot of the tanks in use up to that time, so the decision to have new vehicles for the assault was welcome to most of the troops. However, the change meant that all the tanks would have to return to Lulworth Ranges to 'shoot in' the new tank guns and have all of the gunsights properly adjusted. At Lulworth, gunners would fire live ammunition in the Browning .30 calibre machinegun at a distant target, and then adjust the cross hairs or lines in the gunsight to coincide precisely with the path taken by the tracers being fired. Since the master gun was co-axially mounted with the machinegun in the mantlet, (the heavy steel shield that protected and moved with the guns on the outside of the turret) the path taken by the machinegunfire was also a measure of where the shells from the master gun would fall. Through actually shooting the guns at targets at measured distances, the gunners could further refine the setting of their sights to correspond exactly with where the fire was landing.

The gunsights were of course mounted on the gun assembly; a telescope peering through a small hole in the mantlet to the right of the gun.

The binoculars used by the crew commander were marked identically with the markings in the gunner's sight with extra lines equidistant from each other on the vertical and horizontal axes, called "graticules." These markings allowed the crew commanders to communicate changes in sightings by common units of measurement, to their gunners.

Ken MacLean was much impressed with the empathy between Ron Osborne and Sergeant Chapman, when they "shot their guns in." After only a very few rounds, they were both fully satisfied with the sight settings, and the rest of the crew were impressed with the accuracy of their shooting, as verified and tested in the course of actual firing.

Ken had begun to feel more comfortable in his new role as the loader operator of a combat unit. Normally the first member of the turret crew to enter the tank, he would clamber through the turret hatch and under the breech of the master gun to take his position on the small round seat on the left side of the turret wall, directly behind the .30 calibre Browning machinegun. The loader operator's prime job was to load the master gun with the type of ammunition called for by the gunner, and to feed boxes of belted ammunition into the machinegun as and when required.

MacLean was also responsible for operating the radio equipment in the tank, known then as a No. 19 Wireless Set. This set consisted really of three separate networks; the main "A" set which permitted communication between the tank and all other radios in the squadron or the regiment on the same network, which could extend over a radius of 10 or more miles; a much smaller "B" set which could be used (although seldom utilized) for usually short range communication within the troop of tanks; and the 'I.C.' network, which allowed people to intercommunicate within the tank itself, above the roar of the engines and the noise of battle, through the use of individual head sets and microphones. Netting- in the radio with other radios on the same net was the regular job of the loader operator, along with the maintenance of the radio equipment, which included the various settings used to tune the aerials for sending and receiving on the variometer attached to the side of the No. 19 set. As MacLean came to realize, although maintaining communications was considered only a secondary responsibility for his position in the tank, it added a great deal of stress to his job, because radios could be temperamental, especially when the traveling was the roughest; the weather and noise the worst; and the need for communication the greatest.

Above MacLean's head was a rotating periscope which afforded him a limited view of the outside world in the direction in which the prism faced, but nothing in any other direction. But his job was really inside the turret, where he was usually a very busy man, so his view of the outside was of less importance than that of the rest of the crew.

Ken had it drummed into his head in every lecture he had attended, that a tank is an offensive weapon, built to bring heavy fire into a battle, whether in offence or defense. Consequently, everyone in the tank crew was really there to serve the guns, bringing them into action at the right time and place. The gunner was regarded as the absolutely key man in the crew, since lives depended on his ability to hit his targets and knock them out before the targets could knock Osborne out. The premium for top grade gunnery was high. There was no room for mediocrity. MacLean and the rest of his crew were more than satisfied with their gunner.

Ron Osborne was a short, quiet and laconic man. He slipped into his seat and played his destructive role as if to the manner born. Dark piercing eyes and a strong set to the mouth and chin left a deep impression of a solid, determined young man who had no time for nonsense. The complete ease with which he swung the turret around with the traversing handle in his right hand, while cranking the gun level up or down with his left hand produced a rhythm reminiscent of a smooth orchestra leader. There were never any jerks or yanks as he quickly picked up his targets and ranged on them. One thing he did insist upon was extra care by the drivers in passing ammunition up to the turret from the bins down below, lest the quick swinging of the turret should jam a shell casing while being passed into the turret.

Osborne's feet hovered over the two pedals on the turret floor directly ahead of him, ever ready to depress them and fire the guns whenever opportunities arrived. His head seldom left the padded sight for the guns directly in front of his forehead, when he was using the guns. His periscope resembled all the others in the vehicle, when he was simply searching the foreground, but he used it only occasionally.

Mounted above the breech of the master gun was a mechanical assembly of rods, controls and clamps which connected the gun to the roof of the turret. This was the Westinghouse gyrostabilizer, designed to maintain the level of the gun in a pre-set position, notwithstanding the motion of the tank as it traveled across country. The idea behind the device was to improve the standard of gunnery while the tank was in motion and overcome the necessity to stop the vehicle in order to fire the master gun accurately. The gyrostabilizer was a good idea, but it required considerable further development before Osborne, or any other Canadian tank gunner, would put it to use. It was not yet effective, and created a hazard for the turret crew that none were willing to risk.

Commands to Robinson and Metcalfe down below in the drivers' compartment were never numerous. After "driver advance," Chapman left Robinson very much on his own to drive the vehicle as he saw fit, which pleased both of them. Robinson, a large powerfully built man with thick, black hair and bushy eyebrows, also inspired great confidence. He reluctantly consented to be spelled off infrequently on long journeys by Metcalfe, his co-driver, but he much preferred to do most of the driving himself. He was a mechanical perfectionist, greatly relieved to be away from the Churchill tanks with which he had worked previously. He was almost in love with the engines that powered his Sherman so fittingly. Somewhat put out by the canvas gear attached to the sides of his tank to create its DD tank capabilities, he accepted the swimming role that had been imposed upon all tanks in B & C Squadrons with as much grace as possible. Other than an occasional "Steady as she goes, Admiral," muttered quietly between clenched teeth when the tank was swimming, Allan took on the extra responsibilities that came with a DD tank without complaint.

Jack Metcalfe was the easy-going member of the crew. About 26 years of age, with wavy, brown hair and a pleasant, open face, he took his cues from Allan Robinson, whom he almost worshiped. He was completely adequate as a driver, on the infrequent occasions when he assumed Allan's position in the driver's seat, but spent most of his time helping other people in the crew. As bow gunner with his own Browning machinegun in the hull of the tank, he looked forward to putting his shooting ability to use once the tank landed and the canvas covering was dropped off, but until then he had to bide his time. Jack appeared to be a steady performer, happy to be in the crew he was in, and doing the job he held.

It was apparent from the experience gained during maneuvers, that the crew of Sergeant Chapman's tank, like the others in the regiment, regarded themselves as a separate social unit living together by day and sleeping as a group beside the tank at night. They became interdependent upon one another, each having a role to play in cooking the food, attending to tank maintenance, scrounging special food delicacies, cleaning up the pots after meals, or standing guard duties at night. Rank meant little or nothing within the unit making up each tank's crew, as officers, non-commissioned officers and men talked to one another freely and frankly. A close parallel undoubtedly existed with the crews of individual planes in the R.C.A.F. At the same time, the final decision on matters of consequence was understood to be that of the crew commander, without argument or discussion, and Chapman left no room for doubt on that point.

The new tanks supplied to the Fort Garry's for the forthcoming operation were all M4 Sherman tanks, although they varied slightly, depending upon the Mark issued. Perhaps the most common type issued to Canadian troops was the M4A4, made by Chrysler and powered by five 6 cylinder engines turning a common drive shaft. Known as the Chrysler Multi-bank or 5-bank engine, it turned out to be a dependable and effective power plant, contradicting the many critics who contended that the engines were too complicated and would pose problems, particularly in keeping them all synchronized. There were also a number of Sherman M4A1 tanks of similar proportions, but powered by Continental radial engines, which seemed somewhat less powerful and certainly less dependable than the 5-bank Chrysler engines.

Both of these types were built and delivered with a 75 mm master gun and two .30 calibre machineguns, one firing from the bow gunner's position in the hull, and the other co-axially mounted with the master gun in the turret, as already mentioned. Each of these tanks also arrived from the Tank Delivery Regiment with a large .50 calibre Browning machinegun mounted on a swivel atop the turret hatch, but most crew commanders removed it from this position. Although it was a fine weapon for firing at aircraft or soft vehicles, it necessitated its gunner climbing half-way out of the turret hatch to aim and fire it, an exposure that would assure an early death for him in normal action conditions.

Each of the three fighting squadrons of a regiment like the Fort Garry Horse had four troops of tanks, and one or two tanks in each squadron headquarters. In all of the troops, also comprising four tanks each, at least one of the tanks would be a "Firefly" tank, a Sherman M4A2 in its official designation. These were vehicles that had been significantly renovated by British Army Ordinance in response to the need for an "up gunned" tank that would be able to redress the balance, to some extent at least, with the more recent high velocity guns carried by enemy tanks. The master gun in a Firefly was a long-barreled, high muzzle-velocity gun which fired a larger projectile, weighing 17 pounds; hence its name "the 17 pounder". Other modifications in the Firefly Sherman included a counter-balancing weight installed at the back of the turret, with the radio moved further back to accommodate the greater gun recoil and the much larger and heavier breech. There was also a cut-away in the turret floor to allow for the much larger shells for the gun; and the bow gunner's position was sacrificed to provide extra storage space for the ammunition. This reduced the crew to four from the usual five men in an ordinary Sherman.

The Sherman tanks weighed about 35 tons when fully loaded, and could travel for 100 miles without fuel replenishment, at speeds up to 26 miles per hour. Only the 75 mm Shermans were modified as DD tanks for amphibious operations because the longer-barreled 17 pounder guns made the attachment of collapsible screens impossible. Extra steps were taken to conceal the existence of the Firefly tanks with canvas covers, and even more the DD tanks from prying eyes that might be watching the training maneuvers. The hope was to deliver some complete surprises to the Germans when the cross channel assault took place.

The landing plan for the DD tanks, as explained to MacLean and his colleagues, anticipated that they would lead the landing forces ashore. Once the tanks grounded in water shallow enough to permit them to travel forward on their tracks, the front of the canvas screen could be lowered to permit the tank guns to engage enemy targets, while the rear screen could remain upright to prevent following waves from swamping the engine before the tank was fully ashore. In actual practice, most DD tank crews intended to run their tanks completely ashore immediately, dropping the entire canvas screening away so that they could operate as conventional armor as quickly as possible.

The Firefly tanks would be brought into wading depths by the L.C.T.'s transporting them, after the DD tanks had established bridge-heads with the assaulting infantry.

In the lectures given to the Fort Garrys and indeed to all the tank men who would be in the assault on the enemy coast, relatively little was said about the comparisons between the tanks and guns of the Allied Forces, and those of the German army. The experiences of other Canadian troops, who had been fighting against the German forces for many months in Sicily and Italy, were certainly known to higher command before these lectures were delivered early in 1944. But little if any use was made of this knowledge, whether through ignorance or as a part of a deliberate program to play down or even suppress particulars of enemy strengths. The size and power of German tanks was usually mentioned only along with comments about their lack of speed and manoeuverability, implying that when all characteristics were compared and considered, there was a fairly even balance between the tanks of the two forces. Nothing was said about the new long-barreled 75 mm gun developed by the Germans months earlier. These were matters left to be discovered by the troops when battle was joined.

Lecturers in England did nothing to disabuse their audiences of the assumption that approximate parity existed in the striking power of many of the tanks and anti-tank guns used by the Germans and by the Allied Forces, and that this meant that there would be approximate equality in the use and performance of weapons of the same calibre. It was a considerable shock for Canadian troops to discover that although most of their tanks fired 75 mm shells, many German tanks and anti-tank guns fired ammunition of the same calibre, but with much larger shell casings and more explosive material, which dramatically increased muzzle velocities of their shells to almost twice those applicable to the M4 Sherman tank. The higher velocity shells allowed the Germans to penetrate any armored fighting vehicle opposing them. By contrast, the low velocity Sherman 75 mm gun was at a serious disadvantage against the more heavily armored vehicles opposing them.

Whatever could have been said about 75 mm tank guns, the reputation and fame of the great German 88 mm dual purpose gun was widespread and undisputed. MacLean and his friends had heard about its legendary attributes from veterans from Sicily and Italy. The balance between the descriptions of enemy and allied strengths had to be decided in advance of any major campaign, and in this case, the decision favored an under-emphasis of the enemy's strengths.

The last days at Lulworth for the Fort Garrys for testing and adjusting guns and sights on the tanks passed quickly. They were blessed with pleasant sunshine and increasing familiarity and friendship between all tank crew members. Then it was back to Fort Moncton on the Solent, where frantic preparations for invasion could be seen everywhere. A new sense of commitment to the tasks at hand was evident among the members of all the armed services there.

By the end of May, the scattered pieces of the Regiment were pulled together again. They began moving to what had been previously designated as "Concentration Areas." Training was over, and everyone in the Fort Garrys knew it. The next movement would be into action; to put into execution what everyone had wearied of practicing. There was a certain grimness in the faces of the men around him, MacLean thought, as he watched them pack up and stow their gear. Naturally they realized that for some among them, this would probably be the last time they would ever pack their gear away, but they, like soldiers everywhere, took comfort in the old biblical reassurance, "A thousand shall fall at they right hand, but it shall not come nigh thee."

There seemed a certain hollowness in the over-hearty and extra-jocular exchanges between the tank crewmen, intended to bolster spirits as they went about their routine duties. Beneath the banter Ken thought he could detect a greater seriousness that was not out of place, as men switched their thinking from practicing war exercises to preparing for war. These men seemed proud of their regiment and determined to give a good account of themselves; not just for themselves alone, but for all the others in their regiment that were depending upon them. MacLean considered himself fortunate to be with a unit in that frame of mind. Commanders could ask for nothing more from them.

Major Blanchard, commander of A Squadron, joined with Major Bray from C Squadron and Major Meindl in a series of private discussions with Colonel Morton. These talks were obviously important, because no one was to interrupt them on any count.

Then, all the officers began to attend briefing sessions every day. A thorough water-proofing of all vehicles, through the application of more of the sticky 'Bostic' to all seams and joints was undertaken. Then the tanks moved off to a number of camps set up in the marshalling area in late May, where they were divided into separate loads for specific ships that would transport them to wherever they were going. Ken and his fellow soldiers were all told that movements outside the marshalling area were prohibited henceforward. They were closely guarded by barbed wire barriers to assure full security.

As darkness fell on June 3, each tank crew was told the identification number of its LCT. Sergeant Chapman informed his crew that they would travel in LCT 1402. Following this announcement, the entire regiment mounted their tanks and crawled slowly down toward the harbor at Bay House.

As they crept along, they passed through the small town of Alverstoke, a community they all knew well, a short distance from the hards. Although the hour was getting late, a few people who had been trying to sleep, poked their heads out of darkened open windows, accurately sensing that this was no ordinary training exercise. They knew that they were watching the beginning of a very large venture from which many of those traveling past would not return.

Driver Allan Robinson had to attend to his driving in the darkness, but the rest of the crew rode at ease on the tank deck, leaning against the turret. They waved a hand now and then in response to a handkerchief fluttering from a window. The sound of hundreds of mighty engines, even though running slowly, drowned any possibility of talk between tank crews and civilian bystanders. Nevertheless, there were unmistakable signs of emotion and tears among some of the watchers, as the soldiers passed in seemingly endless lines.

"Do they know something that we don't?" asked Jack Metcalfe from the turret top. "We haven't even been in action yet, but they're sorry for us already."

Sergeant Chapman looked sharply at his bow gunner. "You never know, Jack. They don't know which ones, but they do know it will be some of those they see now, and it saddens them. They've seen more of wars than we have."

As the slowly advancing column of tanks reached the 'hards,' as they were called, the paved docks from which the loading on different vessels would proceed, Allan drove onward along the dimly-lit dock extremely cautiously. He pointed his vehicle toward the ramp to LCT 1402, which he could discern further along, pausing slightly to see the tank ahead of him safely out of the way. MacLean's tank was one of five on their vessel. He was surprized as he and his crewmates looked around them to see the broad panoply of amphibious craft being loaded in the LCT's. They anticipated that since the tanks were supposed to lead the assault ashore, there would be nothing but tanks in the vessels loading at their dock. This proved to be a mistaken belief, because the mixture was astonishing. As daylight spread, they could see ships with tanks in them, all right, but also there were trucks, jeeps, anti-tank guns and infantry-carriers being loaded in other vessels nearby. The variety was mind-boggling.

Once loaded, no one was allowed ashore again. By eight o'clock on the morning of June 4, all of B Squadron had been loaded and their ships left their places along the docks to sail slowly upstream, and tie up to buoys where they all awaited a general moveout.

MacLean and the rest of his crew, with nothing to do until their LCT sailed away, watched fascinated, as ships of all sizes and shapes moved about in Southampton Water around them. Some of them had been given the red band which identified them as part of "J" Force. All "J" force ships had been designated to carry the troops of the 3rd Canadian Division and the 2nd Armored Brigade, to their common destinations somewhere across the Channel.

The sun made several frequently interrupted appearances throughout a fine day. The thousands of waiting servicemen were happy to stare at speeding launches tearing back and forth among the dozens of vessels around them. The wind was sharp and surprisingly strong for a sheltered anchorage. Clouds passing overhead, gapped by wide stretches of blue sky, were hurried along by sudden gusts of wind. Although it was all a day of waiting, no one could be bored with the fascinating, ever-changing scene around them.

There were ships that had once been channel steamers, loaded with infantry in full battle order, easing downward through the crowded waterway toward their anchorage; swarms of landing craft of all shapes and sizes packed with troops and equipment; menacing warships of breath-taking size and description; and big, gray transport ships, all awaiting some magic call or signal to move out of the harbor.

But the ordinary people aboard this amazing array of ships, boats and landing craft had no knowledge of when they might sail, nor even less, of where they would sail. Certainly, some senior officers knew more about it, but they weren't saying. But there was little doubt in anyone's mind that their destination would be somewhere on the French Channel coast.

Still in harbor, tied to the buoys, the multitude of ships with their curious cargoes remained through June 4. The following day was much like it, with even stronger winds blowing out of the west, and banks of consolidated cloud drifting rapidly overhead only to give way to patches of blue sky. Weather reports talked of "unsettled conditions."

Crap games aboard ships began in earnest among some of the troops who had tired of watching masses of shipping move about. The stakes were high, as the dice rolled and tumbled in many nooks and crannies. Although the waiting must have been tiresome on the crowded decks of the steamers, on the LCT's where more room for movement was available, there was little chaffing or complaining.

About mid-afternoon of June 5th, the great mass of the invasion fleet began to move down, away from the moorages. The vessels sailed out past Portsmouth and the Isle of Wight. Everyone knew then that the invasion was "on." The day for which they had all trained, studied and sweated, had finally arrived. As evening advanced, the sea became noticeably rougher for the shallow-draught LCT's. They wallowed in the open channel swell, into which they pointed their blunt, gray painted bows, rolling and yanking about in the strong wind which swept up the Channel. The violence of the weather overwhelmed any lingering sentimental feeling about the final disappearance from sight of British land astern.

MacLean could tolerate, but certainly not enjoy, the yawing and heaving of their LCT. He was in no danger of losing his lunch, but many around him were less fortunate. Some were already running to the rails to bring up, while others hurriedly gulped seasickness pills, futilely hoping for instant cures. It did not augur well for a pleasant channel crossing.

Immediately after passing the outer harbor boom at the entrance to Portsmouth, the officers opened their sealed containers to extract the maps they found in them. For the first time they studied the real invasion beaches on "Juno beach" where the Canadian forces would land. It became apparent why their ships had a red "J" on them. The map displayed the actual place names on top of the code names, the phony names with which they had become so familiar during training. As the force of the wind continued to increase, the rolling of the ship increased as well. A large fraction of the men aboard were falling victim to seasickness, and the squadron commander, not looking notably well himself, became much concerned about the condition of his men. Here they were all expected to make an assault landing on a hostile coast within a few hours, while many of them lay groaning and reeling with the worst seasickness he had ever seen.

Ken MacLean felt distinctly queasy and very uncomfortable as he stared out into the blackness that surrounded the darkened armada, pitching and rolling in the wind-driven seas. He tried to focus his mind upon the comments of Lieutenant Gray, when he spoke to all of the men in 4 Troop gathered around him. He heard a brief repetition of the general information about the landing that they had heard previously. They would support the infantry of the 8th brigade, with whom they had been training. They would have 7th Brigade on their right and the infantry of the British 3rd Division on their left, going ashore. Gray also repeated that the 3rd Canadian Division would land on Juno Beach, and that the beach sector identified as "Nan" on the east side of Juno would be their responsibility.

Lieutenant Gray then singled out the three crew commanders under his supervision to emphasize what he wanted to accomplish with the tanks in his troop. MacLean and the others listened closely to some new information which had just been provided. They heard him say that the violence of the weather imperilled the entire plan for DD tank launching, but if they were to be launched, it would be at a point three or four miles from shore. They were told that they would thread their way in to a landing between Bernières-sur-Mer and St. Aubin-sur-Mer. After landing, they must penetrate the coastal defences and hurry inland in the direction of Bèny-sur- Mer to broaden the bridge-head. Ken was impressed with the comprehensiveness of Gray's briefing. They were told of the roles being played by the Navy and the Air Force, who would be doing their utmost to assist the assault. This would reassure the troops that the planners had gone the second mile in providing a massive bombardment for the beach ahead of them. It would not be a repeat performance of the fiasco at Dieppe.

Touch-down on the beach for B Squadron would be possibly ahead of, but certainly with the infantry assault landing at 08:04 hours. Gray mentioned to them that the Americans would land earlier on Utah and Omaha beaches, well to the west of them, because of differences in tide times, and that the British landing on Gold Beach immediately west of them, would be slightly earlier also. Timing had been established to take advantage of daylight landings when the tide was low enough to expose the enormous array of hostile obstacles, most of them mined, that the Germans had installed along all of the beaches. These deadly obstructions would have to be removed by frogmen and engineers at various locations so that assault craft could pass through, and lanes could be cut across the minefields to permit tanks and infantry to advance ashore.

After the briefing, MacLean wandered slowly to the side of the ship to ponder what he had heard and what lay ahead. He looked with envy at the figure of Jack Metcalfe, snoring peacefully against a bulwark of the ship. Nothing was going to deprive Jack of his rest.

Looking out across a tortured waste of heaving water, through which LCT 1402 continued to batter its way, MacLean's mind dwelt upon how small a figure he was in relation to the enormous enterprise of which he had become a part. It seemed too much for him; too many and too large machines of war surging forward to an inevitable clash with the immense German machines of war awaiting them ahead. He felt that it would have been so much better if the great collision of forces that everyone had planned, just proceeded without him, for he was only one small man in the vortex of a world-shaking event. If this was fear, MacLean knew he had his share of it, and an upset stomach as well. Looking at the faces of his comrades at the briefing, he was sure that they must have felt much the same; if they had played their cards differently, they wouldn't be in this hellish jam now.

But Lieutenant Gray had anticipated their states of mind very accurately at his final briefing a few minutes earlier.

"Every man in this assault, whether in the navy, the air force, or particularly in the army, feels as you men do now," he had said. "It's normal to feel apprehension before going into battle; to feel too small for the events that are too big around you. Remember that the Germans are going to feel the same way pretty soon themselves, when this invasion hits them, only more so, because they're going to receive more bombarding than they have ever had, no matter where they have served before. If the Allies are ever going to crush the Germans, they have to come to Europe to do it. That is what you men have trained for months and years to do."

"There is no one anywhere better fitted or trained to do this job than you are. That's why you are here. So don't take counsel of your fears, however normal they may be. Master them, and you won't let your comrades down, for they are depending on you, just as you depend on them."

The tank crews were greatly reassured by Gray's comments, even though they were a trifle corny. The men were secretly relieved to hear from their leader that they were not alone in feeling insignificant in such a massive operation, and they like everyone else, had the responsibility to conquer this feeling and go on with the job that other men were relying upon them to do. Sergeant Chapman added a poignant comment to the members of his crew; "If you think someone else should be doing what you are doing, forget it. There is no one else. We do it, or it doesn't get done."

As the night wore on, the rolling and swaying continued unabated. Waves of four to five feet drove up the Channel, beating upon the blunt bows and flat, slab-sided hulls of the vessels bearing the Fort Garrys on their southward course to France. MacLean was struck by the difficulties faced by the naval personnel in charge of navigating his vessel, doggedly maintaining their precise station in the immense flotilla, as it sailed across the gale blowing abeam of them. It could not have been easy for them, sailing in the darkness without lights, and probably without much inter-ship communication either, to avoid premature betrayal of their presence off the enemy coast.

Like many, many other soldiers at sea that night with time on their hands, MacLean's thoughts wandered back to his family at home. What would they be doing at that moment, about eight hours earlier in the day? It would be supper time in Edmonton and they would be totally unaware of the events taking place around him for another day or more - a good thing too. Idly, he reflected on the consequences in his family of a notice from the Government that the Minister - "was very sorry to inform you that your son did not survive the fighting ...," and so on. Apart from the normal grief for the loss of a son, Ken's parents would feel confirmation of their worst fears.

From the very beginning, MacLean's family had never understood his interest in tanks. The pictures in the newsreels of armor employed in the earlier stages of the war, which had fascinated him, had had the reverse effect upon his parents. Deeply concerned that he had joined a tank regiment, of all things, they would say, "I knew it would end like this," reviving their horror of the pictures of burning and destroyed tanks that also made the news. There he was, very much alive and possessing the same chances of life, or death, as the many other soldiers around him. He knew it would do no good to ponder thoughts of this kind anyway. He forced his mind back to the scene before him, sitting on the deck-plates of "Bailiff," the name that they had printed in small letters on the left sponson of the DD tank that his crew called home.

Off to the right, some sort of naval encounter seemed to have taken place in the darkness ahead. The sounds of heavy guns firing came to them as brilliant flashes were reflected in the blackness above them. But strangely, probably miraculously, no sign appeared that the great convoy sailing with them had been seen or identified yet. The thought crossed the minds of some of MacLean's crew mates that the Germans might be watching them sail into a deadly trap. Others thought it possible that the enemy might be completely fooled, and that the landing could be a 'cakewalk,' although that possibility was quickly ridiculed and dismissed.

"No one anywhere has ever found the Krauts to be stupid, or sound asleep. Just be thankful that they haven't seen us yet. When they do pick up us, we'll hear from them," commented Mr. Gray to his crewmen, sitting on their tank just ahead of MacLean's vehicle.

Close to dawn, the steady, bass drone of many heavy bombers passing unseen in the darkness overhead, raised the spirits of the men in the boats. Smiles of satisfaction spread from face to face and the thumbs-up sign was exchanged among tank crews, as recognition spread that the heavies were going to plaster the same defences they would soon attempt to breach. The sharper bark of the engines of medium bombers had been heard several times during the night, flying at much lower altitudes on missions of destruction against coastal events west of Le Havre. No one aboard any of the ships toiling southward could say much about the effectiveness of these air raids at that point. They would find out about that later, after the landing. But everyone's hopes were buoyed by the sounds of aircraft: allied aircraft, swarming to their help, flying thousands of missions directly in aid of getting the troops ashore. It looked as though the planners had pulled out all the stops for this attack.

But the sea continued in torment from the blasts of wind driving strongly up the Channel. The stars had permanently disappeared behind the overcast. Smoke from the exhaust stacks of the ships was snatched away by the gale. The rigging on LCT 1402 could be heard slapping and pinging, as the force of the gusts continued unabated. Ken's apprehension continued, as he peered ahead at the rushing swells, pondering what waves that size would do to a floating DD tank.

He became convinced that there would have to be a change; either the wave action closer to the French coast would have to subside, or they would be obliged to abandon all hope of a launching offshore. The swimming tanks with their two feet of freeboard could never survive the combers that hissed past him in the darkness. He even wondered whether the violence of the Channel weather would spoil the plan for the landing generally, causing delays and therefore disruptions for other regiments elsewhere in the assault. No one in the entire armada was happy about the weather.

Very soon after the heavy bombers passed over the fleet, flashes could be observed ahead where big bombs were landing and heavy German flak was replying to the aircraft. Then MacLean perceived a wavering black line below the flashes, which he soon identified as his first sight of the coast of Normandy. Dawn seemed to break very rapidly after this sighting, and the buoys marking the channel in which their LCT had to sail were noticed on either side, exactly where they were supposed to be.

"It looks like the navy was on the bit for this show," said Allan Robinson admiringly. Ron Osborne, though lost in thought, nodded his agreement. "How'd you like to have been one of the poor guys detailed to plant those buoys out there a day or so ago? They're probably getting their thrills today as they try to disarm the mines on the beach obstacles up ahead. Oh to be a frog man eh? They've got to be even nuttier than us."

A gray dawn advanced, revealing waves still breaking above the top of the doors of the LCT, a cloudy sky and a thin mist hugging the water further out to sea. It had not been a restful night for many on board; some still seasick enough to make them indifferent to the arrival of an early breakfast, and others yawning and peering owlishly at one another from tired, blood-shot eyes. Mercifully, there still seemed no recognition by the Germans of the arrival of the invasion fleet, slowly moving into position.

As the hour of battle approached, the last few words of the padre's prayer, given in the pre-dawn darkness to a cluster of men gathered beside the rear-most tank aboard the vessel, still haunted their minds. Quoting, as always, from his beloved Shakespeare, he recited King Henry's words in Henry V, spoken just before the battle of Agincourt:

"O God of Battles! Steel my soldiers' hearts;
Possess them not with fear; take from them now
The sense of reckoning, if the opposed numbers
Pluck their hearts from them ..."[1]

Their gentle padré had always been one for literary references to elaborate on his Christian beliefs, and this one struck home with his listeners. They understood that others before them had implored God to "steel my soldiers' hearts" for a battle about to begin, and had been comforted just to realize that others had felt just as they did.

The gloom of the night nullified the camouflage of the diverse cluster of ships and their contents. Crap games ended and breakfasts were bolted down by those who could eat. All the DD tank crews were attending to a final waterproofing and sealing of their tanks. Radio sets were switched on and radio operators like Ken MacLean checked the radio nets once more, tuning their variometers to make certain they were getting the maximum broadcasting and receiving signal possible. The drill for launching the DD tanks was reviewed one more time in rehearsal, for the particular attention of drivers and crew commanders.

At about 05:15, black and white visibility returned, although it was officially still before sunrise. The planners had estimated that at this hour, the landing craft would arrive within range of many of the enemy coastal guns, even though the misty conditions that morning made it extremely doubtful that they could be seen from the shore.

---

[1] Shakespeare - King Henry V - Act IV, Scene 1, Lines 309 & ff.

Then the naval bombardment began. Bombing by the Lancasters had not long ended when the huge shells of the naval vessels erupted from the ships. No one had ever heard such appalling noise, such thunderous roars, such earsplitting blasts on all sides, as the many grey warships that had accompanied the assault craft all the way from Portsmouth harbor, swung to and fired their main armament. Without pauses or interruption the terrible bombardment continued. Half-smiling; half trembling, MacLean and his friends watched awestruck, as salvo after salvo of mighty artillery bellowed and smoked around them.

The wind dropped noticeably, though the sea was still running sizeable waves. It seemed that conditions were improving, as they moved closer to land. Everyone was still dubious about being launched into the rollers they could see beyond the LCT. Osborne and MacLean strained to hear the signal which would come over the radio, telling them whether to swim the tanks from the present location or wait for the vessel to approach closer to the coast. There were mixed feelings about the lack of a decision. It would be far better to launch in calmer water closer to shore, more like the waters in which they had practiced. On the other hand, the closer to shore they sailed, the greater the chances of being hit by enemy coastal gunfire, which had began to flash from a number of locations along the shore. A well-placed shell would mean that nobody would get off the boat.

After a long and tense delay, word came through about 06:30. The "floater" signal was given, advising that they should prepare to launch from about 5,000 yards offshore, close to where they were then sailing.

CHAPTER V

THE LANDING AND EARLY ATTACKS

Vigorous discussion between Naval officers and senior army officers took place, as the flotilla approached the coast amid a few splashes from long range German guns. The question, of course, was whether or not to launch the "swimmer" tanks. Word of these arguments reached all the way down to the tank crewmen, who were certainly interested in their outcome, having to conform to whatever decision was reached.

It was well known that many navy men wanted nothing to do with DD tanks, considering them unseaworthy at the best of times, and a serious nuisance to the launching ships when they paused offshore to launch them. In the face of the level of the seas running on the morning of June 6, a number of senior naval officers advised strongly against launching "swimmers".

On the other hand, the argument from the army point of view was that the infantry badly needed armored support when they hit the beaches, and the best way to deliver it was through the use of DD tanks, which would lead, or accompany them ashore. Besides, the traditional rivalry between the navy and the army generated the thought in the minds of some army officers that the navy wanted to interfere in the way in which the army fought a land battle, a point of view bound to polarize discussions between the two services.

A shout from someone aboard LCT 1402 drew attention to launchings already under way by the vessels transporting the First Hussars Regiment, and therefore, wisely or not, the alarm button was pressed and preparations to launch began forthwith among the Fort Garrys.

MacLean's tank was the third to be launched by LCT 1402. Much went through the minds of all the crew-members as they clambered into their respective places in their tank, and bid goodbye to the few members of the ship's crew standing about. Ken certainly wondered, and his crew-mates must have wondered too, whether they were seeing the last of the world about them, unsettling and disturbing though it was at the time, as they set out on their precarious voyage. Their apprehensions about getting to shore transcended their apprehensions of what would happen when they got there, but it was time to go, and off they went.

The launching of the tanks from LCT 1402 went surprisingly well. The naval personnel were particularly impressed, watching the un-gainly-looking vehicles waddling into the water with their canvas screens extended. Being accustomed to the substantial steel walls of naval vessels, they shrank from even the thought of putting to sea in a canvas-covered blob of steel weighing 35 tons, especially in a rough sea, with the intention of sailing deliberately toward a hostile shore. They shook their heads at one another, even as they shouted "bon voyage," to the crew commanders disappearing from view and heading out into the surf. All tank crew members already inside their vehicles, hoped and prayed that they really were riding in "floaters," as they were referred to in the battle plan. They had more than 4000 yards to travel, at a speed of about four knots per hour, so their ability to "float" would receive a rigorous testing.

Allan Robinson sat squarely in his driver's seat holding the engine speed to a steady throb.

"That's the speed we want, Allan," called Chapman over the I.C. "We want to keep in line with the other tanks. From what I can see, it looks like all the tanks of our squadron are swimming along, except one. I don't know who it was, but one tank went down the ramp some distance away from us and the flotation gear must have failed. I didn't see anyone get out of it either. There seems to be a hell of a lot of traffic around, and we've got to avoid running into anyone else or getting run into ourselves, or we'll all feed the fishes. Pull her a little more left, Allan."

They picked up their pilot boat and headed for the objective stated for them on the maps issued to all crew commanders, Bernière-sur-Mer, on Nan Section of Juno Beach. None of them had ever experienced seas as rough as these while in training, but once the decision to launch was made, everyone was determined to "give it a try." And in vindication of that decision, all tanks that were successfully launched, sailed unsteadily forward.

Inside the tanks, MacLean looked around the turret for the hundredth time, studying the details of every object he saw, simply to occupy his mind while his period of confinement continued. He fussed with the radio several times to see if he could pick up anything of interest to the crew, but without success. He even tried to resurrect in his mind the play of some of the football and hockey games he remembered from his days back in Edmonton, as a mental diversion. He wanted desperately to take his thoughts away from what could happen next.

Across the turret, he could see Sergeant Chapman's lower half only, the upper half protruding from the open hatch. Ed kept up a steady chatter about what he could see about them.

Ron Osborne sat motionless in his seat, staring glumly across the turret, anxiously awaiting further comment and description from their crew commander. Ron had little to say, preferring to keep his thoughts to himself. It was typical of him and his sense of discipline that he would stoically accept whatever circumstances he found.

Down below in the drivers' compartment, Allan Robinson considered himself lucky. For once, he was the only member of the crew with anything to do physically. He carefully made the steering adjustments called for by Chapman, studied his RPM gauge to assure constant speed from his engines and generally kept his own counsel.

Jack Metcalfe in the other driver's seat was the maverick. Regularly whistling and humming bits of songs that appealed to him, the forced confinement in his compartment seemed to stimulate his desire to share his tastes in music with the rest of the crew. Jack felt this was an ideal time to demonstrate his musical talents, while getting everyone's mind off their obvious concerns.

"From this valley they say you are going," Metcalfe sang out at the top of his lungs.

"What the hell's eating you?" growled Allan Robinson over the I.C. system, to be sure Metcalfe heard him above the noise inside the tank. "Haven't we got enough to put up with now, without hearing you sing the song that the cow died on?"

"I thought a little good music would lighten your day," responded Metcalfe with a grin. "Music has charms to soothe the savage beast," he added.

"Listen Caruso," Robinson rejoined. "I happen to like music at the right time and place. Your bellering is objectionable on three counts: it's not music in the first place; and this ain't the time nor the place for it. Thirdly, I'm trying to get this rig ashore where Ed wants us to land, and I don't need any more bloody distractions, least of all, another of your cowboy song renditions that I've tolerated for years now. Knock it off, right now!"

"Okay, Okay," said Metcalfe. "We have to do something to pass the time while we're in this phoney submarine. I'll just sing quietly to myself here," and turned his back on his surprizingly surly companion, more than a little surprised at the outburst he had provoked from an ordinarily affable colleague.

The argument between the drivers was heard by the turret crew too, when it came over the I.C. system. Ed Chapman decided to say a few words to ease the tension felt by everyone in the tank, a tension which had just boiled over between two of the best of friends. They had often heard Metcalfe singing to entertain himself on other occasions but had not heard him this time above the noise already around them in the tank.

"For those of you that are interested, we're now about half way to shore, as I reckon it," Ed interjected. "We seem to be third in our column of DD tanks. My count says that there are two more missing from the Squadron now. I didn't see them disappear, but I can't find them behind us any more. We have to steer more to the left here Allan, because I want to stay well clear of an infantry landing craft coming up on our right side. We sure as hell don't want any collision in this thing. Hang on men. This is character-building for all of us."

"Only half way in," complained Osborne, revealing that his nerves were taut too. "I thought we'd be a lot closer than that," and he dropped his gaze to his feet and idly tapped the breech of the gun with one finger.

MacLean sat slumped on his small loader's seat, as anxious to get ashore as anyone, but knowing that he simply had to contain his restiveness, just as everyone else did. But it was difficult to keep from shouting up to his crew commander that he too wanted to look out of the turret; that he too wanted to breathe some fresh air; and that he was extremely tired of just sitting and staring ahead in that turret as time ragged by. He did not allow himself to ask Ed Chapman for a few more comments on what could be seen from his hatch, a question that Ed promised to remedy. He wanted to maintain the narrow balance between talking too much on the I.C. system, which might intensify rather than relieve their tensions, and on the other hand not telling them enough about what they felt they had a perfect right to know.

Wave action continued to buffet all the sea-going craft-approaching Nan Beach, to the discomfort of everyone riding them. The L.C.I.'s carrying the infantry ashore provided a rough and unsettling trip for all of their passengers, as they bobbed up and down riding high on the combers and battering their way ahead with their blunt noses, rather than carving a crease through them, like a destroyer or a cruiser.

The DD tank craft, having extremely low centres of gravity, with the weight of a Sherman tank holding the canvas container around it well down in the water, did not bob as much as regular craft. This of course increased the risk of waves sweeping over the freeboard, a hazard which greatly concerned Ed Chapman. He called for the small bilge pump several times, each time creating additional concern among the rest of the crew.

"Will this trip ever end?" MacLean whispered to himself as time dragged slowly by. Nothing changed in any way among the things that he could see and hear. Ron Osborne still looked blankly across the turret at the space below the smoke discharger, his mind a complete enigma. MacLean decided against an attempt at conversation with him, because all the signs indicated Ron wanted to keep his own thoughts to himself alone. Ken thought again of some advice from one of his wireless instructors: "If there is nothing to say, don't say anything." He decided that this was a good time to apply that advice.

Outside, the sound of the barrage increased in intensity, if that was possible. Daylight improved as the time marched on, but they were told by Chapman that the shoreline was still a good distance ahead. He also reported that big shells could be seen bursting among the buildings on the sea front. Salvoes of rockets, fired from special rocket ships, soared screaming overhead, emitting a unique hissing sound as they headed for the shore ahead. Their explosions on landing added shuddering crashes to the sound of battle. The bark of the 25 pounders firing from LCT's that were still well out to sea behind them added to the cacophony, as an immense volume of fire fell on the beach.

The shells from the really big guns of the battleships continued to pass overhead from guns that no one could see anymore.

"They moan and groan like the sound of a great freight locomotive flying overhead," Chapman described it. Even with the headsets in place over their ears, the noise, the colossal roar and din of battle, was far beyond anything they had ever heard or imagined.

Chapman picked up one of his key shore markers as he peered through his binoculars; the Norman building with the gabled roof standing at the edge of the beach, on the left side of their landing target. He also saw several landing craft and DD tanks stationary and awash in the surf, probably struck by shore fire or swamped by the heavy seas still pounding away. The number of tanks still under way toward the beach had definitely diminished, and the shell fire sweeping the beaches from the shore installations had taken its toll among the infantry assault craft making their way inward. Looking back, Chapman could see a few figures swimming in the water. But for all the rest, the crews of the knocked out DD tanks, and the infantry in the smashed assault craft, they must have found watery graves. His strongest impression, which he passed on to his crew below him, was the smallness of the number of men who were actually assaulting

'Festung Europa,' notwithstanding the massive members of men and materials that had gathered in Southern England to fulfil the thousands of tasks necessary to get it launched.

"Let me give you guys something to think about, while you're sitting there on pins and needles waiting for us to reach dry land," Chapman calmly stated on the intercom. "I heard the squadron commander say yesterday that over 31,000 men were involved with getting this invasion mounted, and yet only three thousand men of all ranks are actually involved in the assault landing here. Just as I thought; from now on its just between the few of us and the few Germans in those bunkers and pillboxes ahead of us."

"What does the French coast look like now Chief? Do you see a lot of flashes from their guns?" asked Osborne, snapping out of his funk.

"Plenty of them," came the reply. "The navy is still pounding them with their guns, but that doesn't mean they're all knocked out up there. The bombing probably plastered a lot of targets further inland, but from here you can't see much bombing damage along the shoreline."

Crew members in DD tanks could not allow their thoughts to pause over what would happen to them, if one of these shells from shore burst close enough to rip the canvas screens providing their buoyancy. The fact that, as they well realized, the tanks would plunge to the seabed probably well before the crew could manage to wiggle free of its tight confines was not pleasant to contemplate. It certainly did not matter whether they were good swimmers. It was better that they force themselves to think of other things: about people they hated in the army, or old girlfriends, or splendid meals they had enjoyed; anything but feeling sorry for themselves in their current predicament.

Everyone was thankful for the steady, reassuring growl of the tank engines. A mechanical breakdown at that time would likely mean broaching to in a rough sea, with every likelihood of swamping soon afterward. In spite of their small free-board, as long as they maintained their heading, the craft, to their considerable surprize, seemed able to continue to squirm toward shore.

For the umpteenth time, the question ate at the edge of their minds, however often it was put aside, "would their tank become their coffin, or would they luck out and reach the shore?" Few words were exchanged, except for more corrections in direction from crew commander to driver.

It was Allan Robinson who led off with the remark that relieved a lot of the tension in the tank. Suddenly shouting in his mike, he said, "Good God! Can you smell that? That's old Metcalfe for you. Waits till we are all sealed in like this and can't get away, and then lets a fart that would curl your hair. You must be able to smell it in the turret too, can't you?"

"Can we smell it?" cracked MacLean. "I'd bet the Germans can smell it on shore. They'll complain to the league of Nations that the Canadians are using poison gas."

Osborne turned in his seat and announced acerbically, "I don't mind the smell that much, but it really is hard on the eyes." Returning to the attack, Robinson said, "If we get any more like that in here, I'm afraid it might choke the engine. Aren't you afraid of that too, Skipper?" asked Robinson.

"All right! All right!" shouted Chapman, grinning down into the tank, and pleased with the kidding and horseplay. "Believe it or not, we are getting close to shore. I can see a fair amount of crud being fired out toward us now. This will be a shaky do, let me tell you."

MacLean could hear the crackle of small arms fire developing, above the steady thrum of the tank engines. He was sure that the sounds of cannon fire were audible too. He looked across at Ron Osborne, who was obviously listening to the same sounds with equal concern.

"This is why they pay you all that big money," remarked the laconic gunner. "They want you to control your nerves while you go into battle. We don't have a hell of a lot of choice here, when we're all cooped up in a vessel swimming in below water level. But it sure would be nice to get on dry, hard ground again to fight these buggers, even if we would be more of a target ourselves."

"Amen to that," chorused MacLean and the two drivers from their positions in the hull below.

"You know it strikes me at long last," muttered Metcalfe. "If I had known I was going to spend all this bloody time under water when I enlisted, I'd have chosen submarines in the navy. Too late to change now I guess, eh Skipper?"

"Yep. Too late now," agreed Chapman quietly happy to hear his crew talking and bitching in their normal manner, "No navy in the world would have you anyway, Jack."

There had been grave concern that the still strong onshore wind would increase the depth of water washing inward on the exposed steel posts, tetrahedrons and other beach obstacles that Chapman described for his crew as they awkwardly and gingerly approached them, steering very carefully to avoid touching them. The critical importance of reaching the beach at the exact time planned meant that at low tide many of the mines and obstacles could be removed by the combat engineers; whereas once the water deepened around them only the frogmen could clear the paths needed to get ashore.

No less important to the success of the landing was the suspension of the naval bombardment as the assault craft and DD tanks neared the beach, in order to avoid killing their own troops with short shells and rockets. During the brief interval immediately following the lifting of the bombardment, the plan called for all troops to get across and clear of the beaches, before the Germans reappeared from their bunkers and shelters to man their weapons again.

The arrival of the DD tanks would prove a massive relief to a lot of very anxious infantrymen wondering how they were going to deal with the many still functioning enemy guns.

Suddenly, the tank was rocked by a violent explosion in the water nearby, a blast that shook everyone in the crew. Tattered nerves were given a further strain, as Jack Metcalfe shouted into his mike in the bow gunner's seat:

"What the hell was that?" he demanded.

"I'm not positive, but I think it was a sea mine, put off by another shell or a bullet," responded Chapman as cooly as he was able to speak. "We don't seem to have any damage though," as the tank continued to churn forward, its canvas canopy still in place. MacLean looked uneasily across the turret to Osborne, sitting silently in front of the gun controls. The unspoken question was in both their minds; would this water journey ever end?

A moment later, the tank lurched again, but this time it brought relief and rejoicing. The tracks engaged the sand and gravel of the beach. Cheers were shouted and smiles appeared all around the crew. Robinson quickly cut the speed of the engines, shifted down two gears and tightened his grip on the tiller bars with which he steered the monster. They roared out of the shallow water and onto the beach, without any pause.

"Beautiful," shouted Ron Osborne. "Now drop that damned canvas screen so that I can see to do a little gunnery here," he added.

Without stopping the tank, the canvas screen was dropped all around the vehicle and each of the crew members snatched their first opportunity in what had seemed an endless wait, to steal a quick peek at the outside world through their respective periscopes. They wanted to look out, regardless of how hostile and disturbing the view might be, just to see daylight and land again, the world that only Chapman had been able to see while they waited.

There before them on the sandy beach stood the gabled Norman Inn, their objective ever since launching hours ago. Now it was close at hand, on their left. They could also see infantrymen of the North Shore Regiment racing forward on the beach beside them. Further to the right, men of the Queen's Own Rifles struggled against withering machinegunfire coming from ahead of them. The Q.O.R.'s picked their way precariously through the maze of mines and beach hazards strewn about them. There had been several hair-raising near-misses by their assault craft, before they touched down right on their initial objectives.

Some assault craft had not been so lucky, and the swelling mass of debris washing back and forth in the surf bore witness to their misfortunes. Helmets, weapons, ammunition cases, broken and smashed panels from the sides of boats, life preservers, dead bodies, parts of dead bodies, boots with feet still in them, rose and fell with each surge of the sea, a horrible and shocking flotsam and jetsam from which everyone quickly turned their eyes. Not moving with the incoming tide were a number of stalled or knocked-out tanks, and the hulls of several assault craft, destroyed as they approached the beach and now resting on the sea bottom. Those who saw them were amazed at the carnage accumulated after only a few minutes' fighting.

Sergeant Chapman called for immediate action from his crew, once they were ashore. He could see evidence of heavy damage caused by the bombardment, from the fires and smoke erupting behind the beach front. However, a number of concrete pill boxes and emplacements above them seemed undamaged, and were beginning to come to life in a very dangerous fashion. He heard on the radio that Fort Garry tanks advancing on St. Aubin-sur-Mer at his left had encountered a network of extensive underground tunnels, leading to a threatening concrete fortress at the edge of town that remained virtually undamaged. The extent of the menace presented by these deep tunnels was not fully appreciated by the first troops ashore, as they strove to push through the town and on toward the country beyond, as called for in the invasion plan.

"Take on that pillbox to the right of the inn, Ron," said Chapman. "Give them an AP to open a hole, and then you can fire H.E. through the hole."

Without a word, Osborne looked at MacLean to assure that they had an armor-piercing shell "up the spout." He quickly swung the turret in line with his nearby target. The shell was fired immediately and struck just below the muzzle of the German machinegun which had been firing in enfilade along the beach.

"Give us some H.E. now," said Osborne, and MacLean quickly reloaded the 75 mm gun with a high explosive shell while he held another ready on his lap. The explosion from the second shell's entry into the pillbox was impressive, and there was no sign of life there afterward. MacLean pushed another H.E. shell into the breach, but Osborne's foot swung away from the trigger pedal.

"I think that's one pillbox that's now kaput. Let's save our ammo. We may need it later."

"I agree," said Chapman from the cupola. "Let's head for that road there that leads south to Bèny. Take it really easy though, because we don't want to bypass any strong points without dealing with them. Driver advance."

Heavy exchanges of fire followed between the tanks moving through the village and the guns that were concealed further inland, a number of which had come to life again after the lifting of the heavy naval barrage. Several enemy 75 mm. guns had begun raking the infantry and the flail tanks coming ashore with them. Some Churchill tanks of the Assault Engineers were busily engaged in clearing pathways through the mines and bridging the sea wall.

MacLean had to replace several boxes of .30 calibre Browning ammunition for the turret machinegun as Osborne poured fire into some trenches and buildings overlooking the road along which the Canadians were advancing. Chapman continued to keep a sharp lookout for enemy tanks and anti-tank guns that might be firing from concealment further back along the road on which they were traveling, while his gunner concentrated on nearby targets.

Gradually, the advance took the squadron inland, as the town of St. Aubin seemed to be cleared of enemy. Word was received that the Régimént de la Chaudière had landed and were pushing through Berniére-sur-Mer, along with the Queen's Own Rifles. The Q.O.R.'s had had a very difficult time working their way ashore and inward against extremely heavy enemy fire, with many casualties. The tank support for the infantry on the right, or western end of Nan Beach had been delayed, because their landing craft had hit mines in their approach run. Unfortunately, this left the infantry without armored support for a short time as they tackled the immediate beach defenses. Their casualties rose alarmingly. Finally the badly damaged L.C.T. did land and disgorged its tanks. They found the 9th Canadian Infantry Brigade, which was the remainder of the 3rd Infantry Division, already awaiting them in the streets of Bernière-sur-Mer, and anxious to move on.

All crew commanders had been warned to keep a sharp lookout for gathering enemy armor, for it was widely feared that the German response to the Allied landing, once its location was identified, was bound to be a savage counterattack to drive them back into the sea. As MacLean's tank headed south along with the rest of the Regiment, toward the objectives set for them on the higher ground at Anguerny, the crew felt considerably better about their accomplishments since they were launched from their LCT hours earlier. They had shot up some German infantry in the town, knocked out a pillbox at the edge of the beach and destroyed two anti-tank guns sited further into the heart of the villages. Osborne's gunnery had been superb and morale was high among the crew. They continued to push south on the way to Anquerny, swinging around a bend in the road just in time to catch some German gunners leaping frantically into their positions behind a pair of well camouflaged 75 mm antitank guns, one on each side of the road. The Canadians had surprised their enemy, plunging through the village so quickly after the landing, and they meant to take full advantage of it.

"Driver halt! Let them have it, Ron," said Chapman calmly from the turret hatch. Osborne fed an H.E. shell into each gun pit in rapid succession, before the Germans could get their shells off, a neat bit of traversing while holding his targets in view. The gun crews were decimated, but there was no time to see if anyone survived; that would have to be determined by the North Shore men following behind.

"Driver, advance. We've got to get on to Anquerny," said Chapman quickly. "Keep a sharp eye out for Kraut tanks."

Pyres of black, oily smoke climbed upward above the beach area behind them. Since landing near Berniére, Chapman had counted two British A.V.R.E. Churchill tanks and five Fort Garry Shermans knocked out; all but one burning fiercely, as their fuel and ammunition ignited. Smoke from burning buildings in the town added to the grey-black pall that hung over the settlement. They had passed the wreckage of a Canadian jeep and a scout car, each with dead bodies draped over them in awkward postures, as B Squadron drove southward toward the higher ground.

Word came over the radio that the Squadron Commander, Major Meindl, had been seriously wounded when his tank was shelled while attacking an enemy artillery battery, a loss that the squadron could ill afford. At the same time a warning arrived that some other tanks were encountering snipers in civilian clothes. Chapman's response was to hunch down lower in the turret hatch, to expose less of his head and shoulders. He hated to close the hatches down, thus making him dependent upon only one lens of the periscope for his view of what was happening outside. He concluded he would have to just take his chances on the accuracy of the snipers.

Earlier in the day, they had passed a monster 150 mm German artillery piece set up at the side of the road, apparently idle and abandoned in its mounting.

"I'm glad they weren't firing that brute at us coming up the road," said Osborne as he looked it over through his telescopic sight.

"You said it," answered Chapman. "If we weren't in a hurry, I'd do something about it. It's awesome."

They heard somewhat later that the crew of the big gun later reappeared and commenced firing down the same road they had traveled. There was lesson number 1 learned: there should always be time to neutralize unattended enemy weapons, or you may later see them in action against you when the absent crew returns.

Shortly after arriving at Anquerny, infantry from the Queen's Own Rifles thankfully also arrived to help consolidate a grip on the village.

Machinegun fire still echoed in some streets, and the unsettling crack of snipers' rifles continued, among the crashes of enemy artillery shelling the buildings from comparatively close range. The fight for the town subsided as the day wore on, and it finally fell into Canadian hands just before dusk.

More welcome news arrived on the radio. The men of the Chaudières and the North Shore Regiment were at least holding their own where they stood. Most of the Garry's moved back to harbor at Bèny-sur-Mer, where they planned to spend the night, after a check-up on the tanks. This meant refueling and replenishing ammunition and water, after which some sleep just might be possible.

MacLean's crew gulped a very hasty meal at the side of the road, like every other tank crew, as they settled the order of shifts on guard around the perimeter of the tank harbor on this, their first night in Normandy. Slit trenches were dug, near the side of the tank, in order to create a place of at least some protection in which the troopers could stretch out and sleep, but the digging was extremely difficult. Less than a shovel's depth below the surface of the ground, the digger encountered hard, chalky rock which would yield to only the most powerful blows of a pick. Consequently many men laid down exhausted in extremely shallow slit trenches, warned that they were not getting much protection from shrapnel or bullets sweeping their area during the night, but too tired to dig any deeper.

The irony of climbing out of heavily armored tanks in order to sleep in shallow slit trenches, exposed to the weather as well as anything that might drop on them from guns, mortars or bombers, struck MacLean forcefully, as he watched Allan Robinson slamming the pick into the chalk beneath him. But there was really no possibility of stretching out to sleep in the tank's crowded interior. Ken also recognized that, for the first time since they had climbed into their tanks on the LCT about 15 hours earlier, they could walk on the ground, look into the near distance, and escape the mixed smells of engine exhaust, cordite and stale human sweat that were inescapable in the close community of life inside a tank. In exchange, as they walked around their vehicle, were the pungent smells of burning straw and burning buildings, along with the oily smoke from several tanks knocked out earlier in the day, still burning where they stood, as the last of their fuel was consumed. One stench replaced the other.

Not noticed initially was the relief they experienced from the constant roaring and grinding sounds that accompany any armored formation while it is traveling. Even though head sets muffled the engulfing din to some degree, the roar of the 5-bank Chrysler engines, the almost constant clatter of the metal tracks revolving over the sprockets and idlers and the general clanking and banging of the tank equipment as the vehicle lunged and swayed over very uneven ground, became a wearing burden of noise for the crewmen. And then there was the concentrated sound within the vehicle when the master gun was fired, delivering a jolt to everyone in the crew, to anyone on the ground near the firing, and even to men in neighboring tanks.

It must be said in defence of the tracks which propel tanks forward however, that they made the best of negotiating rough and undulating country. Contrary to commonly held notions, tanks could ride over holes, ditches and hillocks with the least violence to the passengers of any of the army's vehicles. The action of the bogies and the volute springs which controlled the tension of the tracks permitted tanks to "flow over the ground," thus eliminating small irregularities and reducing the shock of larger rolls or bumps in the terrain. On a highway, a tank could provide an extremely stable ride for its crew. However, most battle plans called for off-highway movement by armored troops, across ditches, and streams, and through brush or even walls at times, where the image of rough rides in tanks was created.

The first night in Normandy for the Fort Garry Horse produced a short and troubled sleep, during which the Luftwaffe paid several visits over the beaches and the coastal villages. Ken MacLean and his sleep-eyed crew arose early on the morning of D+1, contented and really a little surprised to be still alive and looking forward to what the day might bring. There had been considerable disruption during the night, caused by some rather indiscriminate strafing and bombing raids about midnight. Also disturbing was the arrival of the tanks of C Squadron as they rejoined the Regiment in the late hours of darkness.

Sergeant Chapman, on returning from the early morning "O" group, told his crew that contact had not been established between the Canadians that landed on Juno Beach and the British 3rd Division which landed east of them on Sword Beach, although a strong reconnaissance had been sent out by the Garry's in search of the British. They had found many enemy units still extremely active in the area between the two Divisions, including a number of German guns that had resumed firing at targets on the beaches. Several well-placed shells from other Fort Garry tanks disposed of these guns in short order, but the situation still looked worrisome, with many German troops continuing to prevent a juncture between the assaulting forces.

About noon, orders arrived for B Squadron to prepare a defensive position at Hill 70 nearby, to meet an expected armored attack from the 21st Panzer Division. That was the unit which had been identified as maneuvering in the area, ready to counter-attack through to the beaches. B Squadron's move took them through Colomby, where the Chaudière's had blunted an infantry attack the previous night, with significant losses of men and machines on both sides. MacLean saw a number of Canadian and German dead lying in grotesque positions exactly where they had fallen during the fighting, a new sight for all of them. While passing through the area, snipers picked off the commander of 3 Troop, Lieutenant Allnut, a popular and extremely effective officer who, like most other crew commanders, stood with his head protruding from the open hatch of his tank, as it passed a partially damaged house. The Canadian troops were learning the sad lesson that snipers were often concealed in the upper floors of buildings, from which they could look down on passing traffic of any kind through curtained windows, choosing their targets carefully and with little risk to themselves.

Three Messerschmitt 109's zipped overhead at low level, firing their cannons at B Squadron tanks, as they moved into position on Hill 70. Luckily, they did not cause any serious damage. The wait for the arrival of the 21st Panzer Division began, as the tanks sat in carefully chosen hull-down positions wherever possible. They found a number of bodies strewn about among the wrecked vehicles, remnants of the battle of the previous night between the Chaudieres and the German reconnaissance regiment. Waiting for the enemy to appear could be a test of the nerves too, as the troops discovered while the day drew to a close without any further action.

The second night ashore in France was another restless experience, as the Luftwaffe returned in greater strength to attack the landings with flares and bombs. The Germans were more interested in interrupting the enormous traffic across the beaches, where supplies and reinforcements were landing around the clock. For the troops inland from the beaches, enemy mortars were busy throughout the night, working over locations where Allied troops had been observed, or sending colored signal flares to one another.

D+2 commenced with a response by MacLean's tank to some sniper fire apparently coming from a house about 1000 yards to their flank. Action picked up during the day as B Squadron became involved with support for the Queen's Own Rifles back near Anquerny, establishing contact with the British 3rd division to the left of them. In the course of this action, a small but spirited counter-attack by tank-supported enemy infantry was repelled. Osborne picked out the mottled outline of a well-camouflaged Mark IV German tank sitting at the very edge of a small copse of trees. He had spotted the intruder, about one thousand yards away, while peering through his telescopic sign in search of targets.

"Ah, I think I see one of them, barely in the bush there to the right of us, Skipper. It's a Mark IV all right."

"I see what you mean, Ron. Maybe about 1,000 yards," responded Chapman. "Let's have AP up the spout."

MacLean remained silent as he eased the H.E. shell out of the breach of the gun and replaced it with an Armor Piercing round. He watched as Osborne elevated the gun barrel ever so slightly.

"Fire when ready," added Chapman.

There was a quick crash of the gun, followed by a puff of smoke back in the turret as the extractors automatically ejected the empty shell casing onto the turret floor. The run-out after the recoil left the gun cocked with the breach open, ready for the next shell. Osborne and MacLean had fired up to eight shells in a minute, in a timed test on the Lulworth ranges before leaving England, so rapid fire from the 75 mm gun was possible. The two of them watched the path of this shell as it arced toward the German tank. Its turret began swivelling rapidly toward them. A flash appeared from the ring where the turret joined the hull of the enemy tank.

"A hit!" shouted Osborne jubilantly. "We hit him anyway. Let's have another AP. Ken."

MacLean rammed a second AP round into the breach and the breach block slammed closed, signifying that the gun was ready to be fired again. There were a few seconds for MacLean to steal a quick look through his own periscope, from which he noted that the gun of the Mark IV was no longer traversing. He stared at the ugly, squat shape of the vehicle, its gun pointing in their general direction. Half expecting to see the flash of the German's 75 mm gun firing back, he stared in frozen fear of the shell that might hammer them in an instant. His trance was broken by the crash of the gun in his own turret firing again. More acrid fumes were sucked back into the turret with the opening of the breech again. Watching the fall of the shot closely, they saw the trace arc swiftly, and then the small spark of the solid shot striking the enemy tank just above the track.

"You've got him," shouted the Crew Commander, watching through his binoculars, as the Mark IV seemed to shudder. A figure appeared, scrambling from the suddenly opened hatch atop the turret.

"There! Watch the bastard burn," said Osborne with real satisfaction, as smoke began to issue from the open hatch.

"I think you got him just before he got us," commented Allan Robinson, who had been silently watching the duel through his driver's periscope down below. Allan, like all tank drivers, had to have an extra amount of self control at moments like that, for he could do nothing but watch and listen, once the tank was stopped to allow the gunner to take on targets beyond them. The tank driver had to try to remain cool, calm and collected in the middle of the fight, while the more actively engaged members of the crew went about the business of determining whether Germans or Canadians were going to die violently. As Allan used to say, "it certainly was character-building."

One of the infantrymen in a slit trench near the road, who had watched the shoot-out anxiously, lifted his arm upward with the thumb pointing to the sky, a clear indication of his satisfaction with the armor that supported him.

"Driver advance," came over the intercom as their Crew Commander responded to an order that B Squadron must next provide relief for the Sherbrooke Fusiliers at Les Buissons, where there had been heavy and costly exchanges of fire between tanks and infantry on both sides since June 6. There they stayed, facing and exchanging increasing fire from mortars, machineguns and AP shot until darkness fell. Darkness that night brought a further emotional shock to the squadron, when word was passed that the very popular Acting Squadron Commander, Captain Jimmy Hall, had been killed by a mortar bomb while checking on the welfare of his tanks during the night. He was among a number of men from the Garry's killed or wounded in the savage fighting that day.

News the next morning also confirmed an exceedingly bad night for the infantry nearby. They reported enemy infiltration on one flank and an increase in fire from all quarters of the front. Several Garry tanks were knocked out, in exchange for a number of enemy tanks destroyed at Les Bussons, making that a memorable destination for all who fought there.

The early days in Normandy followed one another in sad succession, as packets of tanks from the regiment fought their way forward in support of attacking infantry columns, or in defence of hard-won objectives from one tiny village to another, losing tanks and crew members with a regularity that deeply disturbed the army commanders. At the rate of casualties being sustained in these small battles among the hedgerows and along the roads, the tank crews could see no chance of leaving Normandy in one piece, barring an absolute miracle. No one seemed unduly frightened, as the butcher's bill lengthened rapidly. A fatalistic attitude appeared to grip most of the soldiers involved; a feeling that what was happening would continue to happen "until their number came up." They had to support their friends, because their friends did the same for them. They fought because it was their job, their business to fight, and because there really was no alternative there.

At the end of the sixth day of fighting, the most critical of the entire invasion, the regiment moved to a more relaxed location, still within artillery range of the front, but with the exception of an occasional period of mortaring, they were free of the front line atmosphere which had surrounded them every moment since landing.

Some much needed re-organizing became possible to integrate new members of the unit and to review the lessons learned in the fighting to date. The great storm which disrupted everything in the channel on June 12th, interfered with the build-up of supplies and ammunition for everyone. The break in the fighting therefore came at an opportune moment. Although enemy air action took place above them every night, and heavy shelling went on around the clock, the number of daily casualties dropped drastically during the regiment's stay at Anguerny.

Toward the end of June, the regiment began its moves into position for the coming major battle for Caen and the associated Carpiquet airport. Move-ups were made in the darkness and rain to Bretteville, from which B squadron was to support an attack by the Royal Winnipeg Rifles of the 7th Infantry Brigade. They were to drive forward on the right flank of the main attack, to seize the south hangars of the airport. All intelligence reports indicated that this would be a hard battle against powerful defenses, which included concrete pillboxes, communication tunnels, barbed wire entanglements, mines, and all the rest of the paraphernalia which the Germans had prepared and exploited so effectively.

For help in the taking of Carpiquet, flail tanks, AVRE's, flame-throwing crocodile tanks and extra heavy artillery were placed under the same command as the regiment itself. Everything available for a great battle was assembled and the artillery barrage began right on time.

The infantry attack crossed the start line with their tank support accompanying them, almost in text-book fashion. They attracted heavy enemy fire immediately, and the sounds of a savage battle roared and rumbled north of the village. What started out with satisfactory advances by the entire brigade, soon became a vicious struggle to gain occupancy and control of any of the features of the battlefield.

It was with sardonic looks that many of the Fort Garry men read periodically in the few newspapers that found their way forward to the regiment, that the Luftwaffe had been "knocked completely out of the sky," while German bombers droned overhead every night, sometimes several times in one night, doing what they could to help their beleaguered brothers on the ground. Nevertheless, all Allied troops took immense comfort from the knowledge that the Huns were getting much the worst of the air war, particularly during daylight hours when German flyers were especially scarce.

While still moving south from Anquerny, MacLean's crew noticed a number of cleverly constructed Crowsnest lookouts concealed in tall trees, growing in various points along the road, vacant by the time they were overtaken. These helped to explain the uncanny accuracy of some of the artillery fire that had been directed their way since leaving the beaches at Bernière-sur-Mer.

"We're encountering heavy mortar and machinegun fire as well as the fire from at least two anti-tank guns here," said Lieutenant Gray on the blower to the squadron commander. "I can see two of our tanks knocked out and burning here. This reduces support for infantry just when they needed it the most," he continued, as the fight for Carpiquet intensified.

"Can't send any more just now, because everyone is engaged. Try to move forward to south hangars. Watch for Jerry tanks on right flank, because they have been seen there," came the calm and measured response from the Squadron Commander to everyone in the Squadron.

"You guys heard all that," said Sergeant Chapman on the intercom to the rest of his crew. "Keep a damned sharp lookout, especially on the right. The infantry are taking some shelter behind our tank, so we know anyone that moves out there to our front is a Kraut. Driver advance, but slowly."

The tank engines snarled as they accelerated up the short slope before them. Ron Osborne spotted the lurid winkle of heavy machineguns firing on the infantry from a slit trench at roadside. He swung the turret to the right to take on the new target, while explaining what he was planning to do to the Crew Commander. A solid burst put a stop to the flickering from the muzzle of the Spandau ahead, for the moment at least. Its sound had been lost in the rising roar of the battle around them anyway, but it appeared that Osborne's shooting had been accurate again.

"Just follow the side of the road, Allan, and not too fast," came Chapman's further instruction to his driver, as the tank continued to advance beside the narrow road, but not on it, hoping to avoid the mines they were sure had been planted in the roadway. MacLean squinted quickly through his periscope, curious about what was happening on their left, as they pushed ahead. The infantrymen crouched low and followed behind with their weapons at the ready.

Suddenly there was an ear-splitting crash and clangor from the right side of the tank, down in the bow gunner's region of the hull. The tank shuddered and came to an instant halt. Ken looked anxiously over the breech of the gun at Osborne, who turned his gaze away from his telescopic sight and back toward the crew commander, just lowering himself from the open hatch. Then MacLean peered down through the open panel on his side of the turret basket, into the drivers compartment below. With the turret swung to the right to cover targets on that flank, Ken had a clear view of the awesome chaos beneath them.

Daylight appeared through the neat, round hold drilled in the side of the tank, only inches from the ammunition bin beside Jack Metcalf's seat. Had the shell struck the ammunition bin, there would have been a second, louder explosion which would have lifted the turret right off the tank, with instant death for all inside it. As it was, the shell had struck Metcalfe, much like a large-bore rifle bullet would strike a grapefruit. Although there was no time to consider its probable path as it ricocheted about in the lower levels of the tank without emerging on the other side, after thought and consideration led to the conclusion that the projectile must have struck both drivers as it bounced off armored walls, finally ending its flight in the engine compartment at the rear of the vehicle.

Both drivers had virtually disintegrated, MacLean saw as he looked into the charnel house below him. Blood, tissue and exposed bone fragments coated the floor and the rounded cover of the huge transmission which separated the seats of the driver and the co-driver. In the instant of horror that he spent gazing at the ghastly, slimy remains of the two friends who had been sitting quietly below him only seconds earlier, Ken noticed a large stain on his left leg, where blood and parts of the drivers had been splashed on him. He also noticed a fiery streak of light following the drive shaft below the turret, forward to the final drives of the Sherman. Although this was a completely new experience for everyone in the crew, MacLean quickly recognized the immediate sign of a fire which would quickly consume the tank and everyone in it.

"We're hit! She's starting to burn. Let's get out," shouted MacLean into the intercom. Osborne, unable to see what had happened to the drivers from his position, glanced wildly at him as he tried to move the turret with the hand traversing crank, to assure that the gun would be clear of the opening of the drivers' hatches, allowing them to get out too. Chapman leaped out of the hatch and onto the deck plates behind the turret, shouting back into the turret to hurry before the fuel and ammunition exploded.

"They're both dead down there," shouted MacLean to Osborne, to convince him that nothing more could be done beyond getting out themselves, as smoke thickened around them. Osborne quickly spun off his seat and shot out of the hatch behind Chapman. MacLean slid under the gun and over to the open turret hatch above him. There was absolutely no time to waste, if they were to leave the tank alive. With one heave, he climbed clear of the hatch, stood for a second on the deck plate and then leapt into the scrub and tall grass on the far side of the tank. He landed beside Chapman and Osborne, both poised to put distance between themselves and the tank that had brought them all the way from England, but had now become the target of an .88 mm anti-tank gun.

"Let's get out of here, fast. See the smoke starting to pour out of her. She'll blow soon," said Osborne as they began to crawl toward some taller bushes close to the road, where Chapman said he thought he had seen some friendly infantrymen creeping forward.

"I didn't get my Sten gun or a damned thing out of the turret. All I have is what you see," admitted Osborne as he looked glumly at his Browning pistol in its holster. "I wish I could get at my kit in the blanket box. It's right there at the back of the tank. Maybe I could nip over there, just for a minute, and get it out. The fire is still at the front of the tank and in the turret," Osborne said hopefully to Sergeant Chapman.

"If you go near that tank now, there'll be three new faces in hell for breakfast; not just the two we've already lost. That fire probably started in the engine, right next to the blanket box, where you want to go. Besides, what do you think the Krauts that shot us up are going to do to anyone who runs near that tank?" asked Chapman, his temper roused.

As if to give point to the Crew Commander's question, the machinegun that Osborne had fired at before the tank was knocked out, came back into action with a hail of bullets down the ditch ahead of them.

"Do you see that?" demanded Chapman of a chastened Osborne. "Now let's wiggle back to one of those slits where the infantry are hanging on."

It took at least a quarter of an hour for the threesome, armed only with the pistols carried by most tank men, to crawl back to the ditch from which the men of the Royal Winnipeg Rifles were shouting to them. When they looked back, still shaken and not fully appreciating what had happened to "Bailiff" just moments earlier, their instinctive reaction was to try to save themselves. The full impact of the instantaneous snuffing out of the lives of their two comrades within inches of themselves had not yet fully registered with any of them. They were surprised that they appeared to be totally unhurt themselves while the hull of the tank had appeared as if mixed with a giant spoon.

The Canadian infantrymen nearby, as inexperienced themselves, were mute and subdued as they stared at the quick and violent destruction of the two tanks brewing up in front of them. Both poured thick, black, oily smoke into the gray sky above. The sounds of machinegun and .75 mm gun ammunition popping and cooking off" inside the tank could be heard for a long time afterward.

A corporal in the Winnipeg Rifles spoke to Chapman as they hunkered down behind an embankment that gave them some immediate protection from the firing ahead.

"A lot of guys bitch around here about being in the infantry, but I wouldn't trade my job here for a job in one of them tanks fer nothin'. You guys attract big stuff from all them big guns. We only saw three guys come from your tank, where are the other two?"

"Still in it," responded Chapman.

"Couldn't you get them out? Were they hurt do you think?"

"They weren't hurt. They were both dead before the fire started. There was nothing much to pick up. You could bury them both in one ration box," said MacLean through tight lips. "This is some of their blood," he concluded, pointing to the large stain on his left trouser leg.

"Nope. Tanks ain't for me," returned the infantry corporal. "I'll keep my two feet on the ground when I fight. That way, I can get down into the ground when I want. I don't want to be perched up there in one of them big steel buggers, waiting for a shell from an 88 mm to come through the side and scramble everything up. You can have it."

"Well Corp., to each his own," replied Chapman. "We'll have to go back from here to get some new kit and get another tank. Any advice on how to find Brigade H.Q.?"

"We never see none of those bastards up here," replied the corporal. "But if you go back along the route we all came up, you'll find a sign somewhere."

Without further delay, the three survivors crept along the ditch adjoining the road to a road junction several hundred yards back, after which they were able to walk upright behind the shelter of a thick hedgerow. A further walk of about 3,000 yards, past a battery of 25 pounder artillery guns firing rapidly in the direction they had just left, took them to yet a further road junction and a welcome directional sign, guiding them to the Elgin Regiment. The Elgins filled the role of a tank delivery regiment. Their function was to supply replacement tanks and tank crews to the Canadian armored regiments. Quartered in an abandoned school, surrounded by a number of marquee tents, survivors from knocked out tank crews and reinforcements newly arrived from the United Kingdom were mixed together, awaiting postings to armored regiments as required.

Sergeant Chapman and his two crew members, Osborne and MacLean, were documented and issued with net kit to replace what they had lost with their tank. The new kits included a small pack with shaving gear and "housewife wallet" inside; a change of shirt, underwear and socks; a rubberized ground sheet; a "death blanket" (ie. a large, wool blanket long enough to cover the entire body of its owner, and in which he would normally be buried if he should die on active service); eating utensils; and sometimes an extra pair of tank boots with rubber soles and heels. They were told to make themselves comfortable in a nearby tent marquee, where they would remain until assigned to a unit.

"You mean, we may not be sent back to B Squadron of the Fort Garrys?" Chapman anxiously questioned, when the Elgin Regiment clerk gave them instructions.

"That's right, Sergeant," he replied. "We don't set policy here. We just live with orders. We send replacement tanks and reinforcements to the units that need them, when they are required. We can't keep men here who want to be sent to some particular unit which does not need reinforcements, while another unit is in crying need of replacements. We have to process them through. We try to send men where they want to go, but we make no promises."

"I don't like the sound of that, but I guess we'll just have to wait and see what happens," said MacLean. "We can't holler until we're hurt, but leaving all our friends at the Garrys? Hell, we want no part of that."

As it turned out, Chapman and Osborne, after what seemed a lengthy stay with the Elgin Regiment, did manage to return to the Fort Garrys, but it was their long service records with that unit that swung the balance. MacLean, with a much shorter history with the Regiment, did not have the same claim.

"I know you want to go back to your old regiment MacLean," said the Elgin Regiment Staff Sergeant, when MacLean asked for an interview with him. "You must understand that everyone who comes through here has a preference, and we try to satisfy them. And we've just sent some men back to the Fort Garrys who have been with them for years, as you know. But we have to look after the demands from other units too. The 4th Armored Division has just had a rough baptism of fire in France, and they need a lot of replacements, fast! Your name and some others here came up on the list of men going there to meet their requirements. In your case, you'll be going to the Canadian Grenadier Guards in the 4 Armored Brigade. And that's the way it's going to be. You've got a good record in your file so far, and you'll fit in with the new bunch soon enough."

"Is that the last word on it? Can I complain to an officer about getting chopped off from all my friends? And without even a chance to say 'So long,' to men I've lived with right around the clock since early this year?"

"Listen, MacLean. There is no officer here now anyway, but if there was, he wouldn't give you and your sentimental feelings the time of day. When you left your camp in Canada, nobody gave you time to say 'goodbye' to your friends. And the same thing when you left your army friends in Aldershot to join the Fort Garry's . There's no time for that in the bloody army, and you should know it by now. You're going to the Grenadiers this afternoon, and that's all there is to it."

CHAPTER VI

EARLY DAYS WITH THE GUARDS

The small truck that brought Ken MacLean and three other new recruits to the Canadian Grenadier Guards looked spanking new in its fresh coat of paint. This was not surprising, because, like a lot of the equipment of the 4th Armored Brigade, it really was brand new. The driver was hurrying toward his destination, raising clouds of fine dust from the chalky road over which they were traveling. More experienced drivers of vehicles had learned that raising dust clouds attracted attention from German watchers. Their attention was often reflected rather quickly in increased mortar activity or artillery fire. But this time they were lucky - no incoming shells or mortars.

The heat of summer in Normandy was a real surprise to the Canadians. They had not expected the baking temperatures they encountered. The chalky dust penetrated everything; food; water cans; goggles; clothes; map cases; gun barrels; noses and throats. The mud, of which they complained a few days earlier in the rainy weather, had all too quickly turned to the finest of dust, as soon as it dried out.

The truck pulled up near a collection of Jeeps, staff vans and scout cars which represented Regimental Headquarters of the 22nd Canadian Armored Regiment, the Canadian Grenadier Guards. From one of the assembled vans (usually referred to as "gin palaces" for some obscure reason not associated with the making or consumption of any clear, liquid drink), stepped a tall, slim captain, who introduced himself as the regimental adjutant. He gave the new arrivals a very brief introduction to the regiment, mentioning its affiliation with its namesake, the British Grenadier Guards. He also added that the Canadian unit boasted a long and proud tradition dating back some 200 years to the raising of the first muster of militia in old Montreal.

While on the subject of tradition, he mentioned some of the rather small differences between Guards regiments and others in the Canadian army. For example, the different squadrons were designated by numbers rather than letters; the lowest rankers were not "Troopers," but "Guardsmen;" and the foot drill in marching on the drill square, if they ever got back to it again, was noticeably different in some particulars. But overall, the adjutant's welcome to the unit was well received by the new recruits. They learned that the 4th Canadian Armored Brigade, consisted of the Governor General's Foot Guards, the British Columbia Regiment and the Canadian Grenadier Guards, as tank battalions, and the Lake Superior Regiment as a motor Battalion, making it a hard-hitting and powerful force which would fight as an armored Brigade as much as possible. He tried to distinguish between the role planned for the 4th Armored Brigade, and that of the 2nd Armored Brigade where MacLean had fought up to that point, the latter's role being one of fighting in small armored packets in support of infantry units in operations of their own. However, the Adjutant observed that he felt the differences between the operational activities of an armored brigade in an armored division and one in an infantry division were much more theoretical than real.

The adjutant then read out the assignments from his clipboard. Ken MacLean was to be the new loader operator in Sergeant Sandy Forsyth's tank in No. 2 Squadron, parked a short walk away from R.H.Q. MacLean's disgruntlement at being transferred to a strange regiment in a strange division welled up in him again, as he went in search of Forsyth's tank and crew, all of whom would be strangers too. But the thought crossed his mind that the remnants of his old crew were going to face almost the same problems that he had, with a host of new men replacing the familiar faces he had known, many of whom had become casualties in the heavy fighting around Caen. He resolved to keep quiet about it and to accept the changes he was powerless to resist anyway.

Ken's encounter with Sandy Forsyth went well, he thought. Sandy was a large, blond, farmerish man with an open face and gregarious nature, anxious to make MacLean feel at home in the crew. Sandy had been raised in the Eastern Townships area of Quebec, south of the St. Lawrence River and had recently married the love of his life, a Scottish girl, before embarking from England. He appeared to know and be on good terms with everyone in the Grenadiers, in which he had served since the outbreak of war in 1939. He had led his crew through its initial brief experience in action at Bourgebus, while supporting an infantry attack, but the part played by No. 2 Squadron had not been conspicuous in the attack. An indoctrination to heavy action still lay ahead of them, as they were all aware.

The gunner in Sandy's crew was a cherubic, short man with a bushy, black moustache and a warm, ready smile. This was Bill Brown, who hailed from Truro, Nova Scotia. Bill boasted that he had nailed down almost every crooked shingle on the roofs in his home town. Brown had the easy country manners of most men from a small town, and had become an ardent admirer and friend of his crew commander. Apparently, Bill had not warmed to the previous loader-operator in the crew. He had been struck-off-strength due to some serious physical ailment, which left a vacancy for MacLean, when he arrived.

Big Leo Codal was the regular and much respected tank driver, a lean, hard-muscled man with sinewy arms and legs. Leo was another product of the Eastern Townships, coming from the town of East Angus. Though of Francophone background, Leo seemed more at home as an Anglophone, pursuing his trade with a quiet seriousness that pleased all who knew him. His sandy moustache, carefully trimmed each morning, gave him a trim, dapper look, as he went about his duties, checking the tracks and fussing with the controls in the driver's compartment.

Russell Scott, another Nova Scotian, handled the duties of the co-driver and bow gunner. At thirty-one years of age, Scott was older than the rest of the crew. Short and thick-set, he seemed the quiet man of the group, anxious to help Leo in any tank maintenance chore, but not otherwise very communicative. The thought crossed MacLean's mind, watching the other four members of the crew performing their various tasks around the camp, that Scott was really ill at ease around tanks. He seemed unduly jumpy from his short experience in a relatively small action, but MacLean did not want to reach any premature conclusions about the man. He decided to withhold any judgment about Russell until he had seen much more of him.

Word had been passed down the line that No. 2 Squadron would be involved in the next attack, a drive on the village of Cintheaux, assisted by a company of the Lake Superior Regiment in their halftracks. This was to be part of a final push by the Canadians that would at long last penetrate the German defences centered on Caen. They were to straddle the Caen-Falaise highway in a night attack. They would be aided by artificial moonlight, to be created by beaming powerful searchlights forward from the rear areas, thus providing the centre axis for the attack, so necessary if the wild confusion of many night time maneuvers was to be avoided.

The idea behind this novel plan was attributed to the army commander, Lieutenant General Guy Simonds himself, so it had considerable support from the lower level commanders of course. By this means, it was hoped to move powerful forces of Canadian troops in the darkness, troops that could not otherwise get past the great concentration of machineguns, anti-tank guns, mortars and rockets that the Germans had assembled in the defences near Cintheaux.

As explained by several Regimental Officers, at first blush, night attacks appeared to be much the best and safest way to manage an advance past powerful defences which shot up everything they could see. But against this overly simplistic notion stood the experiences of many commanders who had been involved with night attacks and knew all too well the horrendous confusion that they could lead to: total losses of direction by the advancing troops; mistaken ideas of where the attackers and defenders really were located; and a high risk of firing upon friendly troops. In addition to these drawbacks, the ability of armored forces to see in the darkness, even in comparison with other troops, was notoriously deficient, making their contribution to the attacking force unreliable at best and an absolute handicap at worst.

But in the circumstances of late July in 1944, with General Simonds calling for a night attack with the aid of artificial lights for centre-line markers, the attempt was certainly going to be made. The lights were put in position behind the brigade and the attack stormed forward. Some initial local gains were made, but the overall results were inconclusive. MacLean was convinced that he had seen virtually nothing of where they drove, although it must have been over some extremely rough ground, judging from the violent bumps and crashes the tank had taken. They had not been able to tell friend from foe and the attack dissolved in confused orders and counter-orders, leaving them in positions not really improved over those they had left. Sandy Forsyth had not seen a single target to take on with his tank, and his gunner complained that he could see nothing through his sights, even if Sandy had been able to find a target. After a most disturbing night, the German defensive position was still intact ahead of them, notwithstanding the loss of four tanks during the night-time fracas. The Regiment re-grouped at Cintheaux to prepare for the next attack, which was promised to be a big one, but in daylight hours thereafter.

Word had been received of unrelenting pressure being put upon the higher command of the British and Canadian forces to smash their way southward towards Falaise, in the hope of forcing a juncture with the American armies in that area, thereby wrapping a pincer thrust around the German armies fighting in Normandy. It was a bold and ambitious plan, but it did require a massive drive forward by a powerful force through the widest and strongest German defence belt on the Western front. The majority of the British and Canadian troops in Normandy at that time would be combined, in one army to carry out this drive.

MacLean and his comrades heard all about this plan from their new troop commander, Lieutenant Stanbury, in a gathering on August 1. He told them this operation would be called "Totalize," but it was substantially changed from the original plan. When it kicked off, the Grenadiers were to fight, along with the rest of the tanks of 4th Armored Brigade and the Lake Superiors, in a group named "Halpenny Force." named after their commanding officer. They were scheduled to lead the charge on their part of the front. They would start out behind a group of flail tanks. They were to be accompanied by AVRE Churchill tanks equipped to negotiate tank ditches, and "crocodile" flame thrower tanks pulling their armored trailers behind them.

Just before launching the attack, a force of heavy bombers was to fly in a tactical role, in close support of the ground troops. While the troops waited at the start line, the first wave of bombers swept over about midnight dumping a heavy spread of bombs on the German positions ahead. Almost half an hour later the second wave arrived, and before the dust and smoke had completely settled, the tanks, halftracks and infantry carriers of the Canadian Corps lunged forward against the German positions. "Totalize" was under way, proceeding in tightly packed armored columns with very narrow fronts, as if they were going to ram their way through the enemy front.

Immediately, Forsyth's tank ran into tremendous congestion, in trying to move into the battle. There were dozens of vehicles from the Grenadiers, and other regiments in the 4th Armored Brigade mixed up with some from the 2nd Armored Brigade, although they were each intended to have their own separate frontage for the battle. It was a grand scale melee.

Night turned into day and the traffic chaos still milled about in confusion. Commanders swore bitterly. Tank drivers drove "open hatches," in spite of the shooting going on ahead, because they couldn't see anything through their periscopes. MacLean and his colleagues commented sourly upon the planning behind this foul up, as they idled along short of their forming-up area. Orders had been unclear, and some crew commanders, officers as well as N.C.O.'s, had received very little explanation of their roles in the attack.

The next day, heavy fighting broke out between infantry in the 2nd Canadian Division and some skillfully concealed German defenders at May-sur-Orne, creating a bloodbath for several Canadian infantry regiments. Then, to add even further to the confusion and trouble, a wave of U.S. heavy bombers mistakenly dropped their bombs short of the drop line, with devastating consequences for the troops of the North Shore Regiment and the Polish Division who were following closely. Confusion of orders, of objectives and of identifications seemed characteristic of the way in which the Canadian force operated, from the top down, at this stage of the fighting.

Finally, the Grenadier tanks advanced clear of the general confusion surrounding the commencement of the battle, moving forward along the course planned for them before "the fog of war" descended. MacLean cocked the Browning gun and slammed an AP round "up the spout" of the master gun. Forsyth reported that he could see tanks from No. 1 and No. 3 Squadrons in full action against crossfire from anti-tank guns which had been concealed in some woods at the edge of Cintheaux. After losing several Grenadier vehicles and a number of crewmen, Lieutenant Phelan of No. 3 Squadron eliminated the threat with a sudden charge over the hill ahead, catching the defenders unaware.

Meanwhile, No. 2 Squadron under Major Pete Frederickson had been largely left out of the fighting for Cintheaux. All members of the Squadron heard over the radio that their role would be to push on as quickly as possible to capture Bretteville-Le-Rabet that same day. However, about eight o'clock that evening, Lieutenant Colonel Halpenny decided that, in light of the loss of 17 tanks by the regiment during the day, and the dwindling amount of daylight remaining, he would postpone the attack until the next morning. He wanted a delay so that he could "replenish fuel, ammunition and manpower in a regrouping and renetting for the whole of Halpenny Force," notwithstanding the Army commander's orders to "push on straight through the night" and later to "push on steadily regardless," according to the records of the battle. The critical consequences of this failure by Halpenny to press on as ordered were painfully clear the next day. The Germans had used the reprieve given them to great advantage. They moved powerful reinforcements during the nighttime hours, enough to bolster a position which could certainly have been overrun by "Halpenny force" had its commander followed his orders, instead of yielding to the urge to "get some rest at night and attack again tomorrow."

Early the next morning, and somewhat before daybreak, MacLean's crew was under way again, along with the rest of No. 2 Squadron, in pursuit of the objectives of the previous day. Forsyth spoke loudly with the Lake Superior Regiment men clustered around him, as they rode into battle aboard his tank and on most of the other tanks of the Squadron. This was a new departure for the Grenadiers, a tactic which proved ineffective and probably wasteful of lives: it certainly was among the tank-borne infantry. When enemy machineguns opened up, the infantry were cut to pieces in short order. MacLean could faintly hear the shouts and screams of the men clinging to the turret, along with the crackle of bullets hitting the steel castings as the Spandau fire swept the top and sides of the tanks. The few survivors leapt off the tank decks, determined to take their chances on the ground thereafter.

Bill Brown became very active, pouring H.E. and co-ax into the buildings of the village ahead. As MacLean watched through his periscope, Brown poured belt after belt of machinegun fire against the buildings and ground works that Sandy described.

"Keep your head down, Sandy boy," said Brown to his Crew Commander, as fire was returned from the village. Anti-tank guns spoke from the hedges and houses, firing at short range, with lethal results. MacLean could see smoke pouring from three Grenadier tanks, as Brown swivelled his turret to engage targets among the Lombardy poplar trees lining the road.

"Driver advance," came Sandy's calm command, as the momentum of the attack carried through Bretteville. "Get that 'Moaning Minnie' over on the left Bill," he shouted, as some German gunners scrambled in a vigorous but vain attempt to withdraw with their multi-barrelled rocket mortar.

Both Brown and the bow gunner blasted Browning fire at the "Minnie," which was quickly given up for lost. Canadian infantry from the 10th Brigade surged forward into Bretteville-Sur-Orne, marking the end of a bitter struggle which would probably never have taken place at all if "Halpenny Force" had driven onward the day before. The fighting had been severe, as attested by the burned out hulls of four huge Panther tanks, destroyed by rockets from Typhoon aircraft. Nearby was the blackened shell of a Sherman tank, mutely testifying to the action of the Panther tanks before the air force found them. The customary battlefield wreckage was scattered far and wide around Bretteville; smashed jeeps and trucks; broken artillery pieces, discarded ammunition; spent shell casings, and not of the least consequence, the broken bodies of many of the men who had served their weapons, lying in disarray around the village, some in field grey and some in khaki.

The fight for Bretteville was an ill-remembered day for many Canadians. In the tense struggle to reach Falaise within an absolute minimum of time, Bretteville marked a relatively small gain against still formidable defences, in exchange for a large expenditure of men, equipment and valuable time. More bad news arrived with the report that Brigadier Booth, commander of the 4th Canadian Armored Brigade, had been killed in his scout car, in the course of the fighting there. Since bad news usually comes in bunches, what had already been spread about was capped with a further report that responsibility for the relatively poor showing of the newly arrived 4th Armored Division, had been fixed on the Division commander, Major General George Kitching. In consequence of the inadequacies of regimental commanders, a good general was forthwith sacked by Simonds, who had himself contributed to the disorder by constantly changing his orders and plans. In his place, Major General Foster was brought in to get things moving.

Meanwhile, on the level of the ordinary fighting soldiers, whose duty was "not to reason why, but rather just to do or die," preparations for the next day's action were being made. Another hot day was promised for August 10, the day that MacLean and his friends in No. 2 Squadron were to drive for Point 195, a height of land nearby which had proved to be a deadly trap for the B.C. Regiment and the infantry of the Algonquin Regiment attached to them two days earlier.

The tragic tale had circulated widely, of the B.C.R. tanks, straying into an ambush during a thick morning mist, through misreading their maps, a disaster which resulted in the virtual annihilation of the Regiment. Many brave men died trying to fight their way out of the trap. This gave point to the task of the Grenadiers for the following morning, as they pored over their maps, filled their fuel tanks and loaded all the ammunition they could store in their vehicles.

The plan of action laid out for the following day's operations left Sandy Forsyth and his crew definitely unimpressed. The order of march established that No. 2 squadron, led by Major Frederickson, would lead the departure from the completely shattered village of Bretteville, followed by the other Squadrons and R.H.Q., across a railway and on to Point 195. When the move began, reports came in of Tiger tanks roaming ahead, but these were ridiculed by personnel in Intelligence, who insisted there was no basis for such reports. Their scepticism continued until one of the tanks in R.H.Q., creeping along through the morning mist, was torn open by fire from, of all things, a Tiger tank.

Sandy and his crew became much concerned about what lay directly ahead along the road, when their troop officer, Lieutenant Stanbury also lost his tank to the Tigers lurking in the woods to their right. In the violent clash which ensued, eight Grenadier tanks were quickly knocked out, in a hail of fire that shattered the Shermans like so many sitting ducks. Bill Brown was able to fire several well-aimed AP shells at the left side of a Tiger tank sitting nearly 2000 yards away, but his shot merely struck sparks as it hit the thick armor of the 60-ton monster. Penetration was quite impossible at such a distance with 75 mm AP shells, as everyone anticipated. The long barrel of the 88 mm gun on the Tiger began to swing ominously toward Forsyth's tank, as he watched it through his binoculars. This German tank would soon get rid of its tormentor. Sandy ordered Leo Godal to reverse quickly into a small depression in the field, below the line of sight of the Tiger, where he wanted to remain until circumstances changed. There was no sense in deliberately becoming a sacrificial offering.

Although the German defences appeared to have thinned since the destruction of the B.C.R.'s in the same locality not long before, they still held up further progress southward by the entire Brigade. The attack by the Grenadiers seemed disorganized, and forward momentum was lost. On one occasion that day, Halpenny and his commanders were gathered in an 'O Group', away from their tanks, when they were almost overrun by an enterprising German Mark IV tank rambling through the countryside. The Canadians were fortunate indeed to escape without injuries, as the German vehicle withdrew down a short hill, apparently without seeing them at all. The call went back for artillery to try to secure the very modest gains of the day.

The fighting did produce several memorable episodes for those engaged on Hill 195 that day. Sergeant John Andrews was advancing in his tank with the rest of his No. 3 Squadron comrades along the east flank of the hill, when an 88 mm shell crashed through the hull, severing fuel lines and igniting an immediate fire. The crew bailed out quickly and began creeping through the grass and weeds to a safer refuge, away from the pyre behind them. Sergeant Andrews noticed that one of his crew members, the co-driver, Moe Lutsky, was not with them. In the face of considerable enemy sniping and mortaring, he immediately crept back to the burning vehicle from which he had just escaped. There he found Lutsky, still in the tank, and danger-ously wounded, with both feet shot off. Andrews dug him out of his seat and slowly dragged him back to shelter and treatment, which undoubtedly saved Lutsky's life. The award of a Military Medal for Andrews was approved almost automatically.

Hill 195 saw some other episodes that day with less-happy end-ings. The Grenadiers found themselves with only 15 tanks operating out of a total establishment of 58. One of the tanks lost to the fire from an 88 mm anti-tank gun late that afternoon was that of Lieuten-ant Kendall in No. 2 Squadron, driven by Corporal Dave Willey, per-haps the best-liked tank driver in the entire regiment. A good look-ing, sandy-haired charmer, with a warm, gracious personality, he was reputed to have cut a wide swath among the ladies of Crowborough and Brighton before leaving England with the regiment. Willey was driving Lieutenant Kendall's tank across an open stretch of ground near the crown of Point 195 , an area which became a deadly place to travel, judging from the number of tanks already knocked out and burning below them. Several surviving crewmen sheltering behind a low hillock, beckoned wildly toward Kendall's tank to warn it away from the open stretch of ground, but to no avail. When Willey was almost half-way across the "shooting range," as the watching crew-men called it, a sudden, vicious whip-crack from an 88 mm gun told them the German gunner was striking again.

Willey's tank came to an immediate stop with a hole in its side at the turret ring. The watchers waited for the hatches to flip open and the survivors to clamber out. Seconds went by, and a thin column of oily, black smoke edged out of the half-open turret hatch. More time went by, and still no one emerged from the stricken and now defi-nitely burning vehicle. Two men rose from behind the hillock and began to run toward the fire, only to be cut down by a machinegun firing across the hillside.

The fire quickly gained substance and strength in Kendall's tank, as the watchers looked on in horror from only a few dozen yards away. Then they saw Willey's hatch lift upward several inches, and a ghostly hand appear, already burned so extensively that the bones of the fingers were exposed. The hand pushed the hatch slowly upward, amid flame and smoke rising around it. When the hatch was almost half open, the watchers, looking on spellbound, hoped to see the miracle of Willey forcing himself to leap upward and out, even if his clothes were aflame. His fight for life could still be successful, they believed. But the willpower which drove the ghostly hand failed, and the hatch moved upward no more. Then, as they watched, the hatch closed again, and the fire raged even higher through the turret. There were no more screams from the burning crewmen; just a black, oily, evil-smelling column of flames and smoke rising in the summer air. No one had survived; not even Willey. The nicest of all the Guardsmen had gone, along with all the rest of his crew.

Elsewhere on Hill 195, other tank men had other adventures they would long remember. One of these involved a tall handsome Englishman who had moved to Montreal years before and who chose to do his fighting with the Canadian Grenadier Guards in 1940. He rejoiced in the unusual name of Alfred Sheepwash, and enjoyed the popularity that his name and nature brought him in the regiment. Sergeant Sheepwash's tank was a 17 pounder in No. 2 Squadron. He was called into action that day in an attempt to knock out one or both of the German armored vehicles which had been playing hob with the Grenadier tanks on Hill 195.

Alf's tactic there was to conceal his tank behind what appeared to be a barn in the field, while he awaited one or other of the German armored vehicles to reveal itself. Then the Sheepwash tank would rush forward about 20 yards into the open, fire a couple of quick armor-piercing shells at the German vehicle before reversing quickly into concealment again.

All went well to start with, as Alf's gunner knocked out one S.P. gun before reversing into concealment again in the shelter of the barn. But other Teutonic eyes had seen what Alf was about. They promptly fired tracers and H.E. shells into the sheltering building, causing it to blaze up. The smoke from the burning building did not appear sufficient to conceal Sheepwash's tank, if he made a run to escape, so he decided to stay where he was, in spite of the thick smoke. However, the burning building turned out to be, not an ordinary barn, but a storage shed for Rocquefort cheese, and the smell produced by the fire consuming it was a foul, horrible stink, quite beyond any human endurance.

As the nauseating, choking stench intensified, his anguished crew shouted that they would do anything, brave any hazard , run any risk, just to escape the oily, clinging, obnoxious smoke that enveloped them. Alf finally obliged his crew by ordering Bill Thomas, his driver, to reverse rapidly away from the sheltered side of the building, but within the thick screen of smoke pouring from it, until they reached the shelter of some nearby oak trees. When this escapade succeeded without injury to men or vehicles, his crew proclaimed themselves among the most fortunate soldiers on the front, having eluded a stink worse than death.

The Sheepwash tank and crew were considered among the lucky ones in No. 2 Squadron, by those who rated chance and good fortune whenever they sat around a boiling pot for another "scoff" of Compo tea. Only a few days after the burning cheese episode, the crew were standing about, eating a meal from their mess tins in what they believed to be a quiet, secure spot in the corner of a field. Without any warning whatever, an anti-tank gun fired from some distance to their front, and the armor-piercing shell passed between Alf Sheepwash and Bill Thomas while they talked together about six feet from one another. Though the shot precipitated a scramble by the crew into the tank in record time, it was the only shot fired at them by the enemy gunner, for some unknown reason. The Sheepwash luck still held.

By the end of the first week of August 1944, it was estimated that the thrust by the Canadian forces along the road to Falaise had gained only nine difficult miles, and there was still no sign of a breakthrough. The objective was still miles away. MacLean and his Grenadier comrades were given a couple of days to re-equip with new tanks and equipment and try to assimilate the new crews that came with them. A lot of different faces appeared on the roster for No. 2 Squadron, mainly men who had completed their training but had no experience in action. The recruits had much indeed to learn about living a bivouac existence around their tanks, when they weren't involved with fighting operations, not to mention their unfamiliarity with battle conditions.

The routine followed a familiar pattern. If the tank was harbored in a relatively quiet area, where there would still be the ever-present thump of artillery but the likelihood of night-time bombing or shelling seemed to be reduced, the tank crew would tie the upper end of a heavy tarpaulin to the top of the tank tracks, staking the lower end about seven feet out from the side of the tank. This made a dry tent shelter for the crew, where they spread their bedrolls and enjoyed the luxury of being dry and able to stretch out and sleep comfortably, although completely vulnerable to any projectiles or fragments flying at ground level.

In areas of active operations at the front, tank crews were forced to remain constantly in their vehicles, where space was cramped and contorted and sleep was almost impossible, except for an exhausted doze of a few minutes now and then. Tanks were never dry, nor warm, nor comfortable for sleeping purposes.

In cases where tanks had harbored a short distance from the front lines, a common occurrence in Normandy, the crews would dig a pit behind the tank about a foot deep and narrower than the spread between the tank's tracks. When the pit was completed, it was frequently lined with a few sheaves of wheat, for padding, and then the tank would back over it. This arrangement provided protection from airbursts or bomb fragments from above, and some protection from the sides as well, for the crew sleeping in the pit. The digging was necessary to assure sufficient room to sleep beneath the tank without being crushed if the steel monster should settle a few inches in the soft earth during the night, as they not infrequently did. It also permitted all members of the crew, who always slept with their weapons next to them, to get in and out of the shelter trench easily in order to stand their shifts on guard, a never-ending, nightly responsibility.

Rations for Canadian tank crews were supplied by the British army in "compo boxes." One compo box was considered adequate to nourish a tank crew for 4 days. Different varieties of rations were identified by varying designations printed in block capitals, from A to F, on the ends of the boxes. It did not take long for preferences to develop in favour of canned bully beef in Compo A, of Sultana Raisin Steamed Pudding in Compo F, and so forth. Almost needless to add, these preferences were exercised by troops in the rear areas who were the first to get at the supply trucks as they moved forward. The least appetizing were Irish Stew in Compo C, or "M and V" (meat and vegetables) in Compo D. By the time the ration trucks reached the forward units, everyone further to the rear had already had his choice, and these two unwelcome concoctions were frequently all that was left for them.

The idea of having canned food that required only heat to make it more or less edible, was basic to the Compo scheme of rationing, and it did serve to nourish thousands of army men throughout the European campaign. The food was heated on small primus stoves supplied to each tank. As a general rule, one crew member was generally designated as the crew cook to prepare the meal, whenever there was time to stop and cook.

It was about this time that the word "scoff" came into the lexicon of the Canadian Army with a new meaning. In each box of compo, regardless of its letter designation, would be a can containing dry tea leaves, powdered milk and a little sugar, already mixed. A handful of this mixture would be thrown into a small open pot and brought to a boil on the primus stove. The barbarous, steaming grey liquid so prepared, formally known as tea but bearing little resemblance to that noble drink, attracted a great following among the tank crews nonetheless. They would prepare a "scoff" to warm themselves, cool themselves, quiet their nerves, or for any other reason, whenever an opportunity presented itself. It quickly became the universal drink in the army.

Dishes and eating utensils consisted of a pair of mess tins fitted together, a cup, and a knife, fork and spoon. Adequate cleaning of these utensils was seldom possible, with predictable results in the hot days of a Norman summer. The clouds of flies that were attracted to the rotting, bloated corpses of horses, cows and humans in all directions in the Calvados plains country meant that food was often contaminated by the time the eater spooned it into his mouth from an open mess tin. Dysentery became rampant, and regimental medical officers prescribed doses of opiate of mercury or any other palliative to hundreds of men.

On one of those magnificently hot, dusty days of early August, 1944, when the apples reddened and the wheat fields ripened to a golden yellow, the entire regiment harbored close to the battered pavement of the ruler-straight road from Caen to Falaise. MacLean and his crew saw it all happen. A motorcycle dispatch rider, or 'D.R.', came streaking along the road, hooting and ridiculing the many forms he saw on both sides of the road, bent double and groaning as they relieved their dysentery-wracked bodies one more time. The view, as seen by the D.R., was uproariously humorous; a regiment of tanks parked off the road, while most of its crew members crouched in an irregular line and defecated in the field, each with his shovel and his copy of the Maple Leaf newspaper handy.

What the poor devil on the motorcycle did not see, occupied as he was with the off-highway sights, was a steel-reinforced concrete light pole of the type that lined many highways in France. This one had been hit and weakened by the shell fire of an earlier day. It had bent over and was currently leaning across the road ahead of him, about one yard above the tarmac. Warning shouts came too late. With a sickening thump, his chest struck the cement pole extending across the highway. The riderless motorcycle roared onward for about 50 yards before careening into the ditch, the rear wheel continuing to revolve rapidly. The D.R.'s lifeless body was wound around the un-yielding cement pole like a banana skin.

Sandy Forsyth ran forward to offer help or aid to the hapless form, but there was of course nothing that could be done. The eyes of at least 50 hardened soldiers, who had phlegmatically seen death dealt out repeatedly since landing in Normandy, froze in instant horror, as a rollicking, happy-go-lucky young soul, unknown to any of them, threw his life away.

MacLean thought to himself, war was war, with its own cruelly indifferent ways of terminating youthful life; but the death of this D.R. touched them all because it was an accident that need not have happened; completely outside of the fighting and deliberate killing that the war demanded. "The poor bastard," he heard on all sides, "why did he have to get it, when all he was doing was having himself a good laugh."

CHAPTER VII

ON TO FALAISE

The failure of "Totalize" to carve its way through the German defences blocking passage from Caen to Falaise produced a new directive from General Montgomery, telling the First Canadian Army to "capture Falaise, as a first priority, to be done quickly." All Canadian troops were told of the urgency of closing the Falaise gap, between the American armor coming up to Argentan from the south and the Canadian and British armies very slowly approaching from the north. As repeated to the troops numerous times, the plan was to trap the large German forces which had been dispatched to the west in a futile effort to split the American forces at Mortain.

Consequently, MacLean and his comrades found themselves busily engaged in preparing for another major strike southward to implement this strategy. Maps were issued; fuel and ammunition was topped up. All Crew Commanders were told that the objective was approximately eight miles further along the road to Falaise, through a thick screen of enemy armor, infantry and anti-tank weapons. The plan was to run the gauntlet of this awesome defence in daylight, while it was screened off by a curtain of smoke. All the tanks, halftracks and other fighting vehicles available to the 1st Canadian Army were to spring forward on August 14th, on what was to be called "Operation Tractable." The attack was to be heavily supported by artillery, which would be available to hammer any efforts made by the Germans to try to escape the Falaise Pocket, in which they were to be firmly confined. At least that was the outline of the plan that General Simonds favored at the moment, but he could be relied upon to change his plans frequently.

August 12th proved to be another warm and beautiful day, with low winds. The fine, chalk dust rose in pillars behind any vehicle that moved on the wide plain surrounding Maizieres. But a great many movements had to be accepted, in order to get the great assemblage of vehicles into their proper places for the charge that would soon commence.

Ahead of them, at the bottom of a shallow valley ran the small Laison River, described in all the intelligence reports from Corps head-quarters as "a mere stream," fordable by any army vehicles at almost any place. The open plain was dotted with a number of farmhouses and buildings, most of them surrounded by healthy-looking groves of tall trees in full greenery at the height of the summer. Rising gradu-ally to the west, from a series of undulating grain fields, was a tree-covered height of land that extended as a green border along the sky-line. This part of the plains of Calvados lay pristine and beautiful to the eye, for war had not yet marked its course that far. Although the Germans were believed to have concentrated in and around the woods covering the height of land on the right, there had not yet been a heavy exchange of artillery fire between the enemy ahead and the Canadian and British guns to the rear.

Noon was known to be the kick-off time for the advance across the Laison and into the fields beyond. Radios buzzed and crackled as hundreds of operators netted in their radio sets to the control signals emitted by each Regimental Commander's vehicle. The enemy must have heard that too, but the netting drill had to be gone through any-way, if communication was to exist between members of all the units involved with 'Tractable' that day.

Ken MacLean stood idly talking to Len Matthews in the shade behind his tank. Matthews was the gunner for Major Frederickson, in the Squadron Commander's tank, parked nearby. The two had become acquainted a few days earlier and shared interests in many of the same subjects.

"I see you've got a new boss in your tank, Len. What do you make of him so far?" asked MacLean.

"He's not just my new crew commander. He runs the whole damned squadron you know. He was just Captain Cassils in No. 3 Squadron before they promoted him a couple of days ago, and now we've got him. We can't say much about him yet because we haven't been in action with him, but, he has to be a hell of an improvement over what we had."

"I wouldn't know much about Major Fredrickson. Remember I haven't been around the squadron very long. But you've been his gunner ever since training days in England. Fredrickson seemed to be a big loud bugger at the squadron briefings, but now that you mention the subject, we thought it was strange that we never heard a thing from him when we went into action at Cintheaux, or at Hill 195. We did see your tank turning back toward Bretteville when we came past there. What was that all about?"

Matthews warmed to his subject, as he leaned closer to MacLean and dropped his voice to be certain he was not being overheard.

"Let me tell you about him then. The main reason you didn't hear many orders from old Pete was that once the shooting started, he couldn't give orders. Scared fartless! When you saw our tank going back to Bretteville, you'd never guess the reason. Major Smith from No. 3 Squadron came over and asked our exalted commander why he had taken his tank out of action. He expected to hear that we had mechanical trouble or something like that, but Major Fredrickson said he had to go back to the tank harbor because he had forgotten his pistol. Can you believe it? Ordered his tank and all of his crew to head back there, so he could look for a .9 mm pistol! Took a tank out of action to do that! And then at Hill 195, as soon as the action got heavy, he sat on the floor in the turret holding his head, leaving us really without a Crew commander and Rudy couldn't fire the master gun with him sitting there. If he had, the recoil would have hit the Major square in the face. Whatever happened outside, Pete was never going to stick his head out of that turret and give any orders to anyone. A 'cease fire' commander if I ever saw one."

"For God's sake," muttered MacLean in an awed whisper.

"And this after all the bullshit he spread around about his big battle experiences in Italy and in North Africa with the British army, when he was on loan to them. He just makes me sick, Ken. If he can't

118

stand the gaff of fighting in battle, then he could at least be man enough to admit it and get out. But he wanted to bluff his way through, and as a Squadron Commander at that!"

"Major Smith must have seen through him, when he caught him running away to get his pistol."

"Sure he did. Snuffy Smith is nobody's fool. It sure wasn't long after that before Fredrickson was transferred out and we got Cassils. If he's half as good as Amy in No. 1 squadron and Snuffy in No. 3, we'll be in great shape. Good luck out there today, Ken. There'll be a lot of new faces in hell for breakfast after this one; " and Matthews sauntered off toward his own tank with an airy wave of his arm. The time for start-up was approaching.

Noon hour brought forth a sight never to be forgotten. A hot sun blazed down from a cloudless sky. Golden wheat stalks waved gently in the whisper of wind that swept the fields. All of the huge array of fighting vehicles brought by the Canadian Army to do battle in France were spread in a stirring display of armed strength as if on a parade before admiring crowds. Exercise 'Tractable,' poised like a thick, coiled spring, was ready to dash forward the last eight miles to Falaise, where they would hopefully rendezvous at the end of the day. Everyone was cheered and enthused by the awesome concentration of armed might assembled around them; persuaded that they really could be almost irresistible. Engines in hundreds of vehicles ground into gear as Major Hamilton, the acting Commanding Officer of the Grenadiers for that day, ordered "advance now," throughout the regimental radio net. They were off on the greatest armored charge that any of the participants would ever see. The troops called it the "Mad Charge."

Leo Codal drove his tank at the prescribed speed of 12 miles per hour, as he steered at the head of the column near the left side of the great mailed fist aimed at the Germans. He had been told by Sandy, "for direction, just head toward the sun."

The smoke shells which had been fired by the artillery had landed in the proper places to screen off the wooded heights to the right, where the Germans were known to be dug in, but the smoke screen was thin and patchy at best, and certainly not as dense as hoped for anywhere.

They had all heard the gospel from the planners of 'Tractable', that running the gauntlet of enemy tanks, anti-tank guns and artillery in broad daylight on a narrow front could be made quite manageable behind the cover of a smoke barrage. Looking out on what MacLean could see of their "protective curtain," there was certainly room for doubt. But the central thought in all their minds for the moment was to get ahead, maintain the pace of the drive and blast any target that appeared in front of them, for there would be no friends up there. Whether the smoke obscured them from any German guns or not had become completely academic - the charge was under way.

Very shortly after the advance began, the leading tanks of No. 1 Squadron encountered the muddy little Laison, the small meandering stream on the maps, which was supposed to be easily fordable almost anywhere, by tanks or other tracked vehicles. But two of the lead tanks which rushed into it quickly became mired in its muck and water, their crew commander's bellowing profanely on the radio net that they were stuck, and that other tanks would have to locate some safe crossing points elsewhere. "This bloody anti-tank ditch," as someone labeled it, "is quite enough to stick anyone, at least at this crossing."

All semblance of squadron formations was lost and abandoned as frantic searches for fordable crossings of the innocent-looking Laison took place in all directions from the axis of the attack. Fording places were eventually found, and disorganized clusters of tanks from any and all squadrons rushed toward the revised crossings. Then they fanned out in a multitude of tracks, pursuing courses they thought they might have been running, but for the disruption caused by the accursed stream. The initial planned blueprint for locating each of the squadrons in its own area, so that the proper spread of frontage for the charge would be maintained, was scrapped completely.

"Where the hell should we head for, Sandy?" asked Leo Codal from his driver's seat, as he strove to avoid hitting other tanks from both No. 1 and No. 3 Squadrons, all speeding up through the waving grain fields after clearing the bottleneck.

"Nobody knows where they should be in this bloody schmozzle. Just drive toward the sun Leo, and drive hard."

The fog of war had definitely descended upon the entire scene. Clouds of dust rose from the tracks of the churning tanks. The explosions of Canadian artillery shells registering in the wooded areas to the right side of the field could be heard regularly. With the tank still on the move forward, Bill Brown peppered the woods with machinegun fire, where Sandy had seen some suspicious enemy activity. He even fired two H.E. rounds while traveling, just for good measure.

The noise level reached uncharted heights, as machineguns chattered and tank guns slammed in the midst of the charging horde. The crash of incoming shells from the enemy ahead began to intrude ominously, as the advance continued pell mell over ditches and across open fields by the whole 4th Armored Brigade, with some Churchill AVRE tanks of the Royal Engineers close behind. It seemed as if they had all been mixed with a spoon in a giant batter.

The turret crew in Forsyth's tank received a violent shaking and jolting as Leo piloted the Sherman just short of absolute maximum speed, barreling across shell craters, sunken roads, hillocks in the ground, ditches, slit trenches and level stretches in the ripening grain fields. MacLean braced his feet against the ribs of the side of the turret basket to maintain his position on his small, round loader's seat, bucking and swooping beneath him with every lurch or crash of the tank. Bill Brown simply tightened his grip on his control levers to keep from being flung on one of the dozens of sharp, hard corners or projections in the bouncing turret. Quick glances through the periscopes confirmed what Forsyth had been relating to them on the intercom; the German tank and anti-tank gunners were beginning to take a toll among the Canadian tanks, notwithstanding the artillery-fired smokescreen.

Other things began to happen near at hand too. Several of the tanks ran over Teller mines, which blasted the track off in each case and immobilized the tanks. The Germans, true to form, had already set their mortars on the exact location of the mines. Even though obscured by smoke, the unfortunate crews of the disabled tanks discovered that, upon dismounting to repair the damaged tracks, they were the targets of deadly accurate mortar fire directed on them by unseen gunners. The radio reported that the tanks of six troop leaders were already out of action, in a battle not yet half an hour old.

Forsyth directed Leo Codal further to the left side of the force, to get an open field of fire without endangering friendly vehicles traveling in the same group. Brown fired a lot of machinegun ammunition toward some movement spotted by Sandy in the trees, and again attempted to blast his target with a few H.E. fired while the tank was on the move. This sort of shooting of the master gun was more for effect than for accuracy. In the course of their southward rush, they overtook some German infantry desperately trying to move to other trenches. Brown gave them a savage working over, leaving none of them still moving. Next they encountered the crew of an 88 mm anti-tank gun struggling for all they were worth to change the position of their weapon in the weapon pit, so it would point in the new direction from which the Canadian troops were arriving. This time, Bill called for a momentary halt of the tank, to be sure of dispatching the gun and crew with a few well placed rounds at quite close range. Brown made no mistake about the fate of these five Germans.

"That's getting the buggers," shouted Sandy from the cupola ring, as the tank picked up speed again, past the smoking wreckage of the 88 mm gun. "Another minute or two, and they'd have had that Goddamn thing working, and they'd be picking us off just like we picked them off. It's nice to see a battle go our way for a change," he concluded with a big smile, his gloved hands slapping the cupola ring in satisfaction.

It was about an hour after the charge commenced that attrition began to take a lot more of the steam out of the seemingly invincible armored drive. Although no German tanks had yet been sighted by Forsyth or his crew, there was evidence that effective anti-tank fire was thinning out the ranks of the Grenadier tanks nearby. The surviving members of the crews of three tanks could be seen scrambling clear of their Shermans, already starting to smoke as they stood motionless in the wheat field. The turrets pointed in widely different directions.

Visit by the author with his parents in Edmonton while on embarkation leave

Peering back from the turret of the author's tank in the column advancing through a recently liberated Dutch town

The author leaning against front of his tank with other tank crew members at bivouac in north-west Germany

Fellow Grenadiers butcher young calf slung from muzzle brake of author's Firefly tank in north-west Germany

Sherman M4-A4 DD (Duplex Drive)

The DD tanks would be the first weapons to reach the shore. A DD was a swimming tank, powered by the tanks's engines, and kept afloat by a collapsible canvas screen which was lowered on landing, thus permitting the tank's guns to be immediately brought to bear on the enemy defences. Armament: one 75-mm gun, two .300-inch machine-guns, one .50-inch machine-gun. Crew: five. Speed: 4 1/2 knots afloat, 25 mph on land. Land range: 120 miles. Weight: 33 tons

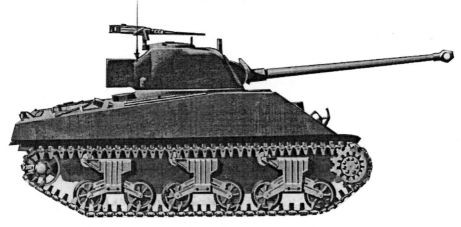

Sherman M4-A4 'Firefly'

The Firefly was the first successful Allied attempt to match the gun-power of the German tanks. This was essential, for the German Panther and Tiger tanks were already known to be formidable – and the result was the Firefly, which mounted the British 17-pounder heavy anti-tank gun on the hull of the well-tried Sherman tank. Armament: one 17-pounder gun, one .50-inch machine-gun. Crew: five. Speed: 25 mph. Range: 120 miles. Weight: 32.9 tons

German Panther tanks in Normandy in preparation for battle

German King Tiger tank moving through downtown European city toward battle

Lt. Col. E. A. C. Amy, d.s.o., m.c.
Officer Commanding 22 C.A.R. (C.G.G.)
1945

Lt. Col. H. A. Smith, d.s.o., m.c.
Officer Commanding 22 C.A.R. (C.G.G.)
1944 - 1945

Two of the bravest of the brave, both sucessive commanders of the Canadian Grenadier Guards in N.W. Europe

DD tanks lead Canadian infantry through shattered village after landing near Berniere Sur Mer, Normandy

Hon. Lieutenant Colonel N.J. Stewart (front) and Hon. Colonel G.C. Meier of King's Own Calgary Regiment on armoured exercise at Camp Suffield

Officers of the King's Own Calgary Regiment on occasion of presentation of the new colors by the Queen, 1990, in Calgary, Alberta. (author 3rd from left, front row)

Heavy artillery shells hurled by Canadian and British guns, could be heard crashing into the German positions in the woods to the left. Past a quartet of burning tanks in the third open wheat field they had crossed, MacLean and his colleagues churned on, following the last known directional order they had heard, "toward the sun". Sandy continued to look grimly out from his hatch, swinging his gaze from left to centre and back again, the part of the field of vision for which he was supposedly responsible.

Suddenly, without any new or additional sound or notice, a gush of blood, with fragments of flesh and bone, splashed down from the open hatch of the turret and Forsyth's bulky body slumped, his fingers squeezing the cupola ring which he had be gripping. The upper part of his head was shot off. An AP shell, fired just inches too high to hit the side of the turret, where it would have killed everyone in the turret, had hit Sandy's head like a giant meat cleaver. As his fingers lost their grip, his body dropped to the floor of the turret amid the spent shell casings, in a pool of his own blood and fragments of his head.

Brown and MacLean stared in shock at the grisly sight at their feet, unable at first to realize or accept the fact that this heap of legs, arms and torso, encased in a khaki uniform now soaked in blood and gore, had been their friend and mentor seconds earlier. They were snapped out of their shock by a massive crashing clang on the side of the hull. The tank shuddered and came to an immediate halt.

"We're hit. Get out down there!" shouted Brown to the drivers on the intercom, as smoke quickly eddied into the turret, brought in by the fan from the engine compartment where the second shot had struck. As Bill turned to climb out the hatch, a tongue of flame leapt forward along the drive shaft beneath the turret, a sure sign that the vehicle was already afire and would quickly become an inferno.

MacLean had to crawl under the breech of the master gun, across Forsyth's bloody and decapitated body on the turret floor, and then up the rear of the turret wall, using Sandy's old seat as a step to climb out of the open hatch. Brown reached back into the turret to help him get out, in the few seconds that would be available before the ammunition would begin to explode. As he jumped to the ground, he thankfully spotted both drivers already crouching beside a track made through the wheat by another tank ahead of them.

"Where's Sandy?" asked Leo Codal, looking desperately upward at the tanks above him, then beginning to burn vigorously.

"He's in that turret, and he'll never come out," responded a shaken Ken MacLean. "He's dead. He took a shell right in the face. That was the first shot from the gun that got us."

"We didn't hear a thing until the one that took us in the engine," said Russell Scott. "Are you sure Sandy's dead?" he added, his brow furrowed and his mouth tight and drawn. He too was loath to accept the statement that his friend and commander had really departed this life, never to be seen again.

"He has no head," said MacLean in a tone of finality. "And we'd better get the hell away from this spot soon or we won't have heads either. They saw us bail out, and they know there are others like us out here. They'll be coming here after us as soon as they consider it safe."

As if to give point to this remark, a Spandau suddenly spat out a tearing burst toward another disabled tank in the field, halted but not yet burning. MacLean and his fellow crew members crawled rapidly down a pair of tank tracks in the wheat field. They attempted to be as inconspicuous as possible lying flat on the ground, in the face of sniper fire from the woods at the edge of the field. Someone had taken some unwise action which attracted the attention of the Germans, because the rifle shots were coming uncomfortably close.

The survivors of all the wrecked tanks in the field were in a real dilemma. They found themselves several miles from their starting point, in strange surroundings of which they knew little or nothing, and quite uncertain of where or even in what direction friendly forces might be located. In addition, they were all poorly armed, having only their personal pistols in their holsters, and in some few cases, no arms at all. This made them easy prey for any well-armed German patrol that might venture out after the armored assault had passed.

In the pause of the firing that followed, MacLean and his colleagues could hear orders being given in German for an infantry sweep, obviously being organized to clean up the survivors hiding in the grain.

"This will be a shaky do," muttered Leo Codal, as the Germans spread out and commenced their advance on foot across the field.

At that moment, one of the survivors of a No. 3 Squadron tank, unknown to MacLean and his crew, stood up across the field and, ignoring an assortment of enemy shots fired at him, dug out the spare .30 calibre Browning machinegun stored in the blanket box at the rear of his tank. There was extra ammunition there too, and he fed a belt into the side of the breech of the gun and began peppering the advancing German infantry. Immediately, the Germans realized that this was not going to be the easy shoot-up of almost unarmed and helpless tank refugees that they had anticipated. In short order, they withdrew again to the trees behind them, not to be seen later that afternoon. MacLean and his friends had been spared to fight again.

For the men lying in the wheat fields, attempting to evade the attention of German snipers, it seemed the beautiful summer afternoon would never end. Instinct and discretion dictated that it was wise to crawl along tracks already made in the wheat by tanks passing through, for two reasons: first, because they did not have to fear creeping over unexploded mines while crawling in a tank track; and second, because it would avoid creating a tell-tale line of movement in the standing wheat, which could attract a sharp-eyed sniper's interest.

MacLean found himself crawling behind Russell Scott in the same track, through wheat stocks only about 18 inches tall. He noted Scott's insistence on crawling on his hands and knees, when a much lower profile was required for real concealment.

"There are too many of us together here Russell," said MacLean. "Why don't you take that track and I'll follow this other one?" he asked when they spotted a fork ahead.

"Right," responded Scott. "I'll see you at that hedge down there below us," and headed off in the new direction, still high on his hands and knees. MacLean continued to edge his way slowly and exceedingly carefully along his track from a fully prone position, as the sun beat down on his back unmercifully. Uncomfortable though it was, MacLean was loath to try any other posture while he wriggled along, lest the extra movement catch the eye of one of the snipers concealed in the trees. Against the background rumble and crash of artillery fire coming from the rear areas on all sides, the occasional crack of a rifle or the burp of an MG42 betrayed the continued German interest in the men still hiding in the fields. Screams or groans sometimes followed the snipers' fire, indicating that some of the snipers were deadly accurate.

Suddenly a wicked "crack" sounded from a larger gun, probably a 20 mm flack gun, of the type being used against aircraft from the German position. An angry streak snapped across the field, directly above MacLean as he lay still in the track.

"My God! I've been seen," he muttered, awaiting the next shot lower down by a few inches, which would surely end his days forever. But the second shot never came. MacLean began to feel that perhaps the flack gunner had just fired a random shot, one that happened to streak across above his chest. After several anxious minutes of waiting patiently, MacLean again edged forward on the track he was following. Progressing ever so cautiously for perhaps a further 50 yards, his head met a pair of boots ahead of him in the same track. Easing himself past the motionless boots to see who was attached to them, he saw the lifeless body of Russell Scott, crumpled face down, in the narrow path through the grain. MacLean quickly realized the reason for the single shot which had so narrowly missed himself. Russell's unwillingness to crawl on his belly had indeed been his undoing, just as MacLean had foreseen.

No ordinary rifle bullet would do the kind of damage which MacLean was forced to study at close quarters. MacLean was certain it had been one of the flack gun's, 20 mm shells that hit Scott. It had almost torn his left leg off and then ripped open his lower back to the abdominal cavity. MacLean took extra care to avoid crawling through the pool of blood surrounding the body. Flies were already gathering, and thousands would follow. MacLean was anxious to get well away from the place, quickly if possible, but without attracting renewed attention from the same deadly gunner. Scott had died without uttering a sound, and MacLean did not want to make it a duet at the same spot.

The crawl continued towards the line of bushes behind them, a completely likely goal for men lying without shade or shelter in the punishing heat of an August afternoon in the Calvados fields. They had had nothing to drink, and no clear idea of where they should go, to escape the enemy ahead of them. Several of them were nursing wounds of varying levels of seriousness, some that needed medical attention soon. All of them wanted to gain the marginal security of a slit trench or even a ditch where they could get below ground level, out of the baking sun and out of the line-of-fire of bullets or shrapnel raking the ground around them.

The crawlers were still short of their goal by about 50 yards, when a 'moaning minnie' was fired from the woods ahead of them. A salvo of wailing, shrieking rockets, passed overhead with their characteristic 'wooshing' sounds, after they climbed aloft. Ken hugged the ground even closer upon hearing the unearthly and unnerving wail, wondering where its rockets would descend. The full salvo landed squarely on the fringe of bushes toward which they had been crawling, decimating every branch and trunk.

"Thank God we didn't crawl any faster," said Bill Brown with relief. "Nobody could live through that. I wonder if any of our gang were hiding in that thicket."

They soon learned from one of the other escapees that at least three men had crawled into these bushes for shelter. One of them was their tank driver, Leo Codal. Bill Brown looked morosely at Ken MacLean, shook his head and dropped his voice to a whisper.

"They wouldn't stand even a ghost of a chance there. The way those rockets explode, you get terrific blast and big chunks of shrapnel that would just cut a man to pieces. Look at the bushes there. All blasted to hell. Nobody survived that shower. And if I'm right, that just leaves the two of us still alive from our crew, Ken. And by God, we're not out of this mess yet either. Look over there. I don't like what I see there."

What Brown had seen was a trio of German soldiers carrying a white flag and wanting to talk to the handful of men huddled in a tiny hollow in the wheat field. The gist of their message, given in passable English, was that the Canadians should surrender to the encircling German forces by 5 o'clock, or they would be wiped out in an attack by all the Germans around them.

A burly corporal from No. 2 Squadron of the Grenadier Guards stood up to talk to the Germans. "You tell your commander that he's got it all screwed up. He can surrender to us by 5 o'clock if he wants, because he's going to be surrounded; not us. We are sure as hell not surrendering while we can still fight."

The three Germans withdrew, talking among themselves, and the threatened attack never materialized.

Shortly afterward, a lieutenant in the 15th Regiment of the Royal Canadian Artillery edged into the small group. He had been riding in a Bren Gun Carrier that had been knocked out earlier in the afternoon. He noticed the presence of three or four men who appeared to be suffering from their wounds, and told MacLean and his associates that he thought he knew of a way to get them back to Allied lines. He mentioned a fitters' service vehicle, (a tank hull will the turret removed to provide room for the tools and equipment of the fitters) that had been stopped in a small valley in the field about 1,000 yards away. He promised to creep over to the vehicle and, if it could be started, he would have it pick up the wounded from among MacLean's group and make a run for it to get them back. He emphasized that the vehicle had a Sherman tank hull, so they needn't fear sniping or machinegun fire once they got into the vehicle.

Without more, away the lieutenant crept, and hope was renewed among all of the group with MacLean and Brown, especially the wounded men, who saw a chance for survival.

Time passed, and nothing more was heard of the stray artillery officer, as an hour slipped by. The scene around them had become definitely quieter, as they awaited the coming evening, hoping that darkness would intervene before the Germans attempted another attack. Suddenly, the sound of a tank engine coming to life came from the direction the artillery officer had taken. Directly afterward, the recovery vehicle appeared, exactly where they were told it was concealed to the surprize of everyone. The driver swung the vehicle in the direction of MacLean's group, gathering speed as it approached. The artillery officer who had returned to the vehicle was perched on the equipment piled in the centre of the hull.

"Thank God for this," said Bill Brown. "These guys can get the wounded men in, and I'm damned if I know how else they would make it."

But the recovery vehicle did not stop, or even pause, as it swept past the expectant group. With its engines going flat out, it rushed past the waving men and across the open field ahead of them, gradually disappearing from sight.

"There they go. They've got the wind up and they want to run whatever chances they have to get out of here, and to hell with anyone else. That was sure a pretty speech we got from that officer, wasn't it. The bastard wanted directions from us, but he wanted nothing to do with helping anyone else out of here, even the wounded men," said Ken bitterly.

"Maybe we'll see the son-of-a bitch again sometime," said Bill Brown. "He was the 4th Division Artillery. I'd like to have a little talk with him on even terms, if we ever see him again," he added, his eyes glinting with menace.

Everyone in the group felt cheated and betrayed. Many an oath was sworn as to what would be done with the rogue artillery lieutenant if he was ever found again, but like most of this talk, little was really expected from it. The men settled down in the hollow to wait and watch events unfold.

Optimism increased as the sniping from the nearby woods died away. This was considered a sign that the enemy troops were steadily moving elsewhere. Within sight of MacLean and his colleagues there were the hulks of eight Canadian Sherman tanks that burned steadily, their fires fed by their fuel tanks. From time to time the steady fires would be augmented by small explosions, as ammunition popped-off in the great heat inside the hulls.

After watching closely, the men became convinced of the direction to take, to regain their own lines, if that should become possible after darkness fell. They would walk toward the sound of the heaviest artillery fire, which they strongly believed must be the Allied side of the fields.

Evening came on, as great shadows lengthened from every tree in the woods along the margin of the field where they huddled. The sky remained bright above them, but visibility on the ground was definitely diminishing. Three German tanks, a Tiger and two Mark IV's lumbered out of the woods and stopped a mere 400 yards away from the awed group, as they frantically sought concealment among some shallow ditches. The German crews, fatigued after what had probably been an intensely busy day, for them too, dismounted from their vehicles. They were talking volubly and too preoccupied to notice, or even to care about, the handful of Canadian soldiers stranded in partial concealment nearby. Their attention was captured by a pair of handsome, twin-bodied P-38 fighters that wheeled lazily over them at high altitude. More to amuse themselves than to make a serious effort to bring the P-38's down, the crewmen of one of the Mark IV tanks swung the Spandau machinegun atop his turret and fired a long, steady burst at the rapidly vanishing fighters without any real hope of reaching them. Then, as darkness closed in around them, all the panzer crewmen re-entered their vehicles and withdrew the way they had come, to the great relief of the men who had been silently watching them.

In the comfort of the early purple and black of nightfall, the group of refugee Canadian tankmen emerged from their ditches and holes to gather around MacLean and consider their next move. Some of them were bearing up well, in spite of painful wounds. They were stoical about their injuries, but quite outspoken in announcing they "wanted to get the hell out of here soon," lest they should be swept up by another group of Germans.

The darkness of night became pervasive, with the exception of the lights cast by several fires still burning in various tanks knocked out in the day's fighting. When MacLean's group decided it was dark enough to attempt the journey back to their own lines, they wearily set out along the tracks made through the grain when they were charging forward. There was a safe feeling in walking in these tracks, in the theory that if mines had been in place along the route, the tanks would have already put them off when they came through. MacLean and some of the others realized that this was a fallible belief, but it gave comfort to many of their colleagues.

"We've encountered Teller mines with a ratchet on the fuse," MacLean observed quietly to a skeptical Bill Brown. "The ratchet required a second, or even a third pressure before it went off. And then there are those damned "S" mines that they put out. As antipersonnel mines go, they are some of the worst. The fact that a tank went through here might or might not snag the wire that puts them off. When they hop up and then explode, they really hammer anyone within 20 yards of the mine. But I think it's worthwhile following the tank tracks anyway, if for no other reason than the fact that they will take us back to where we started from".

After nearly an hour of cautious walking in the general direction from which came the loudest sounds of artillery, hopefully Canadian and British guns, the group suddenly froze in mid-stride. There, clearly silhouetted against the flickering light from a distant fire, they saw the outlines of German helmets on the heads of about six or seven heavily-armed enemy soldiers, moving stealthily across their front not more than 40 yards away. The Germans, probably on a fighting patrol, carrying automatic weapons and lots of ammunition boxes, could not see the Canadians in the darkness surrounding them, but they had heard them, and stopped to await developments. MacLean and his colleagues, weakly armed with a few pistols, knew they would be no match for the German patrol, still seen clearly ahead of them, if it came to a fire fight. After several tense minutes, during which gutteral muttering could be heard by the Canadians, the German patrol got to its feet again and moved off on its unknown journey, probably uncertain of what it had heard and not willing to take the time away from their own problems to find out.

When it was presumed safe to breathe again, the Canadians rose and walked on. MacLean, who was walking beside Brown at the head of the short column, said to him:

"Our luck holds, Bill. I don't know why, but we seem to have it today. Wonder what's next on the program?"

They weren't long wondering, as they continued to cover more distance toward the lines they sought. From out of nowhere, a fighter plane of unknown origin flying in the black void above, dropped a parachute flare, which brilliantly lit all their surroundings. Apparently the pilot could see more than they thought he could, for he promptly fired an extended burst of machinegun fire into the pile of firewood ahead of them. Mercifully, no one was hit, although everyone dove for cover until the mystery pilot flew away. Whether friend or foe, they speculated, but never found out.

Again the group got to its feet after the flare had burned away, and slogged onward, a much chastened group. They began to concern themselves with the problem of approaching their own lines in the darkness, having spent most of the night trying to find their way to them. After some discussion, they resolved to talk loudly and otherwise act inconsistent with an enemy group stealing up in the darkness. They had become deeply concerned about drawing fire from some trigger-happy sentry on their own side.

After a further hour of walking, they were challenged in a thick Scottish broque; "Who goes the-r-re?" With great relief, they informed an outpost of the Gordon Highlanders, in the 51st Highland Division, that they were Canadians. The long trek had ended, and it was time to take stock of who went where, and who was still functioning.

"I wouldn't want too many more days like that one," Brown commented to no one in particular. "I figure the average lifetime in a tank is about five days of combat like we've seen here lately. Hell, we've had casualties among reinforcements who didn't live long enough to become known to the other guys in the troop! I hear no one got out of Anderson's tank after it was hit and they don't know who three of the crewmen were, even yet."

"Yeah. Life is cheap here at times like these," responded MacLean. "We're losing men faster here now than we did anywhere since D-Day. I guess Carpiguet Airport was nearly as bad as this, but this has been the worst to date."

The driver returning them from the Highland Division, not knowing any better place to take his Canadian Grenadier Guard passengers, followed the road signs and let them off at their own R.H.Q. early on the morning of August 15th. The arrival of a vehicle bearing 51st Highland division markings created a certain mild interest among the troops attached to the R.H.Q. Troop. MacLean and Brown climbed down from the small Bedford truck, dirty, unshaven, and without baggage or kit of any kind. They looked owlish and glassy-eyed after a completely sleepless night; really not a particularly engaging sight for a Guards regiment.

No less a person than the commanding officer of the Grenadiers, Lieutenant Colonel William W. Halfpenny, was just emerging from his private van, or "gin palace" as it was commonly called. That was where he slept while quartered at R.H.Q. He was rubbing his hands together and swinging his arms in the brief calisthenic routine he pursued after a good night's sleep, while eying the steaming breakfast that his loyal batman, John Henderson, had prepared for him. MacLean and Brown felt awkward and out of place, deposited almost on their Commanding Officer's doorstep without explanation or a "by-your-leave" so early in the morning. The soldiers could not fail to notice the comparative elegance effected by their commander as he stood before them; his neatly pressed battle dress complete and correct, even to the carefully knotted wool necktie and collar pin in place; and his high brown leather boots gleaming with a fresh coat of polish. It was hard to reconcile this figure, attired and comported as if appearing on a dress parade, with the image of a fighting commander leading his regiment through a bitter struggle with an experienced and formidable enemy. But then, Halpenny had always preached to his officers that standards of deportment, "need never be compromised in any circumstances."

After a baleful and condescending glare in the direction of the disheveled soldiers that had been left standing near his vehicle for some unknown reason, Halpenny turned his attention to his first meal of the day.

"What will it be for breakfast, this beautiful morn?" he asked his batman, with eager anticipation in his voice. The continuous rubbing together of his hands made MacLean think ungenerously of Uriah Heap. Henderson poured hot tea into a cup for his boss and answered, "It's going to be porridge, bacon and toast, sir. I had trouble getting the bread. All we ever get with the rations is hard-tack biscuits."

The continued presence of MacLean and Brown, just standing silently to one side of this almost comic-opera scene, nettled Henderson in the carrying out of his tasks. The colonel could see this, and determined to put an end to it. He called out to them in a voice of annoyance and bother:

"What do you men want here? Why don't you go to your squadrons? Your crews will be looking for you."

"We don't know where our squadrons are, sir, and we don't have crews to rejoin. We are all that is left of our crews in yesterday's attack," responded Bill Brown in a testy, tired voice.

Halfpenny, only slightly taken aback, continued to talk dismissively towards the unwelcome guests. "Go to the adjutant's vehicle. He'll attend to getting you assigned then." And in the next breath he added, "I hope the bacon is crisp this morning John. Make sure that it's almost brown. That's when it's crisp enough."

The Adjutant appeared, without being sent for, having overheard the C.O.'s irritated voice and instructions. He quickly saw that the men of the group before him had had a rough time of it, and needed food, sleep, clothing and weapon replacements in about that order. They also needed directions about where they should go in order to get themselves re-established. But first he wanted them interviewed by the Regimental Intelligence Officer to obtain any useful information they could have, especially concerning enemy locations and strength.

The Intelligence Officer, Captain Hill, arrived at R.H.Q. shortly, and began interrogating the dozen or so men in the group. He asked where they had been knocked out of action, by what sort of weapon, and what they saw or did thereafter. MacLean was one of the first to be interrogated.

"Whose tank were you in, and where is the rest of your crew?" came the first question.

"Sergeant Sandy Forsyth's tank, in No. 2 Squadron," came MacLean's reply. "I was the loader-operator and Bill Brown here was our gunner."

"And the rest of the crew?"

"That would be Sandy himself, Leo Codal our driver, and Russell Scott our bow gunner. We believe they're all dead."

Halfpenny, who could not help overhearing the interrogation, interjected quickly at that point; "Now, be discriminating in what you record in your report of the action yesterday, Captain Hill. You must not assume that the rest of the crew were killed just because one guardsman says they are all dead. That man certainly doesn't know for sure, or he wouldn't put it that way. Maybe all three of them will turn up later. The first exposure to battle conditions often shocks men into some pretty wild conclusions, you know."

MacLean eyed the C.O. venomously, but said nothing more on the matter.

"And what did you see on your way back? I want to know what you can tell me about strengths and positions up there. Try to show me on this map where you believe you were and the route you took to get there," said Captain Hill, continuing his questioning.

Both guardsmen, bent over the map laid out before them, spending a few minutes getting themselves oriented. Then they both agreed upon the location of the field in which they had lost their tank, really not as far away as they had first imagined. Ken spoke for both of them, pointing his finger at the map.

"That's where we lost our tank, Captain. Right there."

MacLean paused, and then said, "Just before we started back, we saw three German tanks, a Tiger and two Mark IV's come out of the bush close to where we were knocked out. They fired their machineguns at some aircraft overhead for a few minutes and then withdrew into the same woods there, where I would guess they still are. We heard them shut their engines off after they disappeared into the trees. It was getting dark by then, so we bugged out."

Again Halpenny interjected. "We have heard nothing to confirm the existence of any German armor that far out on the left flank of the drive, Captain Hill. Reports last evening said that the enemy were withdrawing armor to the south, ahead of the push. I would question whether these men really saw what they say they did at that location, because it's just not consistent with our information from Div. H.Q. Impressions from men new to battle shouldn't be relied upon too much, you know, as I was just saying. Perhaps these men are mistaken about their location yesterday. Our Division intelligence comes from observations by other people, you know, so we can't just ignore their information. They reported no enemy tanks on our left."

"Yes, sir," said Hill resignedly, as he turned to another of the tired group before him to hear his story. Halpenny withdrew to the far side of his vehicle to focus his attention on the breakfast set out for him on a small camp table. "First things first," he had always urged, and the first thing in his mind was breakfast, at the moment.

Bill Brown looked wrathfully at his departing Commanding Officer, and then back to Captain Hill, whom all of the troops rather liked and supported. "The Lawd Jesus," he hissed. "He thinks anyone from the ranks is some kind of moron who wouldn't know a tank from a truck. We have lived with map reading for months, as you know. We are just as able to recognize where we are and what we can see as he is. I'd like him to know that this is our third action since we landed and I back up everything MacLean said. Speaking of experience in action, what the hell does he know about it, dressed up like a pimp at a garden party while he rides around back here in his gin palace? MacLean, by the way, has been fighting tanks here since D-Day, more than two months ago, so I think you can write down what he tells you, without worrying whether he was imagining things because of his lack of experience in action."

"Easy there, Brown," replied the Intelligence Officer in a calming whisper. "We all have to live with our Commanding Officer. Enough said, for now," and he turned back to another member of the group before him, a thin knowing smile at the corners of his mouth. "And what did you see out there, Guardsman Seagrave?"

The troops in need of first aid were paraded to the M.O. at the Regimental Aid Post. For the remainder, as soon as the questioning was completed, Captain Hill led them off along the path to the trucks of the Quartermaster, discreetly parked at the edge of a copse of trees where he could be separated from the supply trucks that hauled the water, ammunition and fuel for the Regiment.

"See what you can do to kit these men out again, R.Q. All they have is what you see."

There followed a rather frustrating session with the Quartermaster, where only a few of the necessities for life in the Regiment seemed to be available. Even these were given reluctantly under the sardonic gaze of a man who acted as if they had sold or wilfully discarded the kit they had lost.

Then they headed for No. 2 Squadron in hopes of scrounging something to eat. Food had become an extremely high priority with men who had not eaten for 26 hours. Next, it was time to sleep. With the blessing of the Adjutant, who showed genuine sympathy for their situations, they all climbed into the hay-filled loft of a nearby stable, there to "sleep the sleep of the damned," uninterrupted by noise, shouts or interference of any kind for hour after hour; a wonderful, relieving and restoring experience that brought them back from the exhaustion they suffered.

Awakening after their much-needed rest, as the daylight of August 15th dwindled away, MacLean, Brown and their other sleep-besotted colleagues were offered food again from the No. 2 Squadron cooks, and told to report for duty with the tanks of R.H.Q. Troop that evening, actively supporting the Regimental advance toward Point 159 on the hill overlooking Falaise.

The Canadian attack had fallen short of its objective by a considerable margin. Although the geographic distance to Falaise was not great, the intervening region was heavily defended by enemy troops and armor trying desperately to keep the escape route open for the many German formations encircled beyond the town. The Germans were well aware that their only salvation lay in their ability to force their way south and east through the Falaise Gap, between the Americans to the south and the Canadians and British to the north.

Replacements were required in Corporal Mel Graham's tank in R.H.Q. Troop to replace casualties and make it operational again. This troop had been working with the tanks of No. 3 Squadron, as they sought to bring fire to bear upon the enemy scrambling along the roads near Epancy. Bill Brown was told that he was the new gunner and MacLean was to be the loader operator. Ed Foley, a veteran driver in the Troop, remained from the earlier crew along with John Gardiner, the bow gunner.

Graham's tank headed back for a necessary rendevous with the vehicles in A Echelon, where replenishment of fuel, water and ammunition was completed. Then it joined a violent and costly scrap with a battery of 75 mm anti-tank guns further along the road to Epancy. Graham shouted his praise for Brown's gunnery, as he blasted a skillfully constructed and camouflaged pillbox strong point at a bend of the road ahead. But they were still three miles short of entering Falaise, when the attack was broken off.

Targets for the tank gunners were becoming numerous, as the Grenadiers inched onward into the Gap area. Brown's 75 mm gun spoke regularly, as he fired H.E. shells into the enemy half-tracks and trucks which jammed the way forward.

There was really no route that would circumvent the awesome mass of wreckage burning and smoking on both sides of the road. The destruction included vehicles, wagons, horses, and men, all mixed together in horrible, stinking heaps, just where the Allied artillery, tanks and rockets had dropped them. No one had ever seen anything like it.

"This is where we get even with these buggers for last week," Brown snarled across to MacLean. Ken continued to feed H.E. shells into the smoking breech of the 75 mm gun as long as Brown kept firing into the shambles ahead. Graham's tank did not have to move for some time, because new targets kept presenting themselves on the crowded road below. He and his crew greatly appreciated the reversal of the roles of hunter and hunted, as they had usually been playing them since landing in Normandy.

Ed Foley sat quietly attentive with his co-driver down below in the drivers' compartment, the engines idling while they waited for orders to move to the next location. They watched closely through their periscopes, as the frenzy developed only about 1,000 yards in front of them. In spite of themselves, they felt a measure of pity for the horses and men being butchered as they persisted in their attempts to force "the Gap." Everyone there thought of the killing room in a packing plant, as they stared forward, horrified by what they saw.

Periodically, some R.C.A.F. or R.A.F. Typhoon aircraft swept over the crowded road, firing rockets or machineguns into the cauldron beneath them. A flight of U.S. Thunderbolts on a bombing mission along the road, unfortunately released several bombs into the region occupied by the Grenadiers, causing several casualties and one death. Although casualties to friendly forces are always especially tragic and demoralizing, the close intermingling of Canadian and enemy troops at Falaise made such an accident much more likely.

The shattered elements of the once powerful 5th and 7th German Armies struggled desperately to force their way along the only escape route still available to them. Out of concealment, and into clear view on the roads came trucks, halftracks, and horse-drawn field guns, all swarming with shouting, gesticulating soldiers, savagely charging eastward to gain some distance in their bids for escape.

A human avalanche was being projected along the road below Graham's tank for two days. Magnificent mid-summer sunshine greeted the gunners in Normandy that August. The noise of battle filled the air, as machineguns and shell-fire stuttered and roared about them. More rockets and bombs hurtled down from frequent fighter-bomber raids on the stalled enemy columns. The bodies of dead cows in the fields, and dead horses and men along the roads attracted millions of flies and scavengers. The rotting, putrid bodies swelled quickly to the bursting point in the great heat of the days. The stench that arose from this charnel house was beyond description. Even the pilots of the Typhoons, Spitfires and Thunderbolts flying over the ghastly scene in the gap, were sickened by the odors.

"This is the worst yet, and getting worse by the hour," said MacLean during a short break in their firing.

"Hell must be better than this," said Mel Graham, his nose wrinkled and his eyes squinting as he peered through his binoculars at the chaos below. "We're going to move down closer to the road there in a few minutes, according to what I heard on the regimental net. They want some tanks down there to prevent any German armor escaping. And we're supposed to stay clear of the fields of fire of the Polish tanks further up on the hill there. The Poles are firing at everything that moves around them; German or Canadian. Be ready to move when we get the order, Eddie."

Graham was a very tall, lanky individual from the Eastern Townships of Quebec, a quiet, farm-bred person who seemed content to do what was expected of him as a crew commander, but always cautiously and without undue risk to himself or his crew. The specific job of the R.H.Q. Troop was to provide armored support and protection for the Regimental Headquarters staff, including the commanding officer. This was an unspectacular role, but a necessary one if the Headquarters were not to be left defenceless in a rapidly moving battle in which the fighting squadrons would be closely engaged in their own pursuits. Graham seemed happily suited to his job in the R.H.Q.

Troop, but the two newcomers to his turret crew were less enthusiastic about their close proximity to the head of the chain of command and the largely defensive role which they would be expected to play there.

For the moment however, there was enough excitement for everyone, including the R.H.Q. soldiers, as they joined heartily in the task of pouring fire into the disorganized enemy ranks ahead of them to prevent their escape. The Canadian forces had been assured that any Germans who did escape from Falaise, and there were bound to be many of them, could be counted upon to re-appear in a future encounter, and probably on grounds more favourable to the enemy the next time.

The battle of Falaise ground on; the intensity of the fighting undiminished so far as the Germans were concerned, although many recognized the almost hopeless situation confronting them and surrendered to the nearest Allied troops. Others fought on fanatically, determined to give no quarter and to ask for none in return, in their unbending determination to break through the crust of enemies surrounding them. Casualties and deaths were inevitably heavy among the encircled masses of the troops, as they took desperate risks to cut their way toward what they regarded as freedom. And the casualties were not all among the Germans. Many Allied units felt the wrath of the pent up Nazi desperation and fury. This was especially true when groups of German troops occasionally gathered around a few of their remaining tanks or other armored vehicles to form a battering ram to punch a hole through the defences gathered around them. The ferocity of the fighting escalated as the pocket tightened around them.

MacLean and his friends were pleased to receive orders late in the day to withdraw from their aerie above the blighted main road to Falaise, and take up a new position at still another contact point facing eastward, covering the road to Trun. It was August 18, and heavy rain fell that evening as they rolled past groups of infantry from the Lake Superior Regiment. They also saw long lines of German prisoners who had been completely surprised by the rapid advance of the Canadians in their sector. Quite inadvertently, they had marched straight into captivity, as they headed into an area they were certain was still occupied by their own troops.

A German liaison officer and his dispatch rider were taken prisoner by Grenadier officers, riding unconcerned along the road toward what they believed to be the H.Q. of the 7th German Army. They couldn't have been more surprised when told by their captors that they were some seven miles behind the Canadian lines.

The next task for the Regiment was to cut the Trun-Chambois highway. There again there were multitudinous targets to fire upon, but heavy fire from German 88 mm guns, and an array of smaller calibre weapons had to be faced in return. MacLean's tank, along with others from the Grenadiers took on a lot of targets seen further up the valley as long as daylight lasted.

After darkness fell that day, the Regiment was told to head through the night to a high ridge, known as Point 259, where they were to relieve a large Polish force which had become isolated, through movements of troops in the 2nd S.S. and the 9th S.S. Panzer Divisions. These two divisions had forced their way out of the Falaise Pocket a day earlier, and then returned along other routes, intending to keep the gap open so German formations still trapped could be released. Through woods and orchards of a countryside not too well suited to tank warfare, the Grenadiers drove on August 21st, past hedgerows littered with corpses, and flanked by smashed and abandoned vehicles, in a general downpour of rain that made climbing the road very slippery in places. The breakthrough to the surrounded Polish troops, finally effected by No. 3 Squadron, was met with great relief and rejoicing. They had been suffering shortages of food, water, fuel and ammunition since they were surrounded by the two large German battle groups. Their condition was becoming desperate when the Grenadiers finally got through to them.

From the heights at which the Polish troops had been fighting, the Grenadiers marched their sullen prisoners, taken from two battalions of Panzer Grenadiers, down past the abject carnage and destruction scattered for miles along what had been a lush and verdant Norman Valley. There were piles of corpses of men, hundreds of dead horses and smashed wagons. Captors and captives saw disabled or ruined tanks, trucks, field guns, cars and livestock lying everywhere, in the open fields and across the roads, stinking, fly-infested, smouldering and ruined. The sickening smells of rotting flesh, burning straw and pools of water rose in an all-pervasive stench that no one there could ever forget. It was defeat for a mighty host; a crushing, unimaginable disaster beyond the experience or imagination of anyone there.

After the relief of the Polish Division, MacLean and his colleagues traveled back to the road leading eastward from the Falaise gap. The gap finally closed on August 22nd. The Grenadiers, with infantry support from the Algonquins and the Lake Superiors, manhandled the German formations still inclined to fight their way out. In the process, they knocked out two more Mark IV tanks, an S.P. gun and several soft vehicles still bent on running the gamut through the 4th Canadian Armored division.

By August 25th, the battle of Falaise had come to an end, for MacLean and all of his comrades. It had been a terrible period to live through, a period of fighting that, for many of those who survived it, remained in their minds as the worst experience they had ever endured.

CHAPTER VIII

A FIRST RETROSPECT AFTER LANDING

Captain P.J. Benson, Second in Command of No. 2 Squadron in the Canadian Grenadier Guards, was feeling expansive. The regiment had just laagered near Chambois, a tiny village east of Falaise, and reinforcements along with new tanks were arriving. Also arriving were mail and parcels from home. The large and totally unexpected parcel for "P.J. Benson, Captain, 22nd Canadian Armored Regiment, Canadian Army Overseas" etc. was enough of a surprise that he decided to open it privately later on.

A small inn had been requisitioned only the day before as a temporary officers' mess, and it was to that dusty old building that Captain Benson headed with his once-read letter and his unopened parcel. There, in the presence of five or six other regimental officers, he began unwrapping a large, cardboard box. After removing two carefully taped and sealed plastic containers, one inside the other, within the box, the prize was revealed - a huge loaf of brown bread!

"How very thoughtful of your relatives, Benson. Bread is the staff of life, and they think you're starving, do they?" asked Major Smith sarcastically. "We could stand some more bread in place of that damned hardtack, but why all the wrapping just to send you some bread?"

"I'm not so sure it is just bread," murmured Captain Benson. "The sender is an old university friend of mine from McGill, and he is not noted for his consumption of bread. In fact I don't remember his ever eating it. See if the cook has a good long knife," he said to Lieutenant Naylor, a new officer in No. 1 Squadron.

With one slice across the middle of the giant loaf, Benson revealed the true purpose behind mailing bread to Normandy from "Somewhere in the United Kingdom." There in the heart of the loaf, which had been carefully baked around them, were two bottles of Queen Anne Scotch whisky, Benson's favorite blend. Absolutely delighted, he proudly announced to the half dozen other officers gathered in the room that the drinks were on him, starting forthwith.

Settling back in a rickety old chair with a glass of "the water of life" as he called it, Benson said he truly felt entitled to be expansive that evening. "And let's not hear any requests for ice or ginger ale in this magnificent beverage. There is no ice available, and if any man here wants ginger ale, he shouldn't drink scotch anyway. Just add water and stir."

As the other officers drew up their chairs, glasses in hands, for a long-awaited and richly deserved pre-dinner drink, Lieutenant Naylor put the brand in the powder keg with his first question.

"Peter, you're a history buff from away back. You studied it and taught it at McGill for many years. And now you've lived through a bit of history being made here in France. How would you evaluate the Canadian Army's performance in Normandy so far, from what we know now?"

Knowing that Peter Benson could never pass up a chance to expound on what the army should have done, and what in fact it did do, in almost any epoch, the other officers in the small group settled down on the assorted old chairs and a small divan that had seen better days, prepared to listen. Benson eyed the level of the whisky in his glass, decided to top it up slightly, and then uncoiled the long legs that carried him about. His deep-set, dark brown eyes sparkled as he tugged at the end of his substantial moustache, brushed a fleck of lint from a well-fitted battle dress jacket and began to speak in his favourite professional rumble. He tried not to appear too didactic, but his sage observations upon what he saw and heard belied the background from which he had come, some four years earlier. After one further puff on his stubby pipe, he began.

"Well gentlemen, it won't be a comforting story. When this thing they called 'Totalize' was being lined up, we were told that we were about to mount an armored punch of almost irresistible strength. They said it would 'cleave through a weakening defensive barrier put up by the Germans still cluttering up the road to Falaise.' I think those were the enthusiastic words used. As you all know, we were supposed to link up with the Americans at or near Falaise in a giant pincer movement that would pinch out two German armies trapped in the pocket created by the pincers. I suppose you could say that that is generally what finally resulted, but it sure as hell didn't fit the timetable set for us by our eminent planners; nor was it accomplished in a way that would reflect much credit on the commanders of the units involved." Being very candid, it doesn't appear, from the rather meagre forces the Americans committed to forcing the Falaise Gap closed, that they wanted to break their asses on this task either."

"For Christ's sake Peter, my men couldn't have fought any harder than they did. And day after day, for a week and a half too," argued Lieutenant Livingstone from No. 3 Squadron.

"I'm not criticizing the efforts of the men, Freddie. They gave everything they had in the way of effort and there are all too many of them missing now as a result. And that goes for the junior officers and N.C.O.s as well. What I am saying is that the plan, if you could call it a plan, seemed to call for nothing more subtle or ingenious than a hammer blow, delivered at high noon, straight into the teeth of the German forces guarding the main road to Falaise. Let's be frank about the results; the Germans, whom we completely outnumbered in every way, put up a hell of stout defence, from everything I have seen and heard. It took us the best part of two weeks to reach objectives that we were expected to occupy in a couple of days. We had to kill a lot of Krauts to get there, but they took a real toll from our side as well, a lot more than would have been lost if we had had a better battle plan and some sharp top commanders to run it."

"But what do you expect from an armored drive?" queried Lieutenant Naylor again. "We had the strategic job of punching through a defence belt six miles thick, to close a pocket around two German armies. How do you act subtly or ingeniously when you have a task like that? I've learned that some disorganization and departures from the basic plan are integral parts of fighting a tank battle."

"Well, to start with, you needn't kick it off at high noon on a brilliant summer day. Sure, we were supposed to be able to compensate for the high visibility by smoking off the German position. That certainly didn't happen, and in the prevailing weather conditions, it couldn't happen. Then it might have been useful to know enough about the ground immediately to your front when you commence the drive, that you don't rush into a God-damned creek that forces all the tanks out of their assigned positions and lines of advance. They all rushed into a number of enormous bottle-necks that developed at the few places where they could ford the stream. From that point on, it was just a mad dash by a hell of a lot of tanks toward the sun, in the hopes of over-running the enemy positions. Not exactly a brilliant tactic against a concentration of anti-tank guns and big tanks with greatly superior guns, with open fields of fire yawning before them, and plenty of ammunition, just waiting for us."

"Our advantage lay chiefly in our excess of both armored vehicles and troops over what the Germans could muster. To realize on those advantages, as the military strategists write, you have to widen your front so that you are able to attack your enemy somewhere that he does not have the resources to defend. We didn't do that. We abandoned our tactical spread, in favor of slugs of troops and vehicles attacking just where the German defences were strongest and most effective. We played into their hands," Benson concluded.

"You make it sound so bad from our standpoint Benson. You never mentioned the fact that our planners could count on a huge superiority in aircraft and artillery working for us in the attack," argued Naylor, who enjoyed a good argument almost as much as he enjoyed a second dram of Benson's scotch. He smiled broadly as his adversary, of whom he really thought a great deal, began wagging his finger at his listeners.

"Sure they could," came Benson's riposte. "But in a highly fluid battle like the start of this one, with tanks scattered from hell to breakfast over miles of country, and no certain knowledge of precisely where the Kraut defences were located until we bumped into them, it was hard to use our superiority in planes and artillery to full advantage on the way to Falaise. Once the pocket became defined, our planes and artillery really worked them over. But until then, we had to fight our way forward field by field; hedgerow by hedgerow, which is damned slow and expensive. We never managed a concentrated, armored drive on a narrow front with sufficient closely integrated tanks and motorized infantry to overwhelm our way through the enemy defences, even though we would have had substantial casualties to men and vehicles in the process. That idea was developed by the Germans, who called it a 'Schwerpunkt', a place of main effort, which is not the place where the principal resistance was encountered."

"Their idea was to keep the drive moving at any costs, always bypassing strong opposition, and fighting only when there was no alternative. The great panzer drives that the Germans mounted in the salad days of their 'blitzkriegs' usually had at least two columns advancing simultaneously, swinging back and forth from one direction to another to achieve almost continuous progress. In this way the defences against them were baffled as to where their columns were headed next. They certainly did not head for the stoutest defences, as they directed their pincer columns."

"Our commanders should have known all this, but never took a step to introduce any such tactics or strategy on our side of the front. They just pounded forward, and the Germans made us pay the price. In an attack by troops and tanks scattered all over hell's half acre, we gave them the opportunity to deal with us piecemeal, bit by bit, and they bloody well did exactly that."

Lieutenant Livingstone then rejoined the fray. Putting down his glass, he asked, "But what about your flanks? How do you protect them when you focus your main thrust in a central drive on a narrow front? Don't you risk getting cut off from open flanks?"

Captain Benson nodded his understanding of young Livingston, and replied, "That's where you employ your aircraft and artillery superiority, as you move forward, without endangering your own troops unduly. The ground commanders could also greatly affect the likelihood of having the "Schwerpunkt" outflanked and cut off by their own manoeuvres. Ideally, they would have two or three attacking columns advancing on more than one road toward the common objective. The columns could then converge in pincers around any force trying to outflank them, and turn the tables on them. Suddenly the defenders find they are themselves out-flanked. The Germans had great success with these tactics when they controlled the attacking forces in Europe. But our army commanders were never taught along those lines in staff college and certainly didn't have the benefit of a powerful General Staff behind them. Furthermore, they didn't learn much from known history either."

Captain Benson paused to replenish his drink and then continued. "You guys think I'm too theoretical and too damned critical of our own commanders. I know. I can see it in your faces, and perhaps you might be a little bit right. But I produced this wonderful whisky for you, so I get first chance to expound my military beliefs before you, and to ask at least a few questions myself. Why do you think the Germans have done so well in fighting against the Allies in Normandy when they were completely outnumbered in troops, planes, tanks, fuel and ammunition?"

"They have far more experienced troops than ours, and their tanks and guns, what they have of them, are just plain better and more powerful than ours," responded Naylor, a note of irritation creeping into his voice.

"I could agree with you about their weapons, but I certainly can't accept the argument that all of their troops are so much more experienced than ours. We have been fighting a lot against the 12th SS Panzer Division, and all the prisoners we ever took from them were from the Hitler Youth; they fought like tigers, and most of them were in their very first action. They did have experienced officers and NCO's leading them, true enough, but our I.O. tells us that the majority in numbers of those guys were new to heavy fighting, just like us."

"Well, what do you think the difference is? Is it the military tradition in Germany that develops a better soldier, or what?" came the questions from a new quarter, Captain Ross of No. 3 Squadron who had idly wandered into the mess and found himself greatly interested in the sermon that Benson was delivering.

"I think that our men are every damned bit as good as any they have, man for man. Give our men the same training and leadership that these Krauts have had, and they would equal or excel them regularly. The difference has got to be in the leadership that the Germans provide. Damn the German government for all they have done to the world if you will, but they provided funds to equip and train a mighty force for years before they pushed them into action. We've read about big military exercises being undertaken in Germany since 1936. We've seen pictures of the German commanders manoeuvering brigades, divisions and armies in training exercises, and later in action. They found out about the logistics and the problems of moving masses of men around in big training exercises, and later in the real thing in Spain, France and soon."

"By contrast, nobody in the Canadian Army, not even its Commander or anyone else, ever handled so much as a brigade on manoeuvres anywhere before the war. Our government believed in starving the military budget, year after year, between the wars. There was never enough money granted to cover the costs of adequate military training and exercises. The only requirement our government made upon its pitifully weakened military leaders was to provide a parade now and then, whenever they might be called upon. There's a price to be paid for that kind of policy, and we are paying it here."

"And so ends the sermon for today, chaps," said Major Smith with evident good humor and good will toward all of his fellow officers. "Now that the dinner hour has arrived, we'll finish off our glasses and bugger off. Captain Benson must be thanked for the lovely libations, but you can see the price we have to pay for it: listening to his sermons about how he would run the army if he was a field marshal, rather than just a captain. However it's a price we are always willing to pay, Peter. You can always lecture us whenever you supply the scotch. And who knows: perhaps you are dead right. I have the feeling, deep down, that we have a lot of people on our side of the fence that have never learned a bloody thing from what they were taught, and even from what they can see happening right before their eyes. That is what I consider unforgivable, when I see the same errors being made time and again. But let's forget about it for a while and join the gang for dinner."

CHAPTER IX

FLIGHT, PURSUIT AND CHANGES IN CAMPAIGNING

The German forces that escaped the cauldron of Falaise continued their flight eastward in search of a new front, behind which they could reorganize and re-establish themselves as a cohesive force. MacLean, along with his fellow Grenadiers, followed the withdrawal of the beaten army eastward from Falaise, and on August 23rd, they arrived at the Seine River in hot pursuit.

It was a wet, cold and windy morning that greeted everyone throughout Northern France. Driving along the roads heading eastward, without much risk of being shot at until they caught up with the enemy again, MacLean, like most of the other tank crewmen, rode on the outside of the turret, where the air was fresh and the view was wide and picturesque.

Crossing the Seine River on a long Bailey bridge at Elbeuf, there were only incidental signs of war around them. Bill Brown and MacLean debated with Corporal Graham where they would be likely to encounter the fleeing Germans once more. There was some small action that developed with tanks close to the head of the column, as they encountered brief anti-tank fire and mortaring when they swung north-eastward from Elbeuf to Rouen, but this resistance was quickly quelled. The tour continued, at highway speeds, past cheering, flower-waving civilians and hyperactive F.F.I. as the French resistance forces were called. They were always and forever eager to demonstrate their hatred toward 'Les Boches.'

At the entrance to Rouen, they saw an incident that reminded them of just how severe the occupation by the Germans had become. A horse, had been shot beside the highway by an FFI member a few hundred yards ahead of Graham's tank, probably to put it out of its misery. It was set upon by three civilians, bent upon carving it up for food. By the time that Mel Graham's tank had advanced to a point opposite the carcass of the horse, a matter of 15 minutes, more or less, only the horse's skeleton remained by the road - every morsel of meat had been stripped off and carried away for food by the starving citizenry. Ken was impressed.

No attempt was made by the Germans to establish a new line of defence near the Seine River, with the exception of a few minor skirmishes with small groups left behind expressly to delay the pursuit. The Grenadiers increased the speed of their column as it rushed through a succession of small French villages all the way to the Somme River, the site of some of the heaviest fighting in World War I. This time an easy crossing was made at Abbeville.

The Germans had hurried on eastward, almost without firing a shot. MacLean heard on the radio that the nearby town of St. Valery had been retaken by the 51st Highland Division. This was a most appropriate development, since an earlier version of the gallant 51st Highland Division under General Fortune had been forced to surrender at the same place to an overwhelming German force in 1940, in the course of the collapse of the French armies.

To gain some time and distance in the rapid pursuit across Northern France at the beginning of September, the Grenadiers, who found themselves at the head of the brigade column, decided upon a night march to bypass a number of other formations following the same centre line north of Aumont. Since no headlights were permitted, all tank drivers were instructed to simply follow the twin pin-pricks of light at the rear of the tank ahead of them to stay on course. The whole column was to be led by the Recce Troop, who were navigating as best they could from a map and an occasional glance at the few road signs seen from time to time en route eastward.

With most tank crews riding on the outsides of their vehicles through the darkness, as they rumbled through what was apparently a peaceful countryside, it was with some astonishment that MacLean saw the head end of a fast-moving armored column approach and pass them going in the opposite direction. Their strong suspicions were soon confirmed by an announcement on the radio that the tanks then passing them were from the head of their own column. Confusion reigned supreme in the darkness that night, but the correct heading was finally established after much profanity on the radios and keen embarrassment for the Recce Troop, whose job it was to reconnoitre new country, using their highly developed map-reading skills.

A further half hour of semi-blind driving passed without any notable event. Then suddenly from the head of the column, almost half a mile beyond MacLean's tank, came the unmistakable sounds and flashes of enemy guns. Major Snuffy Smith's No. 3 Squadron, aggressive as ever, immediately poured gun fire into the tiny village ahead, aiming at the fires they had started with their first shells. Three enemy anti-tank guns were silenced forever, the survivors of their crews having taken instant flight. At least two members of the German gun crews died horrible deaths in the darkness, having first taken refuge in a straw pile that was quickly ignited by the tracer bullets fired into it. Unwilling to come out of the straw piles into the fields of fire of the tanks, they waited long enough for their clothes to ignite. They were last seen running away from their hiding place screaming and burning like two torches lighting up the night.

As the Regiment reformed, more anti-tank gunfire came in from the north and No. 3 Squadron quickly dispatched No. 4 troop to deal with this threat, while the rest of the Regiment sat on top of their tanks in the moonlight, the better to see the show. This time an ammunition truck was hit, and as it exploded, the small force of German troops that had fallen into exhausted sleep at the side of the road, were mown down as they fled. By this time the LS.R. infantry had arrived in their halftracks to clean up the confused situation around them. They quickly brought in over 50 prisoners and several more vehicles.

Corporal Graham, sitting high on the cupola ring of his tank and watching the events unfold hundreds of yards ahead of him, was startled to see a man climb up on the deck plates beside him, totally out of breath and seemingly desperate to get inside Graham's tank.

"Here there. Who are you and what the hell do you want here?" demanded Mel of the frantic climber.

"Oi'm Reston in the Recce Unit," came the frightened response in a strong cockney accent. "Can o'i get in your tank?" he asked in a terrified voice, and then made to climb in through the hatch without waiting for a reply. It was then that MacLean and the crew noticed the hat badge on Reston's beret, the badge of a British Hussar unit which had been providing reconnaissance for the night march of the 4th Canadian Armored Division. This explained an Englishman's presence among them.

"Hell no, you can't get in this tank," answered Graham. "What's the matter with you anyway?" as he barred the way to the terrified Reston. "We're got a full crew here and there's sure as hell no room for any more. What's got the wind up you anyway?"

"We was ridin' along in our scout car, at the head of this bloody column," came the rushed explanation from Reston. "We was tryin' to follow the road in the dark. We had no idea we'd bump into 'Jerry' in 'ere. Suddenly this bloody great gun went off from the ditch right in front of us - only about twenty feet in front of me - and this bloody shell went back about four inches over me 'ead. Never had nothing like that before in all me bloody loife. I leapt out of the scout car and ran. I must 'ave run all the way to your place 'ere. No bloody wonder I was scared. That bastard fired almost in me bloody face, he did."

"Look. I don't know where you can go in the tanks, because they don't have room for any more people in any of them. You must know that much. When this noise quiets down, why don't you just go back to your scout car. It's probably still there on the road ahead," said Graham reassuringly.

"Not on your bloody loife," vowed Reston, still badly shaken. "Oi'm going further back, not up to the 'ead" and he jumped off the tank and disappeared to the rear of the column in the stygian darkness.

"Who the devil was that?" asked Brown after the visitor had left.

"I'll bet I can guess the rest of his story," replied Mel. "He was riding comfortably along in his scout car convoying a night movement of Canadian tanks across country, and kind of enjoying a country tour in the quiet of the night. Then he stumbled into a German

154

outpost, set up where they stopped, exhausted, to get a little long-overdue sleep. Knowing Germans for what they are, they placed their anti-tank gun pointing up the road, loaded and ready to fire on any pursuers before they laid down. When Reston blundered into them in his scout car, he probably got really close to their post before they woke up. When they did awaken, I'll bet their gunner just jumped up and fired the gun in a crash leap. The gun would have been sited to hit a tank, and Reston's scout car slipped under that line of aim. That's why he's still alive."

"He had cause for fright," smiled Brown knowingly. "That damned gun probably fired a few feet from his face, just as he claimed. His feet probably hit the ground running, and he never stopped until he got back here. I wonder how far back he went to get a ride."

"We'll probably never know how far," smiled MacLean, "But if you ask how fast, I believe he was faster than the speed of sound."

It was the day after the all-night march of the regiment to gain time on the fleeing enemy army, that the decision was taken to reorganize for a day or two in a small apple orchard in northern France. Bath parades were arranged and several of the self-styled barbers in the regiment agreed to earn themselves some extra benefits by shearing the bushy-looking heads of a number of Guardsmen who had not had time for a haircut since landing in Normandy. Seats were set up on ammunition boxes, and clippers were brought out of pack sacks, and the shearing began.

Mike Kleza, a tank driver from No. 2 Squadron, and one of the best known and better- qualified "sometime barbers" in the regiment, announced his readiness to begin trimming heads. Mike's greatest claim to fame came, not from a haircut he had given; but rather from one he had received while still in training in Crowborough, shortly before the Regiment sailed for Normandy.

The tale of Mike's notorious haircut, which traveled throughout the unit, had been related about as follows:

One Saturday afternoon in June of 1944, after the Grenadiers had been put upon notice that they would soon be sailing to France, Kleza happened to be walking past the No. 2 Squadron Orderly room, minding his own business. Sergeant Major Blue, often privately referred to as "the Big Stoop," after a not-too-bright character in a popular newspaper comic strip at that time, was hanging around the Orderly Room. He noticed Kleza idly walking past and quickly decided there was something he had never liked about Kleza, and called out to him.

"Guardsman Kleza, tomorrow is a regimental inspection. You get a haircut!"

"But I just got one on Thursday," protested Kleza in mild outrage.

"I didn't ask you when you had your last haircut, I told you to get a haircut. Do you hear me?" roared Blue, his gorge rising at the argumentative reply he had received. He also concluded, from Kleza's contumely tone, that this soldier had no intention of getting another haircut, and therefore should be made an example at the Sunday morning dress inspection, further demonstrating that in Sergeant Major Blue's squadron, 'they had real discipline.'

Kleza, who was no one's fool, reached the same conclusion about his Sergeant Major's intentions for the following day, and decided to thwart them. He returned to his barracks sputtering about the "stupid old bastard who was all hung up about haircuts anyway."

Caring nothing for his image among the locals, because everyone was "confined to barracks" until they sailed to France anyway, Kleza called his pals together after dinner that night for a special haircut that "The Big Stoop" would never forget. First, all the hair was clipped, right to the skin on Mike's head. Then, the top of his head was shaved with a new razor blade, so close that the pinkish skin of his scalp, above the tan on his face and neck took on a distinctive glow. Lastly a heavy coat of wax was applied, a patina that Mike himself buffed up into a brilliant luster with a cloth in his kit. The trap was laid, and everyone in Number 2 Squadron went to bed satisfied and expectant.

Sunday morning dawned a magnificent, cloudless, summer day. What indeed is so rare as a day in June? The band played the troops onto the parade square in splendid martial form, and the big inspection began. There was no doubt about the anticipation in Blue's face when he spotted Kleza marching with the rest of his troop across the square. His tank beret was carefully positioned squarely on his head, as per army regulations, as the band brayed out 'The Standard of St. George.'

They broke into "Greensleeves" for the slow march, as the inspection began. Major Frederickson, the squadron commander, and Sergeant Major Blue, two of a kind on discipline, marched slowly between the ranks. When they reached Kleza's location, Blue glared at him bellicosely.

"You take your hat off!" shouted the sergeant major, confident that he was about to expose a deliberate disobedience.

Without changing expression, Kleza, reached for his beret with one hand and yanked it off. And there it was, for all to see. The sun shone down upon a brilliantly gleaming knob; a polished dome protruding from Kleza's neck; a luminous orb beaming with a shine that rivaled the sun itself. Major Frederickson grunted unintelligibly. Stifled snorts and chortles rose from the troops standing nearby as Sergeant Major Blue gulped audibly, his eyes staring wildly in horror and fascination at the glittering bald pate before him. His mind raced in an attempt to recover his lost dignity and prestige in front of all these men. Finally realizing he had been out-manoeuvred, he gulped and then shouted out lamely,

"Christ almighty, Kleza, you get some hair on there. I don't know how the hell you'll do it, but I'm telling you now, you get some hair on there."

When the laughter subsided in the other ranks, Blue snarled at them to remain steady on parade, while they went on with the inspection. Major Frederickson looked at him with scorn and pity, and the Big Stoop never forgot it, though weeks went by.

As the haircuts proceeded in the field near Rouen, many of the Grenadiers who had been at Crowborough with Kleza reminded him of the caper he had cut with his Sergeant Major on a day that seemed so long ago, though it was really only two months past. Kleza smiled indulgently as his friends inspected the thick stubble making a strong appearance on his head again, as August drew to a close.

At the end of August, the Grenadiers embarked upon the long thrust that would take them across the remainder of Northern France and into Belgium, in the course of which they covered over 200 miles in one week. The uninterrupted advance took the Regiment to the scenic and historic old city of Bruges, fortunately undefended and still undamaged, where everyone was given leave for the rest of the day to explore the town and relax from military duties for a few hours. MacLean and Brown went to a cinema to see an American film. At the end, the lights came on and the packed audience rose in response to the playing of the Belgian national anthem, a poignant moment, since the Germans had not permitted it to be played throughout the occupation years. MacLean and Brown and the few other Allied soldiers present, were stared at and treated like heroes, simply because they joined in the common courtesy of standing at attention during the playing of the country's national anthem.

The Grenadiers then moved on to Eekloo, from which an assault was to be made, ultimately across the Ghent Canal and on toward the Breskens Pocket, in the campaign to liberate the approaches to the huge port of Antwerp.

The fighting in and around the Ghent and Leopold Canals was highly localized, with sharp struggles breaking out in one place after another as the rapidly reorganizing German 15th Army destroyed most of the canal bridges and stubbornly contested the crossings that remained. A long, slow period of successive attacks across individual canals appeared inevitable, a questionable use of an armored division in prosecution of its true capabilities. However, "their's not to reason why," and the infantry certainly required some tank support in the uninviting task before them. So 4th Armored Brigade gritted its teeth and did what it was ordered to do.

It was during this period that the Grenadiers became somewhat better acquainted with the scene around them in central Belgium. Eekloo, a quite substantial town with very little damage, boasted a number of cafes and bars that maintained a limited supply of the dark Belgian beer known as Stella Artois, even through the early days of its liberation. Ken MacLean went with his fellow crew members to sample the local brew one evening, only to find that the beer quota was limited to one glass per patron. Driver Ed Foley, who was fluent in French, was most useful in determining why all the bar maids they saw were wearing cloth turbans: they had all had their heads shaven by the local resistance forces because they had collaborated with "Les Boches," when they occupied the town.

Although little damaged during its liberation, Eckloo was the centre of an area in which the German infantry and engineers frequently demonstrated some of their more devious skills. The placement of booby-traps and concealed mines was developed to an ingenious level in many of the damaged buildings, roads and bridges over the canals. Not content with firing shells into the Lombardy poplar trees that lined every road in the area, thereby creating accurate air-bursts over the heads of advancing tanks and troops, the approach ramps to canal bridges often concealed a necklace of Teller mines or a buried shell from a coastal gun that had been transported to Eckloo. The explosion of any of these super-sized mines could rip a Sherman tank apart, guaranteeing the death of everyone inside.

Booby-traps in damaged buildings were a regular occurrence. The traps could be devilishly clever and imaginative, attached to water-well pumps, isolated doorways, pathways between two thick and impenetrable bushes, or in similar places where people would regularly travel in the normal course of life. Eekloo was also the place where Ken made his first acquaintance with wooden 'shu' mines that could not be located by a mine detector, but could and did smash the bone of any foot placed on them.

Other things happened in the Regiment near Eckloo that Ken had cause to remember long afterward. He could never forget the two notoriously bibulous tank drivers from No. 3 Squadron, Jack MacLeod and Gil McDonald, who could find strong drink somewhere every time the Regiment stopped for a day or more. At Eckloo, in addition to finding a large stock of "coniac" (cognac), they also provided themselves with a magnificent, black Mercedes staff car, which they kept well hidden in a nearby wood during daylight hours. Where they found and "liberated" it was never disclosed. Each day when evening arrived, the two Nova Scotians, once members of the old Halifax Rifles Regiment, could be seen, and heard, easing the beautiful, shiny sedan out of its hiding place and heading toward Antwerp for another night of fun and frolic. Rumors spread from the British Army's Military Police (or MP's as they were known) of the mystery car that made a nightly safari past them and into Antwerp from the Canadian lines, but no one admitted any knowledge of who it might have been.

But as always, McDonald and MacLeod could not stand prosperity for long. Fuel for their limousine was never a problem, for it was easy for them to spirit away a few cans of gasoline brought up to replenish the tanks. It was the fuel for themselves, as always, that proved their undoing. After a few nights of regular carousing they drove the car back to the regimental laager while in no condition to drive anything. The wreck of the Mercedes against a bridge abutment was not total, but a near thing to it. Quite predictably, McDonald and MacLeod climbed harmlessly out of the wreckage with nothing worse than bruises, cursing one another for their inability to drive properly, but not completely certain which of them was in fact steering the car when it wrecked. Many added that, "the devil looks after his own."

There were more wild escapades for the happy-go-lucky pair, of course. MacLean's first direct exposure to them came at Eckloo, after they had consumed a large bottle of Calvados, a very potent apple brandy. They were much the worse for wear, when Ken spotted them in No. 3 Squadron's area; one on hands and knees tightly clutching the grass.

"Why are you holding the grass?" asked Ken quite innocently.

"To keep from falling off, you damned fool," came MacLeod's sullen, drunken response.

There were other episodes involving McDonald and MacLeod, and of course other miscreants from times to time who welcomed a few hours away from fighting tanks and partook of the grape injudiciously in some of the local establishments. However these breaks were brief

160

and they all returned to their duties with the Regiment without creating international incidents.

The campaign by the 21st Army troop under Field Marshal Montgomery to drive the Germans out of strategic locations in Belgium and Holland along the lower Schelde River was moving ahead, but slowly. The rapid armored drive by the 2nd British Army, and particularly the Guards Armored Division, to liberate Brussels and Antwerp in record time had been loudly celebrated by Montgomery. But unfortunately this did not mean that the huge European port could be put to use in supplying the Allied armies because the approaches to the harbor were still in enemy hands. The 1st Canadian Army fell heir to the plodding, unspectacular and thankless problem of clearing the approaches.

"It looks like a long war yet," speculated Corporal Graham, while talking with his crew during a pause near the Leopold Canal. "The infantry needs a few support tanks in these cross-canal assaults, but why the hell put a full armored division in this job? Because we're available, I guess, in answer to my own question. Old Monty really loves the Canadians, especially when a crappy task comes along. We've noticed that."

"And you can get yourself killed just as certainly in one of these small scraps as you can in a big one, if Jerry hits you with the right weapon," added Bill Brown.

"I'd rather stay alive, if it's up to me," Graham repeated for the umpteenth time, "but if I do get hit, I want a quick, fatal shot; one that takes me outright. What I fear is the thought of being badly wounded."

"Well, that's something we can't control," added Ken MacLean wearily, as he did on each of the numerous earlier occasions when Graham had brought up his favorite topics. "In this business you take what you get."

Both Brown and MacLean had made individual requests for transfers back to the fighting squadrons on several occasions, without success. They were much disillusioned by the passive role given the R.H.Q. Troop; by its regular involvement with the administrative people at headquarters; and by the constant bitching which seemed to preoccupy Graham's crew. Mel's testimonial, in which he told the members of his crew about his preference for a quick death instead of long, drawn-out suffering from serious wounds, had been repeated time and time again, ad nauseam.

(Ironically, only three weeks later, while sleeping in the hay in the loft of a barn, Graham was terribly wounded by a mortar bomb which came through the roof above him. He died two days later after dreadful suffering).

Following several days spent in the vicinity of Eekloo carrying out tank maintenance, the regiment prepared to move into action once more. While completing the last parts of stowing the tank with ammunition and provisions, the regimental adjutant, Captain Bicknell, presented himself in their midst, looking for Guardsmen Bill Brown and Ken MacLean.

Addressing Brown first, Bicknell came to the point directly. "We have a spot in a crew in your old Squadron, No. 2, as gunner for Sergeant Brooks. Are you interested in it?"

"Am I interested in it? You're damned right I am," responded Brown. "I'll get my kit over there in 10 minutes. I'd love to become his gunner. I've known him for five years." Then Brown looked at MacLean and became embarrassed, because they would be separating after months of fighting together. "I'm sorry to be leaving you Ken. Maybe we'll end up in the same squadron but just in different tank crews. I'll miss you," he said lamely, realizing that he had been a trifle overjoyed at his own transfer, without regard for what would happen to his friend.

Captain Bicknell broke in. "Guardsman MacLean will not be going with you. He's moving to No. 1 Squadron. I need to talk a little more with you, MacLean. Come over to my scout car here," and he led the way the short distance to one side, before continuing.

"You've had a lot of fighting experience by now MacLean. We also notice that you have an M score that certainly makes you eligible for bigger jobs. Would you be interested in a job as gunner in a tank in No. 1 Squadron for a while? We want you for other things later, but for the present, this will take you back to a fighting squadron, and I understand you and Brown have been itching to get back to one of them."

"Fair enough," responded MacLean without great enthusiasm. "I know the 75 mm gun inside out, but I can't promise to be as accurate as Bill Brown without a lot of shooting practice."

"But you're not going on a 75 mm gun. For now, we want you as a gunner in Hank Maidens' Firefly tank. You would join a good crew of veterans there, but you'd have to learn to handle the big gun in a Firefly. You'll find Hank's tank along with all of No. 1 Squadron over on the left there. Who knows? It may be your tank before long," concluded the Adjutant, with a twinkle in his eye.

MacLean returned to pick up his gear before moving out to No. 1 Squadron, and to say "so long" to the crew he was leaving, most particularly Bill Brown. They had lived and fought together ever since MacLean had joined the Grenadiers several difficult months earlier. Although they had got to know one another better than brothers, their habits and preferences in food and people, their willingness to share everything they had with one another, the parting between fellow crew members was always short and almost cruelly brusque at times like these. Men who would risk their lives for one another in combat were obliged to take leave of one another on a moment's notice without opportunity for expressions of feelings or sentiment. It was the army's way, for time marched unalterably onward.

MacLean and Brown exchanged the usual words of best wishes and good luck, with promises to see plenty of one another at future-get-togethers, even though they knew deep within themselves that this would be highly unlikely. They shook hands, wished each other good hunting and went their different ways.

As it turned out, they never did see one another again. The two squadrons did not fight close together in any actions during the next two months, by which time word had spread that Bill Brown had been killed in action, while his tank fought its way along a canal bank in Holland.

MacLean once again thought quietly to himself; "The originals get fewer and fewer. When does my turn come?" and then he yanked his thoughts back to what lay before him. He had been spared the wild dreams at night that bothered the sleep of many of his friends. So far as he knew, his sleep was never punctuated by wild screams and shouts, like some he knew.

Joining the crew of Hank Maidens' tank was a pleasure. Hank himself was a broad-shouldered, powerful man with a gaunt face and thinning hair. He had worked as a factory hand for years at Lachute, Quebec. An easy-going nature made him a favorite with all who knew him. Hank seemed quite willing to allow MacLean to acquaint himself with the big 17 pounder gun, the special gun-sights and the other equipment installed in the turret to accommodate it, confident that MacLean would make himself an expert on it. Although already in his early 30's, Hank was still the most relaxed and fun-loving crew commander in the squadron.

The loader operator was Tommy Dolphin, also in his 30's. Tom was quiet, reserved and still very much the farm hand from Southern Saskatchewan in many ways. He could be depended upon to do his best at whatever he attempted, according to all his friends and acquaintances. Of average height, with thinning, sandy hair and clear blue eyes, Dolphin's laconic nature fitted well with his steady, imperturbable appearance.

The driver, Henri Brault, was the quintessential campaigner in the crew. A muscular, swarthy man of average height, Henri hailed from Cornwall, Ontario, where he had been a house painter. He took his duties as a tank driver seriously, busying himself with housekeeping chores around his engines, the tracks and the Homelite charger.

All tanks were equipped with a special charger to re-charge the large batteries which supplied the electricity needs of the vehicle. When the tank engines were running, the generators easily handled all the power requirements of the tank; but when the engines were shut off, the drain on the batteries was high, due to the heavy demands for power to operate the radio, the lights, the power traversing gear for the heavy turret, and the starter for the tank engines. When the batteries were drawn down, help was needed from the charging engine. The Homelite charger was a temperamental engine at even the best of times, but Henri Brault gave his charger more attention than most other drivers. His had to work, and work well, or he wanted to know why if it did not. The Homelite became almost his obsession.

Brault scorned the side-arms worn by most of the other tank drivers in the Regiment, much preferring a Sten submachinegun, which he kept in excellent condition on a shoulder strap at his side at all times. Two notches were filed into the barrel of his Sten, just above the foresight. If questioned about these marks, which emulated the characters in the movies about the "old west," Brault would admit that, after being knocked out of his tank in the fighting near Falaise, he had skirmished with a pair of German soldiers in a deadly contest of hide-and-seek around a barn and a wood pile, ending with Brault shooting both of them. Ergo, the notches in his gun. There was nothing of the happy-go-lucky warrior about Henri. He took his job, his regiment and the cause for which they were all fighting with awesome seriousness.

Though quite willing to enjoy a drink away from combat, Henri would never consider any alcoholic beverage before or during any operation. He wanted the maximum performance from all his faculties in the business of war, for himself and everyone with him.

"These buggers that drink that issue rum before they go into action think they're shit-hot; when they're really just ice-cold," he would snarl in his thick baritone voice. "We need a gunner who can aim his gun, not one that feels warm and happy because he liked the rum." And Hank's crew seemed to agree.

In indoctrinating MacLean, Maidens confidentially informed MacLean that Brault had been known to swerve the tank suddenly and without warning, if his eagle eyes spotted the body of a German lying close by the track he was driving. This tactic would take the tank over the body on the ground. When someone asked Henri why he followed this savage practice, his malevolent reply was: "If they're already dead, it won't hurt them; and if they're not dead, they damn soon will be." He had had experience with Germans presumed to be dead, that showed lots of life once they had been by-passed.

Henri Brault much preferred a Firefly tank, where he was the only driver. Utilizing the bow gunner's location for storage of the big 17 pounder shells suited him perfectly. He never quailed about doing all the driving when faced with a long approach, even though most other drivers would be spelled off by other crew members during especially long drives. For Henri, driving his tank was a sacred and solemn responsibility; his alone. He resented anyone else even climbing into his driving compartment, for any reason. He kept it neat as a pin and treated it like his home away from home. There was always a can of white paint handy, for touch-up painting in some of the nooks and crannies of his compartment. Having been a painter in civilian life, the smell and handling of paint seemed therapeutic to him. Stories circulated regularly of the strong odor of turpentine and paint rising into the turret in the midst of combat, when it was stopped but the turret crew were busy with the guns. That would be Henri, painting down in the driver's compartment, to occupy his attention, while the tank was stationary and he had nothing to do. This was a difficult time for any driver, and Brault's response to the tension it generated was as good as any. He remained a calm, steadying influence upon his fellow crew members, even in the most frantic actions.

MacLean began his self-training program as a full time gunner immediately after joining Hank Maidens' crew. Being almost totally unfamiliar with the technicalities of a Firefly tank, he quizzed some of the experienced gunners in the squadron. He and Tommy Dolphin stripped and cleaned the master gun several times, adjusted the head space and the trigger solenoid for the co-axially mounted machinegun, and then checked the power traverse and gun elevating mechanism, really for practice and familiarity with the controls. It was necessary to become fully accustomed to the much more ponderous movements of the largest tank gun on the Allied side. He noted with interest, that the padding attached to the side of the breech of the gun, against which his head would rest when he was sighting

166

through the telescope, meant that the gunner's left ear had to be touching the breech of the gun unprotected even by a radio earphone, when the gun was fired. This assured the gunner of "a hell of a good listen to a real bang," as Tommy Dolphin described it. Little or no thought was given to the effect on the ears of such a tremendous noise focused on the ear lobe, and in such close proximity to it. It was just accepted as part of the gunner's lot in life. It was noticed however that some Firefly gunners could be seen after a particularly active battle with thin streams of blood leading from their ears. MacLean would soon have the experience himself.

The task of testing and adjusting (T and A' ing) the gun sights did not pose a difficult problem, located as they were in a battle zone, where a little extra firing of the guns on local targets could be conveniently arranged. As MacLean quickly learned, firing the 30 calibre machinegun with the customary tracer ammunition aimed at a specific target, was still used to adjust the cross-hairs in the telescopic sight, so that at a measured distance, gunfire landed precisely where the setting on the sight indicated it would. The gunsight also contained graticule markings which could be used for gunnery corrections. The testing and adjusting program for the gunsight of the Firefly proved to be similar to the exercises MacLean had participated in with Bill Brown on the 75 mm gun, but the actual firing of the 17 pounder was indeed a new and different experience. With its long barrel, more than twice the length of the 75 mm gun, and with a much larger shell casing, the propellant for its heartier 17 pound projectile was truly impressive and the velocity of its projectile was dramatically upgraded.

The armor piercing capabilities of the 75 mm gun on a Sherman tank had been found to be inadequate to deal with the heavier-armored German tanks and S.P.'s, traveling as it did at a muzzle velocity of 1975 feet per second (f.p.s.). The barrel had to be elevated by the gunner in order to hit a target at its full range of about 2,000 yards, requiring a considerable exercise of distance judgment on his part. In the case of the 17 pounder, with a muzzle velocity of over 3000 f.p.s., there was little need for the gunner to judge range because the projectile traveled on an almost flat trajectory to its target. Offensively, the Firefly was able to be competitive with the high velocity 75 mm and

167

88 mm guns employed in the German tanks, but defensively its armor was still the same as that of all Sherman tanks.

The firing of all such high velocity guns created a violent buffeting for anyone, including friendly infantrymen, standing close to the muzzle. If fired along the narrow streets in many of Europe's small town and villages, the concussion would often peel the slates off the roofs of the adjacent buildings, to the extreme displeasure of the local residents. They would sometimes emerge into the streets in wild outrage, after the roofs of their homes had been blown away. But MacLean loved the powerful, big guns nevertheless.

After a two day stay near the Ghent Canal to reprovision and reorganize with the new regimental recruits, No. 2 Troop, along with the remainder of No. 1 Squadron moved on northeastward through a succession of small Belgian towns and villages, some abandoned by the Germans without a struggle, and others fiercely defended as they continued their strategy of delaying the Canadian advance by any means possible.

Mines and booby traps proliferated in all the building, encountered in greater numbers in this area of Belgium than anywhere in the campaign. Clearing the roads and villages after years of foreign occupation became a painfully slow and dangerous task for everyone involved. The assignment produced a surprisingly large number of casualties for the progress achieved. One experience in the town of Eupen served as an example of the twisted ingenuity of which the occupying German troops were capable. As MacLean watched, a Canadian engineer pointed to a wire exposed along a door sash, on a nearby house and announced that he had found still another booby trap to be exploded. He proceeded to attach a long cord to the wire at the door and retired to a nearby slit trench, the only shelter handy, where he crouched to avoid the blast when he pulled the cord. But the Germans had out-smarted the poor devil. When the cord was pulled, the blast took place, not at the doorway where the wire was left exposed, but in the lone slit trench in which the soldier had taken shelter, just as the canny German engineer had planned it. The blast was fatal to the engineer.

As Maidens' tank drove further eastward toward the Dutch border, Hank spotted three cyclists pumping hard along a road about 1500 yards away. His binoculars satisfied him that they were indeed German soldiers making their escape, and he ordered Henri to stop the tank.

"There's three Krauts out there at about 1500 yards Ken, riding bicycles. Clear the throat of that gun and maybe you could dust them with an air-burst or two."

Clearing the throat of the gun meant getting rid of the solid-shot AP round always carried "up the spout," in case of encountering enemy armor unexpectedly. In the interests of wasting as little time as possible between sighting a target and firing the first shot from the tank, gunners would often simply fire the shell that was "up the spout". MacLean took careful aim on the two forward cyclists, giving a liberal lead to allow for their movement, set the sight at 1500 yards and fired.

"Christ! Shouted Hank after watching the speeding tracer of the shell. You hit the front one. He just disintegrated when that hit him. Looks like the others just jumped off their bikes and into the ditch. MacLean, I've never seen shooting like that before. We'll call you 'Nimrod' from now on."

Henri Brault, who saw the whole performance through his periscope, was quietly delighted. "Now, let's send a couple of H.E. after the other bastards," he added. It was a simple matter to fire air bursting H.E. to the exact spot where the other two cyclists had jumped, but they never could find out whether they hit them or not.

Dolphin and MacLean, both well aware it had been nothing more than a very lucky shot, smiled in satisfaction to one another. Dolphin, acerbic as always, smiled his narrow smile and said, "Saves ammunition that way, Hank." But MacLean's stock rose with the rest of the crew beyond any doubt. Henri told others how their new gunner had annihilated a German cyclist with a single solid shot nearly a mile away. Everyone was aware of the large part played by luck in a shot such as that, but there was an undertone of increased respect along with it; a few half-kidding comments like "I'm glad he's on our side."

The action in Belgium took them further east along the Ghent Canal. The dike behind which they drove marked the limit of a series of farms, with typical Flemish structures, single brick buildings with high, pitched slate roofs over the house and barn combined under the same roof. Many Flemish farmers wanted to live in close proximity to their animals.

From one of these buildings erupted two German soldiers surprised and terrified by Hank's tank, running flat out in desperate efforts to reach the stone wall of the nearby dike before the following Canadians could catch them. For a moment it appeared as though their bids for safety would be successful too, because MacLean could not seem to traverse his turret rapidly enough to permit him to overtake the fleeing enemy. In fact, MacLean's power traverse was not working, and he had to hand-crank the turret around, to engage his fleeing targets.

It became a thrilling race, as the Germans ran their utmost to stay ahead of the swinging scythe of bullets from the machinegun firing from the tank turret. Shouts rose from the other members of the tank crew; watching grimly as their enemies literally "ran for their lives." Since everyone is forced to admire a game effort in almost any situation, there was indeed some opinion that these two speeding Krauts should perhaps have been let go.

The results of the race were decided with a suddenness that surprised everyone. MacLean was still cranking the traverse of his gun for all he was worth, and the two runners certainly had not slackened their pace, when a sharp blast directly under the runners' feet pitched them bodily in the air, in the midst of a black and purple cloud of smoke. Their dashes had inadvertently taken them across a small mine field, put down by their own colleagues only hours earlier. The smashed bodies of the two runners, their coal scuttle helmets still in place on their heads, slumped lifeless in the grass-covered field.

In war, the object is to destroy the enemy. But in Hank Maidens' tank that afternoon, there were mixed feelings for two enemies, who perhaps deserved something a little better.

The Regiment headed further eastward in the general vicinity of the Ghent Canal to a village called Oedelem, where it laggered in an open farm awaiting the arrival of the fuel, ration and ammunition trucks from "A Echelon." The infantrymen working their slow and difficult way through this "polder" country, surrounded on all sides by canals, dikes and even a few windmills, had to search through every building, barn and haystack. They came from the Argyll and Sutherland Highlanders of Canada and the Lake Superior Regiment. Tanks from each of the Squadrons of the Grenadiers took turns supporting them in their operations.

The night that No. 1 Squadron reached Oedelem, fighting had lasted throughout the day and well into the evening. Maidens selected a place to park the tank close to a grove of lime trees at the side of the road, and near the rest of the squadron vehicles. Many crews had already pitched their low tents at the sides of their tanks and were unfolding bedrolls within them when Henri Brault swung his tank into position. The squadron looked forward to a quiet evening, perhaps catching up on some lost sleep. The sounds of a few distant artillery crumps were audible, but in every other respect, peace had descended.

Just as the darkness of nightfall began to advance among the tall and stately Lombardy poplars, the engine of a Jeep could be heard moving through the shadows and quickly gaining speed, as it disappeared to the south east.

"That's Snuffy and Ned, and I think Tommy Murray from the Lake Soops," observed Hank. "Wonder what the hell they have in mind for this evening. They can't leave well enough alone: have to be raising hell whenever there's a chance. I thought those buggers were up to something when I heard them calling for "Footpad Sunray" on the radio a while ago."

There were nods of agreement from the others idling nearby. Several exchanged knowing smiles, having watched the results of similar "get togethers" on earlier occasions. Then the group dispersed to their own tanks to enjoy some peace and quiet at the end of another troubled day.

About three quarters of an hour later, a muffled explosion boomed out from a windmill at least a mile away. The "boom" sounded very much like a grenade's blast, followed almost immediately by the staccato crackle of sub-machinegunfire.

"That's where they went," stated Tommy Dolphin, as everyone nearby cocked their ears and stared through the gathering gloom toward the source of the racket. One further burp from a Schmeiser was heard, and then an ominous silence. The thought passed through MacLean's mind that perhaps the roving buccaneers had gone to the well once too often.

To the relief of all who waited, well-knowing what could happen on a dangerous raid like this on the German-held windmill down the road, the whine of an approaching Jeep engine could be heard from the direction they all stared. The whine increased with surprising speed. In the last light of day, a Jeep rushed toward the Grenadier laager, a confident Major Snuffy Smith at the wheel, an equally at ease Major Ned Amy sitting beside Smith; and a hulking Major Tommy Murray sitting in the rear of the vehicle between two terrified German Marines, holding onto their seats for dear life. Snuffy ground the Jeep to a shuddering halt, motioning the two German prisoners out of the vehicle. Major Amy pointed down the road, where they all disappeared immediately afterward without a word of explanation or comment to anyone. The two sullen-looking marines, in their blue uniforms, eyed the parked tanks gathered around them as they marched off, looking quite uncomfortable in the captivity of these blood-thirsty Canadians.

The story of the latest escapade of the three majors spread in the Regiment the next morning. Apparently, Major Murray had spotted the local German headquarters at the windmill while on a patrol with his own company in the L.S.R.'s. Easily convincing his pals, Amy and Smith, that it could be taken without much trouble, the plan had called for Murray to lob a grenade into the main room of the windmill, after which Ned and Snuffy would take care of anyone who ran out after the blast. Rumor had it that a German paymaster was visiting the troops, which interested the three majors.

172

Apparently, the raid went much as planned, although the placement of the grenade had raised some differences of opinion, with Snuffy electing to reach into the room after the grenade handle had been released, to move it away from a nearby window so that its blast would be augmented. Smith then dodged back behind the stone wall in the last nick of time. The blast killed three men, wounded a few more, and stunned several others who stumbled outside only to be cut down by Amy's Sten gun. The two Germans, who ran over to investigate the blast at the windmill, were quickly disarmed and became the prisoners brought in on the Jeep. There was very little money found by the raiding party, so they were not pleased with their efforts, except that they did have prisoners to be sent back for interrogation, which always pleased "Intelligence."

To some few men, these three majors among them, their participation in a war, though not by their own choosing, could be converted into a sort of dangerous adventure, in which they regularly played their parts with consummate skill and courage. To say that people of this description enjoyed war is usually neither true nor relevant, because they would really prefer to engage in something else entirely. But once committed to the prosecution of a war, they sometimes could and did relish a contest in which they could pit themselves against their adversaries in mortal combat, and do exceedingly well at it. The lives at stake were their own, as the troops which they led and by whom they were worshiped, certainly realized. In cases such as these, if the three majors ventured themselves in escapades of their own devising, to provide thrills and adventure for themselves, no one wanted to gainsay them and everyone wished them well.

CHAPTER X

A BRIEF INTERLUDE WITH THE PARENT REGIMENT

For the first weeks after MacLean joined Hank Maidens' tank crew, they found themselves chiefly engaged in escorting infantry groups along roads and into small towns, in a series of small but frequently vicious battles. Casualties to both sides were usually moderate, by the standards set back in Normandy, but nevertheless significant. It took brave men to advance along these roads, whether in tanks, carriers, halftracks, or just walking, because they knew they were always under close observation and that they would be fired upon first, usually by an unseen enemy. Infantrymen sometimes envied the armored protection of the crews in the tanks, as they edged along the ditches of the roads. But with the whiplash of an 88 mm anti-tank gun, firing from a concealed position ahead, the infantrymen were usually thankful they were not perched up on a road or a dike, unable to turn off for fear of bogging down in the soft polder, and easy prey for the German gunners firing from unseen locations. Many an infantryman consoled himself with the thought that when the big shells began to fly, they could at least go to ground in the ditches or hollows around them, while the tank crews had to stay atop the road and search out their enemy. And so it went in Belgium, day after day, as the efforts to clear the approaches to Antwerp proceeded. It was repetitive work, boring and yet deadly duty which had to be performed before the great port could be put to use.

On September 12th, the Adjutant sent word that a number of men named on his list, Ken MacLean among them, should be brought to his scout car promptly, with all battle kit packed, to become a part of a group leaving immediately on a short special assignment. Nothing more than that by way of explanation. MacLean, though completely baffled by the unusual order, gathered his personal belongings together and took his leave of Hank and his crew.

On arrival at the Adjutant's scout car, he was told to join a small group of other soldiers from his Regiment, gathered to hear a list of 10 names and regimental numbers read off. This was a verification that the people named on the Adjutant's list corresponded with the people present in the group. The Adjutant then explained his orders, with the only information he had.

"There is an armored show planned for the British Second Army front, north and east of here. Our parent regiment, the Grenadier Guards in the Guards Armored Division has asked for some extra personnel, with plenty of experience who can be brought into their ranks on temporary attachment, as replacements just for this show. You people have been chosen, and you'll leave in this truck pronto."

Requests for further information about where they were going, what they would be doing, and when they would be back with their own regiment, were all stonewalled. All that they were told was that they were being temporarily detached to the 2nd Battalion, Grenadier Guards, in the Guards Armored Division of the British 2nd Army. More than this, nobody seemed to know.

The truck took MacLean and his fellow travelers on a long journey eastward, past Antwerp and on to an open field near Hasselt, in Belgium, where a large laager held the Grenadier Guards and other units of the Division.

Dismounting from the truck, each of the Canadians was taken to one of the squadrons of the parent regiment for assignment.

Ken MacLean was told to join the crew of a Firefly tank commanded by Sergeant Glen Patterson, a tall and lean Britisher from the Midlands of England. He was a strong, affable man in his early 30's, with lengthy experiences in tanks with the Guards.

The tank driver, Douglas Digby, thickset and taller than he first appeared was a quiet spoken flaxen-haired Cornishman, in his mid-20's. Digby looked on MacLean with considerable curiosity, partly the consequence of the drastically different accents of the two men.

Digby had been a Grenadier for more than a year, and fancied himself the unofficial chef for his rather unappreciative crew.

The third member of MacLean's new crew, and with whom he would work especially closely, was Reg Hill, the loader-operator. Reg was shorter than the rest of them and ever so much noisier. His effervescent personality kept the crew in good spirits, but never to the point of overdoing it. Reg had a lot to say but he had no illusions of being an unrecognized public entertainer. He was a serious soldier and Ken came to enjoy hearing him talk of recent experiences in the Regiment and where they had taken place. Hill was a Londoner, a former merchant with a matriculation equivalent education, and four years experience in the army.

Sergeant Patterson called his crew together after an "0" Group of crew commanders, to tell them what he had learned from their squadron commander, Major John Trotter, one of the most popular officers in the Battalion. On a very hush-hush basis, they had been told of an extremely bold and decisive exercise called "Market Garden," about to begin. In this exercise, the British 1st Airborne Division, along with the American 82nd and 101st Airborne Divisions, were going to make a series of airborne landings at a number of key bridges along a road that led ultimately across the Rhine River to Arnhem. If successful, this thrust would breach the last major German defence line in the west, thus exposing the Ruhr Valley, the heartland of German industrial strength, to Allied occupation.

"Market" was the code name for the airborne operation, and "Garden" for the overland drive to reach them, after they landed. Sergeant Patterson seemed enthused with the conspicuous role that had been assigned to the Guards Armored Division - to lead the entire drive by the troops of 30th Corps. They were slated to punch through to the relief of all of the airborne troops dropped ahead of them, leaving an access highway for all the other Allied troops to follow over the next great natural barrier protecting Western Germany - the Rhine.

"Major Trotter told us," he said solemnly, that his orders were to go like hell, and keep going as far as we can. If this comes off as planned, it will certainly shorten the war! It could put the Allies in the heart of Germany. That's good news for all of us, and we, lucky devils that we are as usual, have been selected to lead the drive," he ended with a sardonic smile. "It's a long way from here, with five major bridges to cross if we are going to get to Arnhem, but we have to give it everything we can. It looks like a hairy one."

On the afternoon of September 17th shortly after the announcement to the troops of the plan for the next few days, there arose an awesome roar, the raging sound of hundreds of big guns firing a "stonk" on enemy positions along the Leopold Canal line in Belgium. It was the noise of masses of artillery, beginning the mighty barrage that kicked off Market Garden. The "Eye Division," so called because the insignia for the Guards Armored Division was an ever-open eye, painted on a shield on every vehicle, began moving into position. It seemed to Ken that every gun in the British 2nd Army was firing in this barrage, switching from one enemy target to another. As the sound reached a crescendo, someone pointed upward at waves of large aircraft passing to the north of them, pulling gliders and heading further east and north of their position. The sounds of the airborne invasion were completely lost in the awesome roar of the nearby artillery, but every eye was focused on the never-to-be-forgotten sight of several hundreds of aircraft drifting across the northern sky towards Holland and the battle that would take place there.

Shortly after, the order came to move, and the tanks of the Grenadier Guards headed out on the road to Eindhoven, in Holland. For MacLean the battle for Arnhem had begun.

The immediate plan was to have the tanks batter their way from the Meuse-Escaut Canal near the Belgian-Holland border, across the bridge there, which became famous later as "Joe's Bridge," after Lt. Colonel J.O.E. Vandeleur, the hearty commander of the Irish Guards who led the parade. The road they were to take, which became widely known as "Hell's Highway," would cross important bridges at the Wilhelmina Canal, at Grave and at Nijmegen before the last one was reached at Arnhem. Each of these bridges had to be captured in advance and the approaches held by airborne troops until relieved by 30 Corps ground forces. American airborne troops were responsible for holding the intermediate bridges, but the furthest and much the most difficult to reach was the great Arnhem Bridge across the Rhine itself, for which the British 1st Airborne forces were responsible. Everyone in the "Eye Division" realized that they had a tremendously difficult task before them.

MacLean was unable to see events taking place at the head of their long column, but from the sounds on the tank radio, the Irish Guards did not advance far before receiving a hot reception. The defending Germans had been fully alerted by their own commanders, as well as by what they could see and hear around them. They knew that a major attack was in progress, and they responded quickly and in surprising strength.

Sounds of heavy fighting ahead reached MacLean's tank, a good way back in the long, winding armored column strung out on the highway. Advances were slow and meager at first, since the only means of traveling was on the single, main highway. The problems of moving an entire corps forward on a single road were apparent to the commanders right from the beginning, but there was no alternative if the plan for Market-Garden was to be executed.

Though agonizing to get into the action which they could hear ahead, MacLean's squadron was not able to fire a shot on the first day. The Irish Guards bore the entire brunt of the initial fighting because they were at the head of the narrow column, advancing like a pencil against the enemy defences. They encountered well-positioned and plentifully supplied German anti-tank guns, which knocked out nine of their tanks in short order. Fortunately, the Typhoons were able to render solid assistance to the beleaguered tanks by flying several low sweeps extremely close to the edge of the battlefield.

The fighting was on a front so narrow that only a few vehicles at the head of the column could fire on the enemy. This frustrating situation forced the rest of the Eye Division to await their turns at the front, in "cab-rank" order, idling all of the fire power and mobility that was obliged to stay back in line. As the head of the armored column approached the outskirts of Eindhoven near the end of the first day's fighting, MacLean heard that the Welsh Guards would move to the front of the column on the next day. He found it strange indeed that, like business life in the city, the end of the day brought with it a sense of suspending the fighting and the operations connected with it throughout 30th Corps for another day. There was a pause overnight while the combatants restored themselves with food and sleep, before returning to the fray the next day. He wondered whether the Germans ahead were relaxing in the same way.

He need not have wondered long. The experiences of the Welsh Guards and all the other attacking troops on September 18th quickly established that the Germans had indeed been active during the hours of darkness, restoring many of the defences which had been overcome during the first day's fighting, and bringing a number of additional Panther tanks into position, from which they wreaked havoc. After a day of heavy fighting with determined and well-led German forces, the Guards did reach Eindhoven, pausing only to greet the American paratroops who had landed there and held the road open, before hurrying on northward toward Grave and Nijmegen.

The tanks of the Grenadier Guards led the spearhead the next day. MacLean and his comrades raced across the newly constructed Bailey bridge over the Wilhelmina Canal and onward to the great iron bridge at Grave. There they were gratefully met by troops of the American 82nd Airborne Division, much pleased to be relieved of their responsibilities to take and hold the critical bridge over the Maas River there, one of the principal branches of the Rhine River. Hopes rose throughout the Battalion that they might still cut through to the isolated defenders at Arnhem, already under great pressure there. They were told that the route from Grave to Nijmegen still lay open to them, and Arnhem was only eleven miles further on.

But the speed at which they could move up "Hell's Highway" was dictated very largely by the strength of the defence mounted by the Germans, who still held the key Nijmegen bridge. It was widely reported that the Germans had been seen strongly reinforcing their positions around Nijmegen with additional infantry, anti-tank guns and S.P. artillery. With each passing hour, the defences were augmented. Time became very much of the essence. Word was received that the main road bridge across the Waal River at Nijmegen had not been blown, which certainly spurred the tankmen onward. About noon they entered the outskirts of Nijmegen, where they were split into three columns. The first column was to drive for the bridge on the main road, over the Waal, under Major Gregory-Hood, commander of No. 3 squadron, along with one U.S. parachute regiment of the 82nd Airborne, the infantry that had already penetrated Nijmegen.

MacLean found himself, with Sergeant Patterson and his crew, forming part of the second column, involving No. 2 squadron with the drive for the railway bridge over the river. This drive combined the Guards with more U.S. infantry from the 82nd Airborne Division, under the command of Captain J. Neville.

The third column, comprising tanks from No. 1 squadron of the Guards, some infantry from the 1st Battalion of the Grenadier Guards and a further group of U.S. parachute infantry, headed for the main post office in the city and the large roundabout, with many roads leading from it. Major Thorne commanded the troops in this column.

The Germans were well aware of the existence and position of each of the three columns. They set fire to a number of buildings near the bridges, as night descended on the combatants, to maintain visibility for themselves in the event of patrols venturing against them.

The plan for taking the main road bridge involved tanks from No. 2 squadron, mixed with vehicles from the 1st Battalion of the Grenadiers, and a heavy artillery barrage, all poured fire into the German defenders at the approaches to the bridge.

With all hatches closed down, and his crew watching intently through their periscopes, Sergeant Paterson's tank joined the rest of No.2 squadron's rush on the bridge entrance. They were met by a fusillade of machinegun and anti-tank gunfire from the defenders as soon as they appeared. Patterson very sensibly ordered Doug Digby to drive into a small alcove between some buildings, where he could still use the guns to fire toward the bridge to full advantage.

At one point, an S.P. gun drove up a side street about 500 yards from Patterson's tank, without seeming to notice the Grenadier vehicle.

MacLean and the crew watched absolutely spellbound, as the S.P. gun slowly reversed into the front of a house only a short hike along the street. Its commander and crew must have been intent upon positioning the vehicle in semi-concealment from tanks coming up the street, but oblivious of the existence of Patterson's tank already parked further down the same street and watching them closely. Sergeant Patterson, at first incredulous at the actions of the German crew so nearby, quickly called for an A.P. shot, below the mantlet of the gun if possible. MacLean stealthily traversed his turret into line with the unsuspecting target and cranked the elevation wheel downward. Something warned the crew of the S.P. gun of the danger of their position, for there was an abrupt and jarring jerk to move back into the street again to allow its gun to fire down the street. But it was too late.

MacLean brought the cross-hairs into focus just below the gun mantlet and stepped on the trigger. The Firefly belched a lurid tongue of flame beyond its muzzle break. The concussion of a shot fired by the 17 pounder in the confines of a narrow street like the one where it was parked proved to be breathtaking. The A.P. shot fired by the Firefly could hardly have missed. It drilled a hole into the S.P. exactly as requested. A flickering, orange, purple and black fire erupted from inside the vehicle. One of the crewmen, seemingly wounded, climbed over the edge of the hull and fell to the ground just a second before a tremendous, shattering blast, detonated no doubt by the ammunition in the vehicle, tore the hull of the vehicle apart. An oily pyre of black smoke ascended above it. There would have been no survivors from within that vehicle. Survival was unlikely even for the man who leapt out just ahead of the explosion, his clothes burning fiercely as he attempted to smother the flames by rolling on the ground.

"Bingo! That's the way to hit 'em, Ken," shouted Hill with deep satisfaction. "Those bloody S.P.'s have heavy armor, but when you hit under the mantlet, you penetrate."

"More Jerries in hell for breakfast," broke in Digby from the driver's compartment. "Now, who's next?"

The fight for the main bridges over the Waal River at Nijmegen, one on the road or Hell's Highway, and the other carrying the railway across further along the river bank, became an increasingly bitter struggle between the Germans of the 19th S.S. Panzer Division and the Guards Armored Division. The Americans of the 82nd Airborne Division had fought hard and with grim determination to maintain access to these bridges since they landed in the vicinity several days before. Their pleasure at seeing the arrival of the Guards' tanks was understandable, because they were facing substantiality increased pressure from additional German forces brought in against them from the nearby Reichswald area to the east. It was certainly becoming problematical as to just how much longer the 82nd could hold on, when their relief arrived.

Lieutenant Colonel Goulburn, commanding the Grenadier Guards, announced on September 20th, two days after the fighting for Nijmegen began, that the regiment had finally forced its way across the main highway bridge in the city. The crossing was achieved largely as a result of the outstanding actions of Sergeant Peter Robinson of No. 1 Squadron, then leading a troop of four tanks. His squadron commander, Major John Trotter, had alerted him to make a quick dash for it, along with the rest of his troop across the bridge. Trotter said that the bridge had to be taken at all costs, even if the Germans still held the ground on the far side. Progress was closely watched by MacLean and his colleagues from their position in Hunes Park near the small roundabout leading up to the highway bridge, as houses and other buildings burned fiercely around them. Sergeant Robinson led his troop slowly forward. As they rumbled across the large bridge they attracted heavy fire from the far river bank. All other radio communications within the Battalion were cut off, to assure uninterrupted contact between the squadron commander and Sergeant Robinson, as the crossing was attempted.

There were violent exchanges of fire between the tanks in Sergeant Robinson's troop and the waiting German defenders, as MacLean watched, but the Grenadier gunners prevailed. The anti-tank guns were silenced and the German infantry scrambled into hiding among the bridge girders, where they directed a hail of fire on any and all targets they could see. Fortunately, the demolition of the bridge by explosive charges planted around its supports several days earlier, was mercifully frustrated by some intrepid souls who had crawled out onto the bridge and cut the wires several nights before.

After Sergeant Robinson's taut drama played itself through, MacLean's tank proceeded across the main bridge with the rest of the Squadron to join the Battalion for its next thrust along Hell's Highway. MacLean expected to hear orders to continue the drive, with all due vigor, up the highway to Arnhem, still 12 miles away, once they had cleared the bridge over the Waal. They had been assured by the troops of the 82nd Airborne that the road was clear for several more miles, fully expecting the Guards to hurry onward.

But this was not the order given. Far from an injunction to "go like hell until you cross the Arnhem Bridge," the Grenadiers were told to bolster their defences at the Nijmegen Bridge, while the Irish Guards passed through and onward toward the Arnhem Bridge. Their advance continued agonizingly slowly, on the raised embankment upon which "Hell's Highway" traveled the last distance to the City of Arnhem, exposed to fire from all sides and with no possibility to turn off onto the soft polder on both sides. They fought their way about half the distance from Nijmegen to Arnhem, to the village of Elst, where a vicious exchange of fire took place with the ever-strengthening German forces. The Guards were sustaining heavy casualties, with little indication that they were "giving as good as they were getting." The decision came down from the highest authority on September 24th to halt all further advance.

All the troops, both British and American were mystified by the decision to stop. Whether the top commanders concluded that the problems of supplying an army corps, fighting ever further forward in an exposed finger on a single road system were becoming unmanageable; or that the rapidly stiffening German defences covering the last twelve miles of Hell's Highway to Arnhem were just beyond their capacity to penetrate; or a combination of the two, was never disclosed to the fighting troops.

Well into the night, discussions and arguments continued between commanding officers, staff liaison officers and others all the way down to members of tank crews concerning the change in strategy that halted the Guards Armored division where it stood. Many of the men in the tank crews had relatives and friends in the encircled Airborne Division and felt very strongly about terminating the drive which appeared to be abandoning the 1st Airborne men to their fate.

"We've got one road, and one road only, to move the fighting formations ahead, keep them supplied with ammo, fuel and food, or get the wounded out again," said a staff captain in heated fashion with several Grenadier officers. "The system is too vulnerable to out-flanking, and can't stand any more pressure forward. It just has to be bloody well stop, because it's too narrow a front to punch through all the defences ahead of it."

"A typical staff analysis, with many numbers to support its con-clusions, I am sure," growled a Grenadier Captain. "And we know the Jerries are augmenting their defences up there every bloody hour. That's to be expected, because they know exactly where we are now, where we want to go, and the only route possible for us to get there. So they just double up on all of their weapons and defences," he continued.

After looking about him, he returned to his theme. "But what's really new in any of this that brings forth a change of strategy now, for Christ's sake? Long ago when the planners first conceived this entire scheme, it was obvious that the 'Garden' part of it, where we would push forward to relieve the Airborne people, would have to travel on only one road system. That was the time to give detailed thought to how far you could extend your drive with only one road to feed it. Don't wait until after you have rammed your way within 12 miles of the objective, only to find out you can't punch the rest of the way home. We have hit some bad luck that held us up, but we've also had some damned good luck at times too, so it's not just luck. It's really a damned poor plan, ignoring good military logic from start to finish. A lousy gamble, in my mind."

After further bitter discourse they dispersed and went to bed. The news from Arnhem was not good. German tanks had finally forced their way onto the Arnhem bridge, where they were consolidating their hold.

The fact was, the forward movement along the corridor to Arnhem was blocked, almost within sight of the last bridge to cross, and there was no other path for the armor to follow.

MacLean saw and felt the bitterness of all the men around him, as the realization swept over them that Market Garden was a failure. Grim faces betrayed equally grim recognitions that Hell's Highway had not taken them to Arnhem, after all their efforts. Some tankmen had relatives among the garrison at Arnhem and felt they were deserting them.

In his own mind at least, MacLean concluded that, faced with the defences which had been encountered, the entire scheme was hopelessly optimistic. It came as almost a relief as well as a pity when word was finally received that the Arnhem garrison had collapsed on September 25th, more than a week beyond the period they were expected to hold on. Those unable to escape across the river became prisoners of the German Army.

"A bloody fiasco," said MacLean to his fellow crew members, when word passed around of the estimated number of troops wounded or killed in the fighting for Arnhem, and the number that had "gone into the bag."

"That's not what Field Marshal Montgomery said in the report I heard," replied Sergeant Patterson. "He said that the battle had been a decided victory. You mustn't judge the strategy of the whole battle on the basis of the part that you saw, Ken. We don't know how much damage the Germans suffered from this attack. If the top command say this was a victory for their plan, then that's enough for me, even if we didn't reach our objective."

"What the hell else would Montgomery say?" came MacLean's choleric reply. "He planned this whole damned thing, or at least approved the plan for it. He sent, we don't know how many thousand, airborne troops in masses of aircraft, manned by further thousands of air force people, to a place more than 80 miles from the closest army outpost, accessible by only one highway over the polder and across five big bridges over major canals or rivers and God knows how many smaller bridges over canals and streams. Then he sent more thousands of soldiers charging down this single highway in tanks and trucks and God knows what all else, to try to reach the paratroops. It sure looks to me that there were a hell of a lot more Germans and German armor in our area than we were told to expect by Montgomery's intelligence types. And all for what? We lost thousands of people in killed, wounded, and prisoners, when you count the air force losses, the airborne losses and certainly the army losses. And we didn't get to

Arnhem. If Montgomery says that's a victory, we can't stand many more of them! He's just protecting his own ass, for Christ's sake."

"That's a pretty strong statement Ken," said Patterson. "How do the rest of you feel?"

"I can't argue with what Ken said," replied Doug Digby. "He said nothing that ain't true."

"I'm for a change of commander," offered Reg Hill. "Ken MacLean for Commander-in-Chief, and Bernard bloody Montgomery for gunner in the future, but not in my tank. I don't think he could hit the bloody ground with his hat."

"Sounds as through you have some supporters," said Sergeant Patterson. "Well, the war isn't over yet, and we have to get on with it. Let's get moving."

On his return to the Canadian Grenadier Guards, MacLean was happy to find himself once again the gunner in Hank Maidens' tank, and the crew glad to see him returned from the parent unit. He was told there had been fighting by the 4th Armored Brigade in the smaller battles along the Leopold Canal throughout the last half of September, the overall objective still being the clearance of the Germans from the approaches to the harbor of Antwerp.

MacLean tried to be forthcoming in answering the many questions put to him about the Guards Armored Division and his experiences there from all sorts of interested men in his own regiment, all the way from curious Guardsmen up to the level of the adjutant himself. He left his listeners in no doubt that in his humble opinion, there was a great deal of power and willingness-to-fight left in the German army, and that the airy hopes of winding up the war before winter, were nothing more than idle dreams. MacLean told his inquisitors that he found the parent Regiment quite willing to accept him when they found his level and length of battle experience was at least the equal of their own. He added that, in the circumstances on Hell's Highway, the Guards had fought as strongly and skillfully as any soldiers could hope for, but it was just beyond them to advance any further than they did. When their front consisted of one roadway defended by powerful enemy armored units skillfully positioned to destroy any force that advanced against it, further progress was out of the question.

In turn, MacLean was told of the loss of the much-admired Major Cassils, Commander of 3 Squadron, during his absence. Cassils had been shot dead by a member of the Waffen S.S. while attempting to aid another wounded S.S. man. It was another senseless killing, which again raised the old question among the troops of whether help should ever be offered to S.S. soldiers. Cassils had been done in while offering a simple act of human kindness to a man with a terrible injury: the S.S. soldier looked on Cassils as an enemy to be killed in any circumstances, and seized an opportunity to shoot him before he died himself. The usual arguments for and against reprisals were exchanged, without conclusive answers, as always.

The Allies continued bringing all of their arms and supplies for western front operations through distant ports in Northern France, because the approaches to Antwerp were still menaced by the remains of the German 15th Army. The Germans, located on a number of islands as well as on mainland fortifications which overlooked the lengthy approaches to the great city, were partly in Belgium and partly in Holland. They were in most cases top grade soldiers - paratroops from the campaign in Normandy and men from the Hermann Goering S.S. Panzer Division. Short advances were all that MacLean and his comrades could anticipate in this type of warfare, with the infantry clearing out the bazooka-men from the many pre-dug slit trenches that lined the roads, while the tanks took on the machinegun nests and artillery. If soldiering in action had ever been considered a 'pleasant' activity, the campaign to clear the Scheldt Estuary and the approaches to Antwerp was one of the least 'pleasant' parts of it.

Hank Maidens and his crew, along with the rest of No. 1 Squadron, worked their way painfully forward along a road which took them northward on the polder flats through Esschen in the Netherlands, as October expired and November limped in with more fog and rain. Major Amy led his squadron into a bridgehead among the moats and canals which isolated Steenbergen from the rest of the land. A blown bridge across one of the canals caused still another halt in its drive forward, and 4th Division Engineers dashed forward to put a new Bailey span across the water, in the midst of a shower of mortar fire and shrapnel from a concealed German position further along the road. MacLean, along with the rest of his crew, sat in the relative comfort of their tank watching the completion of the last stages of the bridge through their periscopes, with ever-growing admiration for the men toiling on the structure in the soaking rain. The engineers were completely unprotected from any enemy action against them. As soon as the assembly was completed, they waved cheerily toward Hank, a sign that all was finished and he could take his tank across in pursuit of one more struggle.

"Look at those guys out there. Mortar shells raining down here, and they work in it anyhow," said Hank. "Then they give us a big wave and run back off the bridge to let us go ahead, as if we're the brave ones going on ahead. Meanwhile they go back to the delightful task of lifting mines somewhere, just to keep their interest up. If they don't get killed up here building a bridge for us, they risk getting their heads blown off by an exploding mine. Those guys have more nerve than anyone else around, and get less credit for it too."

"Amen to that," added Tommy Dolphin, as the tank lurched forward across the just - completed bridge, down the ramp and onto the road on the other side. "I wonder how many hundreds of Bailey bridges have been built by engineers over rivers, canals, creeks, and chasms all over Western Europe to keep everybody moving. God alone knows how we'd ever get across the country without them."

CHAPTER XI

BILLETS IN HOLLAND

The gradual occupation of all the territory within the Nijmegen bridgehead by British and Canadian soldiers was virtually complete by mid-November of 1944. They were certain of a reduced level of operations, as the core of the winter months confronted all the Army commanders. The Canadian Grenadier Guards were withdrawn from Steenbergen, the area in which they had been operating, for a period of rest, refitting and regrouping. They drove their tanks eastward, near Tilburg, to the small town of Kaatsheuvel. To the surprise and delight of many of the Grenadiers, kit and baggage trucks from B Echelon rejoined the combat squadrons, bringing supplies of new battle dress, and replacement of worn-out kit and weapons. Bath parades were held and in some cases there was even leave granted for a few fortunate members of the Regiment, but that for only one day in Antwerp.

Unknown to Ken MacLean and his fellow soldiers, a delegation from the Regimental officers, including Bill Glansdorp, born in Holland and fluent in the language, although more recently a resident of Montreal, met with a number of the good burgers of Kaatsheuvel. The subject under discussion had been the possible billeting of the tank crews in various houses in the town, with the families living in the town. The incentive to accept the soldiers was an offer of fuel for the stoves in any house that accommodated them. The response was prompt and favorable, since the availability of fuel had become a serious problem for the half-starved Hollanders.

The winter of 1944-45 was a cold one in western Europe, with snow on the ground and ice in the canals. Henri Brault demonstrated his versatility by attaching a pair of the old-fashioned Dutch skates with high curleques at the front of the blades, to his army boots, and going for a widely-cheered skate on a nearby canal.

When the regiment arrived at Kaatsheuvel, all the tanks were parked in a field near the town, and the crews walked the short distances to their respective billets. All that was requested of the Dutch residents was enough space to unroll bedrolls in the ground floor rooms of the houses. All troops were warned that proper behavior was expected, with serious discipline for any misbehavior.

Hank Maidens' crew was fortunate indeed. They were directed to a handsome, medium-sized brick house owned by the Chief of Police in the town who lived there with his wife and six children, ranging in age from four years to young adulthood. The Police Chief, who rejoiced in the impressive name of Antoon van den Dungen, was a handsome, solid figure of a man. The Canadian visitors were much impressed with his appearance when he presented himself on his bicycle (one of the few not confiscated by the Germans) impressively attired in his black uniform with silver piping and braid around the shoulders. With the black and silver piping mounted on his forage hat, he looked quite the picture of a field marshal, though this was characteristic of the police uniforms in many European towns.

MacLean and his crew were welcomed into the van den Dungen family, told to call the proprietors "Pa" and "Ma," and joined them in their joint explorations of backgrounds and experiences in a strange mixture of English, Dutch and French which became somewhat comprehensible to all.

The tank crews provided their own food from the Compo ration boxes distributed to each crew. When the host family insisted on cooking and preparing the meals as a kindness to the soldiers billeted with them, this favor was accepted with alacrity by Hank and his crew members, glad to be rid of the task. But much to their surprise, they began finding indications of additional food being added to what they had grown accustomed to seeing in the "M&V" cans or the "Irish stew" cans. Extra bits of meat appeared in the stews, and real bread was presented instead of the regular hard tack biscuits.

"What's going on here?" asked Hank incredulously, as he fished out of his evening stew a sizeable wedge of beef. "We're told that these Dutchmen had no food supply of their own, and haven't had for the past month. Yet we keep getting grub that never went in any compo rations. Do you think they believe we are short of food or something?"

"That's got to be it," replied Tommy Dolphin. "We have to get it across to them that we have plenty of our own food. Good God! I've seen some Dutchmen picking over the garbage we leave at the squadron cook's truck. They must be damned near starving."

"Ken, you seem to speak the best Dutch among us. Tell Ma this has to stop, or we'll have to move to some other house," said Hank. "We don't want the reputation of taking food from people who don't even have enough themselves."

MacLean wandered into the kitchen, looking for Jeanne, a young daughter still attending school, when school was in session, who had a reasonably good command of the English she was learning.

"Jeanne," began MacLean, who had become somewhat of a household pet at the house because of his efforts to learn to speak "Hollands," as they called the language. "Your mother and probably your older sisters have been putting some of their food in our stews, when they mix them up. You don't have enough food of your own anyway, and then Ma takes some of yours and gives it to us."

"Nay! Nay!" replied Jeanne. "Zat is not true. Zey just cook the food you bring."

MacLean gave her a disbelieving glance. "Well Jeanne, I am not calling you a liar. But if that happens again, we will probably be moved out of this nice house of yours. Hank says that is final."

After some considerable discussion between Ma and her daughters in Dutch, in the course of which Ma became quite agitated, the conversation trailed off and everyone went their own way. But there was no further evidence of extra food being added to the diet. That mission was accomplished.

They enjoyed the friendship and confidence of Pa and his family while billeted in his house. The crew recognized the position in which Pa found himself; the father of four attractive young daughters and one young boy, all living in a house in which four foreign soldiers were temporarily living also. It was a not a particularly enviable situation for Pa and Ma, but their confidence in Hank's crew was never abused. A friendship grew between Ken MacLean and the Police Chief, nurtured through correspondence and later visits, which lasted throughout Pa's life, notwithstanding that neither spoke the other's language.

Pa informed the crew that the same people in his town that were extending the most enthusiastic welcomes to the Canadian occupiers, were in the forefront of welcoming the German intruders in 1940, a fact that MacLean and his crewmates thought over and considered very seriously. It had taken courage from old Antoon to make such a statement of his own town.

Christmas was impending, raising expectations among most children, but the distribution mechanism throughout the countryside was "kaput," as they phrased it. Pa and Ma were desperate for some expedient that might be understood as a gift from St. Nicholas, for they still had two children young enough to believe the legend.

Early in December, the Dutch observe the tradition of a visit from "Zwarte Pete," or "Black Peter." Pa van den Dugen's family took it very seriously, and the tank crew were curious about what it involved. Certainly Pa's youngest daughter, Liesje was concerned about it, although the Canadians, lacking an understanding of the Dutch language, were unable to gauge how important it was.

About 4:00 p.m., as the afternoon died on December 10th, there was a knock at the door, and when answered, in stepped a person dressed in cheap, black sack cloth. The face was blackened too. This was Zwarte Pete, carrying another big bag with a number of switches in it. Liesje was reduced to terror and tears immediately, and Benny, the next oldest child seemed full of apprehension too. After a brief conversation at the door, Pa smiled knowingly and Zwarte Pete withdrew to visit other homes.

The mystified Canadians were later informed that the tradition called for Zwarte Pete to deliver switches to all the children who had not been good during the past year, and that would be their Christmas gift. Liesje had escaped this dull fate.

Talks took place across the dining room table each evening between MacLean and his colleagues, and as many of the Dutch family as wished to participate.

Daughter Jeanne was regularly called upon to translate enough words to make understanding possible. It was quite surprizing how much could be brought into the conversation between people who did not really speak one another's language. The price of homes in Canada, the price of cars, the level of wages, the amount of crime in Canadian cities, and many other subjects were talked about to the interest and bemusement of the van den Dungens.

One thing brought to Pa's attention which absolutely astonished him, was that the Canadian army overseas was entirely volunteer, or "vrijwilliger" in Dutch. He had never heard of a volunteer army and expressed genuine surprize that men would come all the way from Canada, without compulsion, to fight the Allies' battles against the Nazis.

The other daughters, Ria, Annie and Lia, in ascending order, must have caused Pa and Ma some anxious moments. All were in their late teens and of course interested in men, with a crew of men living in the same house with them. However the eldest, Lia, had already become engaged to a local swain, who paid close attention to her and seldom let her out of his sight. As it turned out, Hank's warnings, and indeed the threats coming down from R.H.Q. were obeyed flawlessly, and Pa and Ma van den Dungen need not have worried. They became sentimentally attached to the crew billeted at their house and seemed to have enthusiastically accepted them.

From the bosom of an admiring family in Kaatsheuvel, where they stayed for about nine days, Hank's crew was finally withdrawn and returned to the tasks that brought them to Holland, as the month of December grew short. With appropriate farewells, the regiment moved out of Kaatsheuvel, parked their tanks in a large laager and became amateur infantrymen along the dikes bordering on the nearby Maas River. For many miles, this river marked the frontier between German and Allied forces in Holland. Guard picquets were set up to prevent incursion by German patrols on the Allied side, and it was soon decided that patrolling should begin across the Maas to gain information about the German forces located there.

The weather remained severely cold by the winter standards of Holland, and many of the Netherlanders suffered considerably as a result of poor or inadequate food, insufficient warm clothing or an almost total lack of fuel for their "kackels," (stoves or heaters). The Grenadiers continued to patrol the dikes along the margins of the Maas River to assure no German penetration to the south of the Maas. December dwindled down to the last few days before Christmas, as the bored troops continued their listless pacing, night and day, on the roads that topped the dikes. The whole of the 4th Canadian Armored Division was caught up in the same mindless pacing, with a few fireworks on occasion to break the tedious monotony. By day, there was very little activity to observe anywhere along the front. Tough German paratroopers, dug in across the river on the reverse slopes of the dikes, paid little or no attention to the indirect "shoots" of the regiment from time to time. These "shoots" were organized to familiarize new recruits with the use of armor as additional artillery, in cases where the tanks could be lined up to augment an artillery barrage on fixed enemy positions.

On one occasion, after a number of tank shells had been fired indiscriminately into German-occupied countryside on one of these "shoots," the exasperated Germans had hoisted a large hand-made bull's eye target between two trees, to accommodate their enemies' shooting practice. Not all Krauts were without a sense of humor.

Then on December 18, the Regiment received some very important news. The 4th Armored Division would commence an immediate move into south-eastern Belgium, to aid in the defensive back-up being developed by the Allies near Liège. A surprise enemy attack had penetrated deeply into the Allied front and alarmed the army commanders with its strength and speed. The preliminary move to block this offensive eliminated any plans and hopes among the Canadians for a peaceful Christmas with friendly Dutchmen. The tanks had to be readied for action again, which meant removing all the parcels mailed from home, with cakes, cigarettes, etc. that had been packed into the sponsons of the vehicles, (the storage spaces in the sides of the hull of the tank) in preparation for a Christmas celebration. In place of the gifts, extra ammunition was packed in and the regiment moved to the village of Sprang-Kapelle, awaiting orders to travel on-ward to Breda and beyond.

Faced with the necessity of disposing of all of the contents of the parcels, Hank's crew immediately realized that perhaps their problem could be an answer to the question bothering Pa and Ma about Christmas presents. Clearly the supplies would not closely match the desires and expectations of the van den Dungen young folks, but they would certainly help. The extensive supplies of cigarettes would receive wider appreciation from the Dutch people than would be possible in Canada, because the use of tobacco was extremely wide-spread, and begun at a very young age in Holland. And so it was decided to try to help those who had helped the crew so willingly.

MacLean was chosen to be the messenger who was to bring the parcels to the van den Dungen household from Hand Maidens' tank crew.

He bicycled back after dark, laden with a number of bags of Christmas parcels. This seeming generosity would put Antoon in possession of a few things to give his family at Yuletide after all. Some received a fruit cake; others got cigarettes, gloves or candy. It was a strange and often not very suitable assortment for some of the recipients, but it got a very kind and considerate gentleman "off the hook," as MacLean described it later to his comrades. It was just a little thing, they all knew, but it was gratifying to them to be able to do something nonetheless.

When Ken arrived at the house, it was occupied by some soldiers of the Polish Division, as he noticed through the curtains. In spite of the loud piano music coming from the living room, which drowned out the sounds of any knocking at the door, Ken was finally able to attract the attention of Ma at the rear door. In the darkness there was little that could be said or exchanged by way of communication between MacLean and Ma against the thunder of the passionate piano playing Pole. Ken simply handed all the bags to Ma in the darkness, to her complete surprise, and said;

"Have a good Christmas, Ma. "Dank u ell" (Thank you for everything)."

It was at this point that daughter Jeanne appeared at the back door of the house, in the shadows surrounding her mother and Ken. Jeanne quickly appreciated the fact that Ken was only in Kaatsheuvel on a flying trip, which he was most anxious to resume. Translating for her mother and for Pa, who was not at home at the time, she said,

"Ken you go away now. Maybe forever. If you get back to Canada will you write? We promise to write back if you do."

"If I get home, I promise to write," said Ken, waving to them on the doorstep as he disappeared in the darkness, to hurry back to Sprang, where his regiment awaited him.

And strange to relate, correspondence did commence between MacLean and the van den Dungen family, some letters in Dutch and some in English, which continued to nurture their friendship for many years afterward. But that is really another story.

MacLean's return to his crew in Sprang, and the news he brought of their friends back in Kaatsheuvel, was eagerly listened to by all of his crew.

As it turned out, the Ardennes offensive was exhausted before any Canadian units got into action, because the expected drive by German paratroops on the Canadian front did not materialise. The Canadian Grenadier Guards had their Christmas dinner after all, in a field south of Breda. All of the troops joined in singing a few carols, followed by a full, Canadian-style Christmas dinner with all the trimmings served, as tradition called for it, by the regimental officers. They were undisturbed by any enemy action throughout the day. After dinner, a number of announcements were made, some of which covered changes of personnel. Most welcome was the statement that everyone's hero, Major "Snuffy" Smith, would forthwith become a Lieutenant Colonel and the new Commanding Officer, replacing Lieutenant Colonel Bill "Bogey Wheel" Halpenny, who was packed off to Canadian Armored Corp headquarters. Other consequential changes, included the move of Major E.A. Amy from Commanding Officer of No. 1 Squadron to Second in Command of the Regiment, another very popular move.

Lieutenant Ellis, the new troop officer, announced some promotions in his Troop, one of which made Ken MacLean a corporal and crew commander. MacLean was pleased to receive the upgrading in rank, but much more pleased to be able to take command of his own tank, and do the things he wanted to do with the crew assigned to him.

Then followed almost a fortnight of training, organized by the regiment on a tract of sandy wasteland near Tilburg, called Loon-op-Zand. The practice periods were used to emphasize and improve armored tactics and moves in cooperation with infantry, for the benefit of all new reinforcements, who would be expected to work effectively in joint packets of tanks and infantry in the future.

At the end of the training session, the regiment was once again brought into action in a variety of minor armored roles along the Scheldt Peninsula until mid-February of 1945. With the commencement of the Battle of the Rhineland, they joined in the fighting which had already commenced south-eastward from Nijmegen toward Wesel and the Rhine.

Ken was pleased to have command of the same old tank in which he had fought with Tom Dolphin and Henri Brault, who remained with him from the old crew. Hank Maidens had been transferred to another troop with another crew. A new gunner in the person of Bill Seaton, a mature and experienced soldier who had been brought up from A Echelon of the Regiment, took MacLean's old gunner's seat by the 17 pounder gun. Seaton was a large, strapping-looking man with dark hair and a carefully trimmed military moustache, who looked as though he had been a successful broker.

In recognition of the fact that a laager of tanks was surprisingly vulnerable to enemy infantry penetration at night - when havoc could be caused by a few intrepid foot soldiers armed with panzerfausts, bazookas or other hand-held rocket projectors, it was of great assurance and comfort to the tankmen to have some of their own regimental members, operating as if they were just friendly infantrymen, prowling around their laagers at night. Each tank crew was responsible for keeping one man on guard in the vehicle for two hour intervals throughout the darkness, in any event, but he usually served his time inside or close to his own tank, thereby providing only a modest amount of security. Noticing this shortcoming, Sergeant Al Hubert organized a group in A Echelon, with the absolute blessing of the commanding officer, taking on the responsibility of a real and effective platoon of heavily armed guards who roamed around the perimeter of the laager area, during the hours of darkness. These men became known as "Hubert's Commandos," and they took real pride in their membership in this group. Bill Seaton had been an enthusiastic member of these Commandos.

Sergeant Al Hubert was himself a most interesting specimen of a Canadian soldier, and his subordinates were always willing and eager to follow him. A tall, handsome man with jet black hair, a steady nature and endless good humor, he was a natural leader of men. He had seen a goodly share of tank warfare in his day too. He was one of the few officers and N.C.O.'s sent on secondment to units of the 8th British Army fighting in North Africa in 1942, for the purpose of gaining battle experience, before returning to his own unit in Europe.

Hubert had had a difficult time of it. He had been knocked out of three tanks in quick succession, in the desert fighting. The loss of his third tank had left him badly burned and wounded out in the Tunisian desert, where he laid up for three days before being found and rescued. Months of hospitalization and surgery in England had almost restored his appearance to the striking looking man he had once been, but a few vestiges of his physical ordeals still remained. He still had papery thin skin covering his badly burned hands. Anxious to return to the regiment as soon as possible, he was welcomed back like a long-lost brother. He was the subject of many discussions among his admirers for months afterward. Even recruits who had never before heard his cheery, "Hi mate! Are you Hortus?" with which he greeted everyone, were soon among his friends and admirers.

The non-word "Hortus" was one of a series of pseudo-words used to indicate satisfaction with life among his friends. They did not appear in any dictionary, nor did they have any esoteric connotation. They simply meant that Al Hubert was bestowing a term of friendship upon comrades he valued and respected. They all joined with him in this private version of double-talk, which really meant little more than "I see you and wish you well, friend of mine."

Soon after dawn on New Year's morning, it was apparent the Germans had something special and different planned. As the Grenadiers stared northward through their binoculars, the buzz and whine of many engines attracted the attention of the Canadian troops. It was a loud and increasing roar of aircraft engines not commonly heard from the Germans anywhere on the western front at that time.

"What's all the racket over there?" MacLean asked, looking inquiringly toward the increasing roar. "It sounds like a big raid to me."

Within two minutes, the answer was provided. It was still early in the morning, but all of the Grenadiers paused to look north. Rushing toward them was a tremendous fleet of Luftwaffe planes of every size, shape and age, rushing southward at low altitude on a huge "search and destroy" mission. It seemed to include every plane that could fly in the German air force. The planes were low enough that individual crew members could be clearly seen from the ground; pilots moving controls and tail gunners swinging their machineguns back and forth, preparatory to going into action.

There were Dorniers and Heinkels, Junkers JU88s, Blohm and Voss seaplanes, Focke-Wulf 190s, Messerschmidtt 109s, Arados, antiquated Stukas; anything and everything that could fly that day, scrambling southward. The Grenadiers were too surprized to fire effectively at the flying armada passing over them at such low altitude and with no advance warning. They had few ack-ack weapons which could have engaged the air fleet anyway at that time in the war.

The Germans did not bother even firing at the few, scattered army targets which they must have seen below them. Their objectives were the crowded Allied airfields near Brussels, Antwerp and elsewhere across the Low Countries. The allied air forces had become careless about proper storage of their planes during the months of their profound control of the air.

The Germans bombed and shot up hundreds of aircraft and installations at these airports, taking advantage of a lax attitude toward grounded planes on New Year's morning by the Allies. They found what they were looking for, and enjoyed a field day.

They shot up enormous Allied installations and created havoc in the rear areas. It must have revived memories of earlier days when the Luftwaffe controlled the air above the battlefields, with plenty of planes and fuel to meet their needs. At the end of the day, the Allies had undoubtedly been dealt a severe blow, of a kind not experienced for many months past.

The surprise raid stung the Allies into a greatly improved level of protection, for their aircraft on the ground thereafter, which was probably a good thing for them. Although the army troops watched the aerial antics above them, and shot down a few planes, they were largely left out of the spectacular actions which marked New Year's Day in the Low Countries. It was the Luftwaffe's day to howl, and they did.

CHAPTER XII

THE RHINELAND AND AFTERWARD

The big attack through the Siegfried Line was begun by infantry-men on February 8, 1945. MacLean listened attentively to the BBC news reports of the desperate fighting which developed in the flooded areas, beyond Nijmegen, the men wallowing in thick mud which had to be traversed in coming to grips with the enemy defences in the Reichwald. This meant the capture of the fiercely defended towns of Cleve, Goch and Gennep. The Germans grimly withdrew in the face of the onslaught, to the next line of fortifications, which included Udem and Calcar Ridge. The 4th Canadian Armored Division, along with two British divisions, were brought into the fighting at this point.

The move into Germany from the Nijmegen Salient started out in complete radio silence. There were no lights of any kind along an incredibly rough series of muddy roads and trails. Even though the drive was supposed to proceed without halts to the destination at the edge of the Reichswald forest, a number of halts took place neverthe-less. No one seemed to know the reason for the halts, but as darkness fell, the struggling column of tanks still rumbled forward through heavily-treed and completely unfamiliar country. It became increas-ingly difficult to avoid rear-end collisions with the next vehicle ahead in the all-engulfing blackness of the night.

Forbidden to transmit on the radios, there was nothing to prevent the operators from switching their radios to 'receive', and listening to any broadcast program available. MacLean and his crew were enter-tained by a program of magnificent symphony music which Tommy Dolphin had located on a German radio station. It was the Eroica, by Beethoven and it had never sounded better, in spite of the background growling and grinding of the tank engines as they powered their way inexorably through the soupy mire and over the bumps and holes. Ken mused about the incongruity between the beauty of the back-ground music and the circumstances in which it was being heard and enjoyed. It was almost midnight, and Henri Brault was still driving solo, fighting off exhaustion, staring ahead through muddy goggles in an attempt to steer his tank in the tracks made by earlier tanks ahead of him in the column.

Suddenly there was a terrific shock, a violent crash like a collision, which jolted the men completely off their seats. One of the tank tracks mounted what they assumed was a massive boulder in a muddy depression in the road. MacLean shouted and Henri stopped the tank to look down upon whatever had caused the crash.

"Lord God! What was that?" roared Seaton from the gunner's seat.

"You wouldn't believe it, but we've just run across the deck of another tank, sitting all by its lonesome in a bloody great hole here," responded Ken.

"The hell you say!" responded Seaton. "You mean we drove over another God damned tank?"

"By Christ, I've seen everything now," murmured Brault from the driver's hatch, as he shifted into low gear and drove slowly forward again. "A real tank, driven into that hole so that it could become part of the road. And not only that, but a crew with the tank. Who would believe that?"

The paradox that Brault described, really did exist. Easing his own tank forward and off the deck plate upon which it had climbed, he then increased his speed to regain his position in the long column moving deeper into the Reichswald. The astonishing presence of an old British Valentine tank placed in the hole behind them had been a deliberate action by the Royal Engineers, who had been responsible for creating and maintaining the trail they were following. The people responsible for placing the old tank in the hole as a filler, were part of the famous British 79th division organized by the innovative General Hobart, and known throughout the army as "the funnies." This division included such unconventional vehicles as flail tanks, flame throwers, bulldozers and fascines (tanks carrying huge rolls of wooden posts to be unrolled as filler into ditches or holes). In this case, "the funnies" had had to deal with a particularly large and deep hole which could not be circumvented. Having access to a discarded Valentine tank, they simply drove it into the hole and back-filled dirt around it, to bring the level of the road even with its deck plate. Had the earth remained in position, many who drove over it in the darkness would not have known how they negotiated the muddy holes in the road. But between the steady rain and the tearing action of many tank tracks, some of the dirt had been churned aside, exposing the steel deck beneath.

The three British Army soldiers standing in the gloom beside the old Valentine, probably the men who had placed it where it was, directed a stream of extremely colorful profanity at any tank which made contact with the turret of their Valentine, because this greatly added to the violence of the noise and shock they had to tolerate. Yet missing the turret was more of an accident than otherwise, in the rain and the darkness surrounding them, though no one deliberately attempted to hit it.

"Well for Christ's sake!" exclaimed MacLean. "I've seen it, but I still can't believe it. A Limey tank made into part of the road, and its crew still sticking with it. Isn't there any other place in the world for them to go? I guess, until they get new orders, they stay where they were sent. I don't think you could count them as friends of the Canadian Army just now."

The crews of the Canadian tanks were not exactly comfortable either. Contrary to common belief, tanks were not dry and warm shelters against the rain and the cold which battered people exposed to the elements. Water found its way around the hatches and periscopes of Sherman tanks, and dripped persistently upon all the crew members within, regardless of what position they were in.

Furthermore, the ventilation for the engines was provided by a number of vents in the hull of the tank, through which air was drawn by a large, four-foot fan placed at the front of the engines and immediately behind the turret, rotating whenever the engines were running. In addition to cooling the engines, this fan would exhaust the foul air, smoke and fumes from the tank interior. This meant a constant gale of air being pulled through the tank, an assurance that everyone would be cold in cold weather. Comfort for the occupants was apparently not a major consideration in the design of the Sherman tank.

The tiresome and exhausting drive into position for the commencement of the battle for the Siegfried Line brought the entire Regiment into a pleasant grove of Linden trees high on a hill at the edge of the Reichswald Forest. To the east, the ground sloped gently downward across a wide valley, studded with church steeples, that poked up from the surrounding greenery. Each church marked the location of another quiet, country village, all apparently innocent of any involvement with the fighting. In the far distance, a faint shimmer, barely discernable from the height of the Reichswald, marked the location of the Rhine River.

The forest itself was attractive too, almost totally free of undergrowth among the tall and stately lime trees. A large monument had been erected in a lonesome, shaded corner, since overgrown with ivy, to commemorate a long-forgotten battle fought early in the previous century between the French and the Germans. Paths meandered through the park-like surroundings, where people had once wandered in idle enjoyment of a lovely, sylvan setting overlooking the countryside for many miles around. But of course, that was before the Siegfried Line was even a thought in the minds of German military engineers.

On the 26th of February, the Canadian Grenadier Guards, part of a much larger group, drove out of their concentration area to commence the assault that would kick off their participation in the battle for the Siegfried Line, the fabled defensive system of fortifications, dragon's teeth tank obstructions, and minefields which the Germans had labeled the "Westwall." It had been the subject matter of pictures in magazines, newspapers and movies all over the world for over a decade. It had become a household name. Little had MacLean and his comrades dreamed in those far off days that they would have the dubious pleasure of leading the assault on a part of this forbidding line, the part near Cleve.

The town of Cleve had been razed by artillery and heavy bombing earlier in the month. Within its boundaries was a brick castle on a hill at one end of the town, damaged but still standing defiantly where it had been for centuries past. From this castle had come Ann of Cleve, one of the unfortunate early wives of the English King Henry VIII, as former history teacher Lieutenant Ellis reminded his Troop. He added that Ann of Cleve had not enjoyed a long life.

MacLean and his crew, riding "open-up" in their tank in the approach march to Cleve, were much encouraged by the plenitude of artillerymen and support service people, who lined the road in the early part of the move, all waving and wishing the tank men well as they rumbled past. They couldn't help feeling encouraged by the large numbers of troops they saw, that they were bound to smash their way through the famous and formidable defences ahead of them. But as they neared the start line for the actual assault, the number of well-wishing spectators dwindled dramatically.

"When you get to the 'sharp end,' the number of spectators and well-wishers dwindles, here or anywhere else," noted MacLean to his crew, as he gestured toward the empty route ahead of them.

"It'll be just the infantrymen and us from here on," added Tommy Dolphin. "I guess we have to have all them other guys we saw along the road to support us, but I sure wish to hell we had more bayonets and not so many spear-carriers when we hit the German lines. It gets kind of lonesome at times, just us and the Krauts at the front end."

"It was ever thus," responded Bill Seaton, "but the more mechanized the force, the greater the ratio of support people to actual combatants. I heard somewhere that it's about six to one now, and getting worse."

"In the next war, we should get into the bunch that make up the six, not the bunch that make up the one," concluded Dolphin with a hollow laugh.

The passage through the ruins of Cleve was not a pleasant one. Although the Germans had experienced a severe bombing by waves of Lancaster bombers, a raid that had driven them out of the town by the time the 4th Armored Division passed through it, immense piles of debris stood high around the canyon-like road they followed. Huge grey mounds of broken stonework, smashed boards and woodwork, shattered glass, and here and there a part of a body, horse or human protruded from the mountains of debris. Fortunately the temperature was low, so the general smell of the battlefield was not further horrified by heat, flies and the stench of rotting flesh. "Sufficient unto the day was the evil thereof," thought the tank troops passing through as they stared in silence at the hell that lay on all sides around them. Men, even those hardened by exposure to numerous earlier sights of death and destruction, became silent in the presence of the levels of destruction they witnessed in Cleve. The Lancasters had been called in to add their massive loads of explosives to the carnage that had already been caused by days and nights of artillery fire on the town. Bulldozing a track, for that is all it really amounted to, through the debris had been a difficult task.

The dragon's teeth type of defensive line which had been encountered by the American forces further south, along the older portions of the Siegfried Line, had no counterpart at the northern end. Instead, the Germans had elected to develop a more flexible plan, consisting of heavily fortified trenches, buildings and pill-boxes among naturally strong topographic contours in three mutually supporting lines of defence, which proved to be extremely formidable. The German towns of Cleve, Goch, Calcar and Udem were all integrated parts of this system.

Only one lane or roadway had been cleared so far through the devastation of Cleve, when MacLean's tank passed through the town, along with the rest of the tanks of his regiment. There seemed to be no walls left standing anywhere, other than those of the castle, at the higher end of the town. The casualties to civilians as well as soldiers must have been extremely high. As MacLean's tank slowly growled its way forward along the cleared stretch of road, he noticed the upper torso of a dead German soldier lying at the side of the road; the lower half of the body having been pounded into the dirt by repeated passages of all kinds of vehicles over it, along the same track on the ground. No driver wanted to follow a new track lest he drive over one of the mines left behind by the enemy. Therefore they slavishly adhered to the same paths as every other driver, each passing over the same corpse.

It shocked MacLean to look down from his turret and see two glazed, half-open eyes staring straight upward from a part of the road only two feet from the rut that his tank was following. It was at least as much of a shock for him to return about two weeks later, along the same stretch of road, after a fortnight of bitter fighting further eastward, to see the same torso in the same spot, still unmoved or attended to. "Some mother's son, even if he was a Jerry," he mused sadly, realizing that it could just as well have been himself or anyone else among his friends lying there, denied the dignity of even a decent burial, and in fact becoming just another part of the road.

Leaving Cleve behind, the Grenadiers, then led by their redoubtable new commanding officer, Snuffy Smith, in a grouping with infantry from the Argyll and Sutherland Highlanders of Canada, or "Ash Cans" as they were familiarly called, commenced their assault early next morning. MacLean headed his Firefly tank, along with the rest of No. 1 Squadron, across the fields leading to Udem and Calcar. It was a sea of sloppy mud, churned up by the tracks of dozens of tanks ploughing through it, as the rain continued to fall. They even had a few flail tanks at the head end of the drive, to detonate the mines that everyone expected as they penetrated deeper into the German defences.

Right from the start line of the assault, they attracted a wicked amount of fire from 88 mm guns. Reports from the Recce Troop indicated the presence of several Tiger tanks and two S.P. guns, among a nest of anti-tank weapons ahead of them. In addition, there was plenty of small arms fire directed at the assault troops from the German infantrymen concealed in slit trenches close by. Immediately, one of the tanks from No. 1 Squadron lost a track on a mine. Soon afterward, two tanks from No. 2 Squadron were knocked out in quick succession by the anti-tank guns.

To overcome this opposition, Colonel Smith ordered a direct charge, to overwhelm the guns that were tormenting them. He was certain that each of the attacking tanks would be knocked out methodically, one at a time, if they continued to advance in column formation. Most unfortunately, the first vehicle knocked out when the charge began, was Smith's own tank, leading the rush on the guns.

The 88 mm shell from the Tiger tank smashed completely through the Commanding Officer's tank, killing some of his crew and severing his right leg. Some of the steam went out of the charge with the loss of Smith, but the drive continued advancing slowly. The day's objective, the Udem-Calcar Ridge, was finally reached after hours of bitter fighting.

MacLean's tank manoeuvred to the flank of the drive across the fields, to get an oblique look at the source of the German firing. As gunner Bill Seaton studied his frontage through his telescopic sight, he spotted a massive S.P. gun changing its position slightly to improve its field of fire. This was necessary sometimes for S.P.'s, because their ability to traverse was narrowly limited. It was the movement, small though it was, that attracted Seaton's attention.

"I've got that S.P. right in the cross-hairs, Ken. What range would you say?" asked Seaton over the intercom.

"Driver halt," replied MacLean. "It looks like, maybe 1400 yards. Try that, but be ready with more A.P. Tommy, because we have to get him before he gets us."

Seaton adjusted his elevating control and fired. The tracer in the back of the shell passed just over the top of the S.P. gun. Tommy Dolphin slammed another A.P. round into the fuming breech as Ken and Seaton both shouted. "Down one hundred," together. Bill instantly dropped a notch on the elevating wheel, steadied the big gun for a second and then stabbed the trigger on the floor again. Everyone watched tensely as the tracer raced toward the target at more than three thousand feet per second, considerably faster than a rifle bullet.

"Got the bastard!" shouted MacLean, as sparks leapt into the air from the hull of the S.P. Smoke began to pour out of its half-open hatch but it did not explode. One or two of the crew could be seen scrambling out of the side hatch of the knocked-out vehicle, and running to join the rest of the paratroopers that inhabited the small bushes along the far edge of the field.

"Driver advance, and quickly," ordered MacLean. "We can't afford to stop for long or we'll get hit ourselves. We have to work the whole of those bushes behind that S.P. with the co-ax, to put a stop to some of that firing going on against our infantry."

Resumption of movement forward was none too soon, for the whiplash crack of 88 mm shells passing close overhead followed soon afterward, making MacLean pull his head down.

"Drive zig-zag a bit Henri," he added. "We're in the line of fire of one of their bloody guns somewhere. We have to keep moving as fast as this mud will let us, but not in a straight line. I can't see who's shooting at us, but let's move on."

Brault did exactly as requested, and, although MacLean was certain that at least two more very near misses whistled past them, they were not hit. They ploughed their way to the ridge ahead, where the business of clearing buildings had already begun. Prisoners were being taken and marched to the rear areas, but some trenches near the buildings were still occupied by German troops anxious to fight for the Fatherland. The arrival of so many tanks and infantry seemed to crush their enthusiasm, and surrenders became widespread.

As the day wore away, the expected counter-attack from the Germans arrived, and was repelled with the loss of one Sherman tank from No. 1 Squadron. The tally also included losses among the counter-attackers: one large S.P. gun and about a dozen infantrymen. It was no surprize that each of the vehicles burned well into the night, as men from both sides prowled about, patrolling in the darkness.

With the evacuation of the dangerously wounded Colonel Smith, a new commanding officer had to be appointed. The mighty mite, Major E.A.C (Ned) Amy was promoted to Lieutenant Colonel immediately from 2 I.C. and took up his new appointment. Certainly the smallest man in the regiment physically, and beyond any doubt, the largest of them all in terms of fighting ability, Amy's promotion was universally popular. MacLean and other men in No. 1 Squadron who had served under him when he was their squadron commander, were delighted to see "their man" get the commanding officer's job. Many were the tales and recollections of his nerve, of his "derring-do" when the opportunity arrived. He was equally well-known for his compassion and consideration for the lives of the men that depended upon his judgment and expertise. He and Snuffy Smith, his predecessor and closest friend, had shown the men beneath them by example how the quintessential tank warrior should conduct himself. MacLean and his colleagues were convinced that they would never serve a better commander.

The Regiment moved on from the Calcar-Udem Ridge toward the Hochwald and the railway line which traveled on the high ground through a gap in the forest, all the way from Goch, west of the Rhine, to Wesel on the east side of the river. The remnants of many German divisions were pressed into the desperate fight for the last defences west of the River. The weather was atrocious and the mud favored the defenders. Only a part of the tracked vehicles and none of the hundreds of wheeled vehicles could negotiate the mire at the beginning of what was to become one of the most savage battles of the war for the Canadian Army. The struggle for the Hochwald Gap, brought forth all the horrors of a very large land battle, through seas of mud. It was fought against carefully prepared defences, skillfully manned by absolutely determined defenders. It was much like some of the worst battles of the First World War. Armored support was provided in those places where tanks were able to penetrate and move forward. But many more tanks simply bogged down near the entrance to the Gap, leaving to the few that did get ahead the full burden of attacking against dug-in anti-tank guns and hull-down tanks or S.P. guns.

The thickly tangled trees of the Hochwald, among which the worst of the hand-to-hand fighting took place, became additional hazards. The wily German artillerists fired their field guns with delayed fuses into the upper branches of the trees, creating deadly air bursts above the troops struggling from slit trenches to ditches to ridges in their climb toward the hogs-back above them. Men who were somewhat protected by a parapet of earth ahead of them, were raked by a rain of shrapnel, as air-burst after air-burst exploded over their heads. Indeed, more than one tank commander was struck by the shrapnel from shells or mortar bombs exploding forty or fifty feet above him.

Friendly artillery did its best to boost the infantry forward in the hell of the Hochwald, but they had great difficulty in laying an effective barrage on the German positions without menacing the Canadian infantry fighting only a few dozen yards from the enemy positions. There could be no air support in the thick, low-lying, clinging mist that accompanied the steady rain.

On March 1, the second day of the Hochwald fighting, MacLean and his comrades from No. 1 Squadron had pushed forward, under extremely difficult conditions to the western end of the Gap. Some huge shell craters were being carved out by large-calibre German guns firing from positions on the far side of the Rhine. This long range fire was being directed by enemy observers watching every development of the attacking forces from nearby concealment. A shell from one of the 155 mm guns arrived every three or four minutes. If one of these monster shells landed nearby, it would destroy any tank, along with everyone inside it.

At the height of the battle, word was received by MacLean and the rest of his squadron that Colonel Amy's new headquarters were established in a large brick building which combined house and barn at the side of an extremely muddy road leading up the Hochwald Gap. From this building, his commands crackled out over the radio net to the entire Regiment.

It was later established that Amy had been wounded in one foot before secretly moving into the brick barn. This explained his wearing a huge German jackboot on one foot, sliced open at the side to accommodate the hastily bandaged wound. MacLean had heard from other Crew Commanders that no one was to betray the location of "Sunray," as the commanding officer was called, lest the Medical Officer, who had heard rumors of Amy's wound, should find him and evacuate him from the battle he was so enthusiastically guiding. Suitably vague communications were exchanged as a consequence.

MacLean's tank became severely bogged down in the mud by mid-afternoon. Though still able to fire the guns, the tank had high-centered in the sloppy mire, unable to crawl further up the soupy, slimy slope ahead. Fortunately, some few tanks from No. 3 Squadron had approached the entrance to the Gap from a ledge at a higher level and managed to continue their progress upward along the roadbed of the single railway track, to provide support for the hard-pressed infantry.

Enemy artillery fire was awesome in that area. High explosive shells plastered the ground around MacLean's tank, and anti-tank gunfire cracked and crashed among the other tanks struggling in the quagmire around him. The grey curtain of rain continued to fall. About 50 yards away was a line of slit trenches, several occupied by infantrymen from the Algonquin Regiment. They sensibly stayed close to the bottom of their trenches, as the fire from many guns roared above them. The moan of nebelwerfer rocket launchers added to the din, inducing everyone not already inside a tank or nestled in the bottom of a slit trench to stay under cover until the current "hate" ended.

Seaton became much amused by the arrival within his range of view of a flock of six or seven farm geese, wandering aimlessly past the tank in the midst of all the shooting and shell explosions. MacLean, who could see a wider spectrum from his hatch, explained that on the other side of the tank he could see a handful of refugees from the destruction of the farm buildings in the area, taking a few pitiful belongings with them, as they tearfully worked their route through the mud. They were following their geese forward into the very vortex of the battle for the Hochwald Gap. Pity welled up in the hearts of all who saw them, terrified and soaking wet, and headed for the very spot where the fighting and firing was reaching a crescendo. They disappeared from view beyond a fold in the ground ahead, and were not seen again; more innocents cast up in the wrong place at the worst possible time. Dolphin had seen them through his periscope and shook his head slowly.

"That's when you know that war is hell," he said sadly.

On the other side of the tank, one of the Algonquin Regiment infantrymen leapt from his slit trench and, with one swipe of his rifle barrel, picked off the last errant goose, as it wandered giddily through the middle of the battle. He quickly took it back to his slit trench with him. The irony of his position struck all who watched his gambit. He certainly would not have risked any appearance above ground level until the geese appeared. But when they did, it appeared worth any risk to capture his own goose. Everyone hoped he might live to eat it some day.

MacLean noted that five tanks had been knocked out by anti-tank gunfire coming from a battery located higher up in the Gap. No fire had been directed at his tank, so far as he was aware, so long as it remained in the exact position in which it stood. He was unable to advance, because of the slimy mud slope ahead, but he was capable of reversing down the slope behind. However, as soon as his tank reversed about 20 yards it appeared to come into the angle of sight of some enemy gun further up the Gap. There would immediately be several shells whistle past MacLean's head as soon as reverse was attempted. This was not to be ignored.

"My God Henri! Don't back up. Some gun on the hill over there picks us up as soon as we go back a few yards. Let's stay where we were and try to live a bit longer." Henri instantly drove ahead again to where he had been stuck before.

This cat-and-mouse game played on for the rest of the dim, foggy afternoon that day. Then just as daylight began to fail, MacLean decided to chance a move out, in hope of getting into another track which would lead up into the Gap. That was where the remainder of the Squadron's tanks were fighting their way toward the Rhine. With a quick surge, Henri reversed all the way to the bottom of the gentle slope, without attracting fire from the unknown enemy gunner up the Gap. MacLean directed him to the track followed by the other tanks successfully into the mouth of the Gap, and they managed to follow the same route.

About 300 yards along the track, MacLean's tank passed several more slit trenches which had been dug weeks or perhaps even months before, by German troops or by members of the Todt organization, for emergency shelter from the ever-present Allied Air forces. To everyone's astonishment, a helmeted German soldier in a paratrooper's jacket suddenly stood up in one of these trenches which everyone believed to be vacant. He was only 40 feet from the side of MacLean's tank, when he aimed his panzerfaust rocket launcher at the approaching vehicle and fired it. From such a short distance he could hardly miss.

The cone-shaped projectile arched forward, striking the front of the hull about two feet below the turret ring. There was an immediate, sharp explosion and a flash of flame at the point of contact, as the cone welded itself to the outside of the tank. Instantaneously a tongue of white hot gas burned its way through the steel plate of the hull, characteristic of the action of all "heat weapons" of the day. This jet of super-hot gas could cut a hole through many inches of solid steel plate. The hole was relatively small on the outside of the tank, not exceeding about two inches in diameter. From the inside, the hole expanded to between six and eight inches. All the molten metal created by the explosion of the heat weapon's projectile, as it burned its way through the hull of the tank, became a blizzard of small pieces of steel inside the vehicle, tearing their way through flesh and bone, or even thin steel plate, as it ricocheted about.

MacLean's tank staggered to an immediate halt in the middle of the road, with a thin column of black and brown smoke emerging from the crew commander's open hatch. Ken, who was standing half out of the hatch of his turret, was shocked and momentarily blinded by the blast in his tank. Instinctively aware that he had to get out, he climbed over the cupola ring to leave the turret, just as a further sharp explosion flung him clear of the hatch and he dropped to the ground. Looking up from where he landed, he appeared groggy but apparently not injured.

"That was the ammunition starting to go," he yelled at two men from Corporal Moody's tank immediately behind him, who ran up to help get any survivors out of the tank before it blew up.

MacLean's words were barely out of his mouth when a massive blast inside the turret sent pieces of metal, scraps of wire, flames, black smoke and pieces of human bodies hurtling into the air through the crew commander's hatch. Directly afterward, the hatch took on the appearance of a chimney from the furnace within. MacLean stood for an instant completely dumbstruck, staring at the raging inferno from within the tank where he had been standing only moments before. Then he noticed the German paratrooper who had stealthily fired the panzerfaust. He was advancing slowly toward him, a sickly smirk on his face. His hands were in the air, signaling his desire to surrender.

214

"Now you want to surrender do you, you Heinie bastard," snarled MacLean. Still somewhat in shock at the instantaneous loss of his tank and his friends, he still had sufficient presence of mind to dig for the Browning pistol in his side holster. He needn't have bothered.

From the tank immediately behind MacLean's vehicle came the stutter of a short burst of fire from a sub-machinegun. Corporal Moody's gunner, Ed Melfort, riding on the top of the turret of his tank, had seen everything as it happened just a few yards ahead of him. Powerless to do anything to prevent the panzerfaust bomb striking, once it was launched, he had kept his Sten gun within easy reach. Hatred blazed from Melfort's eyes as he stared at the man who had stealthily awaited his opportunity to fire his weapon at close quarters, and then, after killing three men who were in no position to defend themselves, wanted to surrender himself so as to be spared further jeopardy. Melfort fired a burst of five or six bullets into the chest of the surprised German.

"A son-of-a-bitch like that should make up his mind, if he's going to surrender," Ed shouted to his crew commander. "If he wants out of the war, fine; let him put up his hands and we'll take him in. But he can't expect to pull his bloody surprise killing right in front of our eyes and then become an instant prisoner of war to save his own rotten skin. To hell with that. If he wanted to shoot other people he should expect to get some back too." And Melfort put his Sten gun back on the turret.

'How are you, Ken?" Moody shouted down to MacLean. "Have you been hit too?"

"I don't think so," replied MacLean. "Maybe a bit in the ankle, but nothing else," he concluded after looking quickly at his legs and arms. The tank he had just left was burning fiercely and more ammunition was beginning to "cook off" in the intense heat generated by the burning fuel in the hull. MacLean scrambled away from the burning tank, crouching low and running along the ditch beside the road, as several mortar shells arrived from the German positions ahead. They had been aimed at the oily pyre of smoke climbing upward, hoping to get any escaping crew members in the area around the fire. It was not a healthy place to stand around.

After retreating several hundred yards, MacLean came to a substantial dugout in the side of the road bank, open at the top to the drizzling rain, but dug deeply enough that men could stand erectly in it, as they peered sourly across a wet and dismal scene. Three members of the Algonquin Regiment, a sergeant and two privates huddled in the dugout, their Bren gun on its bipod pointing toward the enemy.

"What's going on up there?" the sergeant asked. "I see they got one of the Grenadier tanks. I hope the crew got out all right."

"No they didn't," answered MacLean wearily. "They're in there brewing up now. They never had a chance," he added, his voice trembling with the dawning realization, gradually taking possession of his shocked mind that he would never see those friends again.

"Well, where were you? You're wearing a Grenadier hat badge. Why the hell are you walking back in this muck and corruption?" continued the sergeant.

"I was in that tank. I shouldn't be alive now either, but I was almost half out of the turret when the bazooka bomb hit us. There was nothing I could do, and they're all gone now," MacLean answered, quietly shaking his head in utter melancholy.

The infantrymen fell silent, staring at MacLean and sympathizing with him. Finally Ken broke the silence, saying, "I've got to be off. Have to get another tank back up here. Keep your heads down men, and good luck to you."

As he hunched forward in the deepening darkness, he looked for any sign that might assist him in his search for R.H.Q. His mind kept returning to the repetitiveness of his current dilemma, even though he kept drumming it into himself that he had to get his thoughts on other things. The irritation and annoyance of returning to Q.M. stores for still another kit did bother him: a new personal weapon; an explanation of how his tank had been lost; and perhaps a recounting of why no one else got out of his tank after it was hit. No one would say, "If you got out, why didn't you get anyone else out?," but he knew it was in their minds. He even began to wonder whether what he thought he had seen with his own eyes, really did happen the way his reason told him it had.

Since the rocket had penetrated the hull close to the driver's head, there could be no doubt that Henri had been killed immediately by the storm of steel particles blasting inward. The last glimpse of Tom showed a man hammered back against the wall of the turret, and speckled by hundreds of pieces of flying steel that had blasted into his face, head and body, making him immediately unrecognizable. Ken imagined that Bill Seaton must have looked the same as Tom Dolphin, for he would have received the same blast of steel fragments on his side of the gun as Tom had on the loader's side. It was because MacLean was standing above and behind his gunner that he had been protected from the blast; Seaton had taken it all for him. There was never the slightest sign of life in any of the other crew members after MacLean was blasted out of his turret. It was certain that had he or anyone else attempted to enter the tank after the first violent explosion, they would have shared the fate of those already inside. MacLean could not imagine any other explanation of what had happened to his crew.

What continued to stir the nethermost depths of his thoughts, once he reasoned out for himself what must have happened to his crew, were the old questions; "How many more times can you be a survivor? Can you still take some more of this?" He knew that most combat soldiers must ask themselves these questions from time to time, and he forced himself to the resolution that he could take a lot more. There were some around him, like the inimitable Al Hubert, who had definitely survived more than three lost tanks, but that was not what seemed to get to him. It was rather the fact that, three men had escaped from the first tank he had lost, away back at Carpiquet Airport; two survived the loss at Falaise; and now just one, himself, at the Hochwald. "Maybe it would be like baseball," he thought: "three strikes and out." Food for thought, sometime but not just then.

When he did reach R.H.Q. later that evening, luck seemed to be with him. The Q.M. Stores people were accommodating without their customary sarcasm. The questions from the Intelligence officer were routine and easily answered. And an experienced tank crew in No. 1 Squadron needed a new Crew Commander, their own having become a casualty a day or two earlier.

"This is a 75 mm gun tank, not one of your beloved Fireflies," the Adjutant explained, "But you'll like the crew, and I think they'll take to you." MacLean agreed, pleased as punch to be remaining in his own squadron.

MacLean's new crew were certainly not strangers to him, but he was keenly interested in becoming better acquainted with them.

Alex Clark, the driver, was a heavy, balding man in his mid-30's with an excellent record as a responsible soldier, dating back to his landing on D-Day with the First Hussar Regiment. Alex, who patronized MacLean to an extent because of Clark's age and MacLean's lack of it, left Ken in no doubt that he did the driving, all the time, and that his co-driver and bow gunner, "Inky" Blackwell, a large and much less-experienced man, would really act as Clark's helper but never his alternative driver.

The turret crew included Jack Sutherland, a pleasant, handsome and intelligent young man from New Brunswick, with many months of experience in the Regiment as a Loader Operator.

The fourth man, and the key to their success as a crew, was the testy but very capable Joe Mroz, a short, tough little man, greying at the temples and looking very much his age, 32 years. Joe enjoyed the reputation of being a crack tank gunner. He was always miserable when awakened for guard duty, and spent his first hour in each morning snarling like a terrier at anyone near him. But when he was fully awake, Mroz could be a pleasant companion.

And so, after an interval of two days, during which two of the tanks of No. 3 Squadron, with associated infantry support, forced their way up the Hochwald Gap, MacLean and his new tank and crew joined the Regiment for the last few days of fighting in that area. As they did so, to their pleasant surprise, the rainy weather cleared and the sun made a welcome, long overdue appearance. The bogged-down tanks became mobile once more; the Typhoon fighters reappeared overhead, and the war went on.

MacLean and the rest of No. 1 Squadron fought in the armored drives against the heavily fortified villages of Winnenthal and Sonsbeck, located closer to the Rhine and incorporated into the third belt of the Westwall fortifications. The fighting was bitter and the casualties, particularly among the infantry, were severe.

Sonsbeck was the site of the Grenadiers' principle exposure to the full fury of a large concentration of 'Nebelwerfers,' large rocket launchers built in banks or mattresses grouped next to one another. When fired, the rockets traveled rapidly through the air making unnerving, wild, screaming noises while aloft. They caused terrifying surface blasts when they struck, but did not penetrate deeply into the ground like artillery shells. 'Moaning Minnies' fired projectiles that broke into large, cruel-looking metal shards upon exploding, with awesome capabilities to maim or kill anyone within range of the explosion. Mercifully however, the range of travel of these shards was relatively small.

The capture of Sonsbeck on March 10th, 1945 with all its array of new rocketry hardware was followed by the surrender of substantial numbers of enemy troops in the local garrison, the last one west of the river. For the Grenadiers, it was the end of fighting in front of the Rhine. The bridge across the river at Xanten, one of the main bridges in the area, was destroyed by the Germans the same day. This meant that a new bridge would have to be constructed across the great river before fighting could resume.

CHAPTER XIII

THE LAST STAGES

Directly after the collapse of the German defenses west of the Rhine River, the Canadian Grenadier Guards withdrew from the Cleve, Goch, Calcar area, to the more friendly ambience of Holland, for replenishment and reorganization of the regiment. Although the route seemed long, the men were happy to arrive at the city of Tilberg. All of the Regiment's supplies in A and B Echelon were brought along, and everyone enjoyed changes of uniforms, bath parades and meals prepared by the Squadron cooks. Billeting in houses, for the second time for the Grenadiers, was again well organized, and MacLean and his crew were pleased with their quarters and their hosts, who opened their hearts as well as their homes to them.

The cleaning and refitting proceeded well in Tilburg. An uninterrupted spell of warm, sunny spring weather marked a most welcome change for citizens and soldiers alike, from the dismal weather of the past weeks. On the third day in Tilburg, MacLean's crew was excitedly summoned into the house about mid-morning by their Dutch host. Quite at a loss to understand the cause of all the beckoning and waving, they entered the parlor, to find that they had been invited to listen to Radio Eindhoven, just returned to broadcasting for the first time in weeks.

"It's Beniamino Gigli!" whispered their hostess, urging a reverent silence while everyone listened to the recorded voice of a sorrowing Italian tenor.

"Who the hell is Gigli?" asked Joe Mroz, not really expecting to be fully understood.

"He is the greatest tenor alive," murmured the host. "We are hearing Santa Lucia now. He will sing 'Marta M'Appari' next. They have no program at the radio station, so they play only recordings. Everyone in Holland loves Gigli. He is good, no?"

As the power of the great voice surged out, they were deeply impressed, almost in spite of themselves. Though none of the Canadians could call himself an opera buff, the sheer beauty of the music they heard seemed to fill a void that none recognized as really existing. They all stayed for the remainder of the singing before trouping back outside to their work.

The Dutchmen were pleased that their guests from Canada had heard what they themselves adored. MacLean and his crew were surprised and pleased to have been asked to listen, and greatly impressed with what they had heard. Perhaps it was the contrast with the coarse voices, the crashing noises, and all the violent cacophonous sounds of war which assail the ears, that stole the hearts of these men. Unconscious of it, even those who had never enjoyed serious music before felt that their souls had been starved for anything of beauty, whether a painting or a lovely song. It had been a good day for them.

After five days of enjoyable recreation and reconditioning of men and weapons in Tilburg, orders arrived on March 24th that the regiment was to return to Germany and to the fighting that awaited them there. The plans called for a short range artillery barrage, which the 4th Armored Division was to fire across the Rhine at Rees, in support of the assault crossing by Allied infantry at Xanten and Rees.

As they approached the Rhine River valley, the troops of the 4th Canadian Armored Division watched another sky armada pass over them in cloudless weather carrying some 15,000 troops to their landings over the Rhine, near Wesel. The opposition to the landings was spirited in a few locations, but overall, it was an easy landing. The troops fanned out from the landings, joining those who had made the assault crossing on the river, to make a very large and expanding bridgehead on the east side.

The Grenadiers crossed the Rhine at Rees on April 1st, on a very long bridge constructed by army engineers, utilizing 85 pontoons that had been carefully anchored in position in advance. To avoid excessive strain on the floating bridge, individual tanks were separated by substantial gaps. They encountered no defensive fire from the Germans in the course of their crossing.

The next axis of advance for the entire 4th Canadian Armored Division was to be northward and eastward, through Almelo in Holland and then back to Germany, passing through Meppen, Friesythe and Oldenburg, all German towns. MacLean and his comrades from No. 1 Squadron crossed the Ijssel River, amidst enthusiastic celebrations at Anholt, welcoming the end of their German occupation. The drive was to take the city of Almelo as its next objective.

The size of Almelo rather surprized the Grenadiers, and when No. 1 Squadron moved in with a company of the L.S.R.'s, they found themselves moving along fully urbanized streets. MacLean noticed that there did not seem to be much organized resistance in the city, but there was a good deal of wicked sniping coming from upstairs windows of houses and other buildings - shots fired from very close range at tanks with open hatches from which crew commanders peered.

As No. 2 Troop of MacLean's squadron headed along one street, they moved toward a bridge which was still intact, across a canal cutting through the city. The tank ahead of MacLean's in the advance was commanded by Barney Boyce, a popular veteran of years in the Canadian Grenadiers, who had recently been promoted to crew commander. MacLean watched with mounting dismay, as the column moved slowly forward beneath rows of open upper windows, from which curtains fluttered in the wind. Some civilians leaned out to cheer the arrival of their liberators. Many milled about in the side streets as well, convinced that because they were not wearing uniforms they could not be hurt by the occasional shooting that was taking place. MacLean crouched enough that only an absolute minimum of his head, above eye level only, appeared over the hatch. Barney Boyce, on the other hand, new to the job in the turret, stood upright on the turret floor and peered around him.

Suddenly a shot rang out, and Barney jerked violently, clutched at his neck and flung himself out of the hatch and onto the deck plates behind, where he kicked and writhed. Obviously seriously wounded, from the amount of blood which gushed out onto the deck plates, Barney had been shot in the throat by one of the still-active snipers. Although it appeared that Boyce would not live long, he was removed from his tank quickly and brought to the regimental aid post. Miraculously, he survived, and was one of the early returnees to Canada after the fighting ended.

Resistance from the Germans in Almelo continued sporadically, with instances of vigorous celebrations beginning in one street, while fighting proceeded one block away in another street. MacLean's crew had several experiences with pockets of Germans that were still prepared to fight hard for any land they occupied, and their encounters in and around Almelo were typical. Although a large number of prisoners had been taken by the Regiment, a German S.P. gun knocked out several trucks bringing supplies up to the Regiment. Spandau machineguns roared into life, cutting down the advance men of the Lake Superior Regiment in their carriers. The S.P. gun escaped the L.S.R.'s, but was knocked out by another Grenadier tank later in the morning. A number of German anti-tank guns and infantry had been located in the centre of Almelo. They were there, it was later discovered, to provide protection for the quite extensive local Gestapo Headquarters. Their defence of that establishment was vigorous and effective; but they were completely overcome by the arrival of light tanks from the recce troop, along with several Shermans from No. 3 Squadron.

The Germans surrendered quickly when it became apparent that their defence was hopeless, but several members of the hated Dutch S.S., located in Gestapo Headquarters, attracted keen and excited interest from the civilians nearby. A lynching was certainly going to be proceeded with, when Lieutenant Tomlinson from No. 2 Squadron, took the arrested S.S. men into protective custody with his P.O.W.'s There was no doubt in MacLean's mind as to the fate of these men, if they had been left in the hands of the local "Oranje" battalion.

The "Oranje" fighters in Almelo were led by several particularly officious members, who gave orders in loud voices to the civilians crowding around them, meanwhile brandishing a motley collection of weapons they had assembled over many months. Some of these weapons were ancient and probably a greater hazard to the men firing them than to anyone else. Others sported Schmeissers and Walthers which had been recovered from surrendered or dead Germans. These latter weapons could be deadly efficient and effective, as their bearers realized.

MacLean had seen photographs in various magazines and papers strewn about in Dutch houses, showing drafts of young Dutchmen who had been recruited by the Germans in the early 1940's for service in Dutch S.S. units. They fought in the "Viking Division;" along with Danes and Norwegians who had been converted. They had all been persuaded by German propaganda that life with the S.S. would be adventurous, romantic, and rewarding, with smart uniforms and plenty of food. This was in the days when it appeared the Germans would win the war, and those who did not join would be in for hardships and misery. It was no surprise to learn that there was a significant enlistment of idle, young Dutchmen into the German forces, just as there would have been in almost any other country in similar circumstances. MacLean found however that, throughout Holland, the vast majority resisted the German occupancy and vented their spleen against anyone who supported or collaborated with them.

After Almelo's liberation, the Grenadier Guards headed northward in an effort to stifle and block the returning of large numbers of German troops from the northeastern corner of Holland. The Regiment crossed back into Germany, over the Bailey bridge that straddled the wide Ems Canal at Meppen, where a short and sharp fight took place with a number of army stragglers, gathered there.

The number of casualties dropped remarkably throughout the Regiment after the Rhine crossing. The reception accorded by the German civilians was bleakly inhospitable, and in sharp contrast to the delirious welcomes extended by the villagers of Holland. Enemy country with enemy civilians glaring around was new to MacLean and his comrades. Everyone was warned that all-round defence policies were in effect, and that extra caution had to be exercised everywhere.

Gunner Joe Mroz was particularly sensitive about the small groups of people in civilian garb that stared out coldly from damaged buildings, as the tank columns headed north-eastward. Many of the men in these groups looked suspiciously like recent members of the Wehrmacht, who had simply changed into civilian clothes to avoid the P.O.W. cages. Indeed on April 9th, there had been a vigorous exchange of fire between a tank in No. 1 Squadron further ahead on the road through Sogel, and one of the remnants of the German Army that had chosen to man an anti-tank gun with supporting infantry. Some so-called civilians had become strongly partisan in that community, helping to carry ammunition across the gap between two houses where an anti-tank gun was half-concealed. Mroz also pointed to the stir of activity behind several of the houses at Lorup, the next small town on the road to Oldenburg, where white flags waved from the windows. A belligerent attitude blazed from the eyes of the scowling citizens on all sides.

It was also at Lorup where MacLean received a small wound in his left hand from shrapnel slashing down upon them from an air-burst above the tank. A pause in the fighting for the town was seized upon by Ken to go back to the regimental aid post, or R.A.P., to have the shrapnel removed and the hand dressed. The short trip was memorable, not because of the medical aid provided, which was simple and straightforward, but because of the substantial number of enemy wounded, who were receiving treatment there. Some of the enemy were definitely suffering stoically from serious wounds that had to be attended to promptly. MacLean and two Canadian infantrymen with quite significant leg wounds, stared in disbelief as a rough old German sergeant-major, seriously wounded in one foot, ranted about his ill-luck in getting so close to home, only to have been wounded by soldiers in the amateurish Canadian Army, an army that he considered unworthy of any serious comparison with the professional soldiers of the Wehrmacht. His rave was cut short by an orderly at the R.A.P., who ordered silence from him as he was taken into a side room where a Canadian surgeon commenced the task of attending to his injured foot. Everyone in the big waiting area, whether friend or foe, seemed to feel that the war was winding down, but the small outbursts of fighting along the road toward Oldenburg could be just as dangerous as a large-scale action, for those directly involved.

Upon returning to his tank and crew that evening, MacLean was told that the Squadron Plan was to continue clearing the villages and towns along the route to Oldenburg, commencing at Friesoythe, the next town on the road, where rumor held that some 500 paratroops were awaiting the Canadians. Although Mroz did fire a lot of machinegun ammunition, added to by "Inky Blackwell" with his bow gun, when a number of bazooka men appeared ahead in the streets, the heavy battle anticipated did not materialize, for the paratroops had melted away. At the same time, news arrived that men from the 2nd and 3rd Canadian Divisions had forced their way north in Holland all the way to the North Sea, thus liberating the last region of that country.

On April 19th, the regiment's attention was brought back to the current war, rather than what everyone assumed to be the imminent armistice, when it engaged the enemy in a sharp fight to force the Kusten Canal and destroy the S.P. assault guns bolstering the defences there. Several tanks from No. 1 Squadron ran over mines planted in the roadway at Bad Zweischenahn, with casualties to three crew members, among whom were two regimental fixtures in the Grenadiers.

Sergeant Henry McDonald, long established as one of the best Crew Commanders in the Regiment, frequently taking over the full command of any Troop of tanks in No. 1 Squadron that was short of an officer had been hurt. His steady hand and cautiously exercised courage became lost to the Squadron when he was seriously wounded after climbing out of his tank following a mine explosion, almost before MacLean's eyes as he waited on the roadway.

Corporal Donald "Tiny" Fraser, another venerable Crew Commander with lengthy experience, had often mentioned that he had a horror of going through another fire in a tank. He had lost one in Normandy in an encounter with a Panther tank, in the course of which he had been extensively burned, and still bore the signs and scars that resulted. But the blast of a necklace at Bad Zweischenahn under Fraser's tank ignored his oft-spoken preference. The immense explosion lifted one side of his tank enough to rupture fuel lines in the engine and a great fire enveloped the vehicle in seconds. Tiny was again burned seriously before being rescued from the blazing turret of his tank, along with the rest of his crew. Taken back to the R.A.P. for emergency burn treatment, MacLean watched the stretcher men carry his large and groaning friend into an ambulance, but never saw him again.

The entrance of the Grenadiers into the outskirts of Bad Zweischenahn unmasked the presence of a number of belligerent German infantrymen still in the town, backed by two Panther tanks on the far side of the railway. However, the failing light at the end of the day prevented MacLean, and the commanders of the Firefly tanks from dealing with them that day. During the night, the German force withdrew, and Joe Mroz had to be content with some desultory firing at a few snipers encountered as they advanced through the town.

Several unattended roadblocks were met, as the Regiment drove northward along the road past Oldenburg to Wilhelmshaven, with the railway as a right boundary. Good progress was made by the column of 30 tanks, one flame-thrower tank, and one bulldozer tank for clearing obstructions on the roads. They also had two Bren gun carriers full of infantry from the L.S.R. After disposing of an anti-tank gun and its crew, the way seemed open to advance without opposition.

About mid-afternoon, Jack Sutherland, the radio operator, heard a message broadcast to all units. The squadron commander ordered that No. 1 Squadron would conform with the others in holding their present positions, with the infantry in place nearby. He said further fighting would cease as of 0:800 hours the next morning, May 5, 1945. The 1939-45 war in Europe was ending.

Strangely, the end of the fighting did not bring forth the wild rejoicing that might have been anticipated from the combat troops around Ken MacLean. Unquestionably, there was a sense of profound relief that the sounds of gunfire and bomb explosions had ended; the never-ending inner tensions that involuntarily grip people who live in war conditions could relax. Some men shared feelings they described as almost mild surprise, to find themselves still alive, apparently healthy and functioning, though the war that brought them to Europe had terminated. But the wild elation, the cheering and the joyous abandon that characterized the victorious conclusion of the First World War, was missing from the victory scene in Germany in May of 1945. The sentiments were definitely different.

Probably the principal reason for the more subdued behaviour of the men who put down their weapons in Europe was the fact that the

Second World War had not ended: only the European part of it had reached an armistice. The war against Japan would have to continue, probably with some of the same people who had fought so hard to overcome the Germans.

Another reason for the restraint demonstrated by MacLean's comrades when victory in Europe was announced, was the cynicism that had developed in the minds of a majority of the people of military age in 1945. Even though their most formidable enemy had been defeated, complete "peace on earth" was perhaps still more of a dream or a hope than a reality. People could easily recall the disappointments that followed the "war to end all wars," when the League of Nations was organized to deal with all future international disputes. Equally unsettling was the belligerent stance of the Soviet Union, the erstwhile ally that had become so difficult and menacing in all of its dealings with the west, as the war wound down to a surrender by the German government.

Nevertheless, MacLean felt a deep pleasure and satisfaction in the fact that he had lived to see the Allied cause prevail in Europe. He could remember many times when he had felt this conclusion to be extremely unlikely. It was a great day to be alive.

CHAPTER XIV

LAST REVIEW FROM A HIGHER PERSPECTIVE

Near Bad Zweischenahn, was a small airfield surrounded by a collection of grey-painted buildings. They had been used by the Luftwaffe as a storage and supply depot for aircraft engines and parts. There were also a number of modern barrack buildings and administrative offices, all constructed during the previous couple of years. The whole complex was taken over by the Canadian Grenadiers complete and undamaged, as they pushed northwestward toward the port city of Wilhelmshaven. The enemy had cleared out hours before it was overrun, taking only their personal kit with them.

When the ceasefire order was given, this airfield was eagerly seized by the Adjutant as a highly suitable location to park the tanks, accommodate the troops and open a mess for the officers, until orders arrived for final location and distribution of the men and the equipment.

The Officers' Mess was established upstairs in a large conference room in one of the administrative buildings. It quickly established itself as a comfortable focal point at which officers could gather for a drink before dinner and some relaxed conversation. In short order it also became the scene of some spirited discussions, and even heated arguments, enjoyed and usually led by one of the Squadron Commanders. Both the past and the future were hashed and rehashed, amid thick clouds of tobacco smoke and the aroma of spirituous drink. Convivial feelings overrode partisan positions as a rule.

"A damned shame it was that we never got a heavy tank on our side to match the Panther or the Tiger," argued Major Carlisle, his glass half full of brandy and water. "My God! What we could have done with a real competitor."

Captain Sanderson, the tech adjutant shifted his pipe. "I can remember the bumpf we used to get in England about how slow and awkward the German heavy tanks were, and how much faster and more manoeuverable were the British and American tanks. This started back in the days of Cruiser tanks in 1940 and '41. The Americans were taken in by this same myth. All this 'manoeuverability' talk had little to do with fighting an armored battle. If you want to dash around looking for the enemy, send out your recce troop. But once you find him, you need armor and firepower; and that's just what we lacked. We all know the Germans had some teething problems with their first heavies, both Tiger and Panther, but they sure as hell got the job done, after they worked out the initial troubles. They were twice the tank the Sherman ever was. We had the Firefly, true enough, and the 17 pounder was a hell of a good gun. But it was still carried by an ordinary Sherman tank, with its thin armor, its high profile, and its narrow tracks. We needed a real heavyweight. What kind of mentality did they have in ordinance, to keep on making an inadequate weapon?"

"They say the Russian T34 was damned good, and it wasn't all that heavy, compared with the German tanks," said Lieutenant Brown, one of the younger troop leaders.

"Yeah. They were good because they were low, powerful and had a strong gun," replied Captain Sanderson. "The Russians put wide tracks on them and sloped the armor, already thicker than ours, so that they were a hell of a lot harder to penetrate with anti-tank fire. But the biggest difference was in their firepower. They weren't buggering around with a pop gun like our 75 mm guns. They had a 76 mm with about a third more muzzle velocity. That made the Krauts respect them."

Major Shepard, commander of No. 1 Squadron and well known as a thinking officer, cleared his throat and led into the discussion. "You know, gentlemen, the Sherman was not a tankman's dream. But another thing you know is, that there were lots of them. A hell of a lot of them, and no matter how many were lost, there were always more coming up: enough to keep us supplied all along the western front, in Italy and even in the Far East. Maybe the grand strategy was to capitalize on something the Allies could do better than the enemy; we could out-produce them, without any doubt. O.K. then, supposing they said, 'the Sherman is not the best tank in the world but it is the best one we have, and we can out-produce the enemy by a terrific margin, if we keep producing substantially the same vehicle with the same engines, the same thickness of armor plate, and basically the same suspension. And that's really what the Americans did. They could upgrade the armament somewhat, and build in a few other improvements, but it all fitted into the same basic vehicle that they built by the thousand, just like jelly beans."

"Getting down to real basics, the German heavy tanks were tremendous weapons, particularly on defence, but when you have a horde of less capable, but still reasonably adequate tanks attacking in armored division strength over open fields, you may overwhelm the smaller number of heavy enemy vehicles. Fundamentally, that is what we did. But as a battle strategy, it is hard on tank crews. The turnover in armored regiments fighting with the Allies must have been a multiple of the German experience, battle for battle. With all Germany's heavy armor and mighty guns, if the Allies could deliver to the battlefield four or five times as many tanks on a sustained basis, and they did do that, ultimately the Germans would lose."

"You are saying, we really out-produced the Germans and beat down with volume, what we never did match with quality, on a vehicle by vehicle comparison," said Lieutenant Brown. "I think that has to be admitted."

Major Shepard nodded thoughtfully. "We beat a hell of a strong fighting machine, in my opinion gentlemen, really because they had too many enemies. They trained their people longer and better than we did, even after the war began to turn against the Nazis. They equipped them with better weapons and tanks than we did. Compare the Schmeisser and the Spandau with our machineguns. Compare the tank guns in the Kraut tanks, period by period through their development with the Allied equivalents. For the 88 mm gun there is no comparison. Compare the Sherman, the Cromwell, and the Churchill tanks with the Mark IV, Mark V and Mark VI German tanks. Not much doubt about which were better. But the Krauts still had a lot of horse-drawn transport, even toward the end of the war, while we were fully mechanized. I don't think that, man-for-man, the German soldier was any better than ours, but if he was better-trained and equipped with better weapons, he damned soon concluded that he was a better man than his enemy too."

"What do you think of the way our large numerical superiority was utilized by our top commanders?" asked Major Carlisle, seeing a chance to keep a lively discussion going.

"More brandy please," said Captain Sanderson to the mess corporal as he settled himself down into one of the three leather-covered arm chairs, smiling happily as the warming effect of the brandy spread through his body. Major Shepard adjusted his legs over the foot stool and continued.

"Not much, if you think about our experience in Normandy. We attacked where the defences were the stoutest. Look at our record around Caen and Falaise. The strategy was to drive straight ahead, right where the German defences were expecting us; that's where they could make us pay the dearest for anything we gained; that's where our greater numbers were of least advantage. We didn't spread the enemy out to the maximum width of front and then hurl a thunderbolt through at some point where we would have had a huge comparative advantage. We were held up for weeks by an enemy with only a fraction of our numbers and firepower. You think that's great generalship, do you?"

"I wonder that we even won the bloody war, to hear your account of it," remonstrated Major Carlisle.

"Look at the intelligence reports we have already," responded Shepard, with real relish. "Our top commanders never demonstrated the kinds of battle strategy that the Germans utilized time after time when they held the whip hand in the early years of the war. They used armored divisions as they should be employed, locating a 'Schwerpunkt' where the main effort was made to crack through the enemy's lines at some point on a narrow front. And they usually sent several parallel formations tearing into the rear areas, moving constantly forward. They tried to bypass strong points of resistance; traveling on roads as much as possible to keep up the momentum of the blitzkrieg. They didn't worry too much about flank protection because they used the attacking columns to swing out on unexpected routes and then converge as pincers on enemy groups, making the enemy worry about his own flanks. This strategy worked extremely well wherever panzer divisions could be employed on a reasonably broad frontage. It was soon apparent that it was Germany's enemies who had to worry about their flanks."

"By contrast, look at where our commanders chose to fight. With all our plurality of tanks, they were nevertheless used mainly in direct support of infantry attacks on German strong points. Look at Caen. Look at Falaise. Look at the Siegfried Line. Every God- damned time, our drives pointed directly at the heart of the resistance ahead. We had no suggestion that Canadian armored formations should emu-late the successful efforts of the Panzer divisions by tearing through hard-pressed and badly outnumbered German formations, when the opportunities presented themselves. Really smart battle leaders manoeuver around an enemy rather than face him in pitched battle, whenever possible. But that wasn't the way with our commanders."

"We beat the Germans in the race across France, not because of any better plan or strategy, but because we had lots of wheels and tracks left, while the Germans lost most of theirs at Falaise. We didn't out-manoeuvre the enemy, in any way that caught him off balance, or spared a lot of bitter fighting by our soldiers. We just stormed for-ward, straight ahead because they didn't have enough arms to stop us."

Major Carlisle broke into the discussion again, clearly irritated with what he had just heard. "Listen Bill. I don't buy all you say against our army commanders. It's easy to stand back and throw bricks like you do, when you don't know what the pressures were from the very top, and from the politicians as well. You're not being fair to them when you say they never showed any ingenuity." A reassuring smile flickered around Carlisle's mouth as he looked benevolently at his old friend and protagonist in many a friendly argument between them.

Major Shepard leaned forward in his chair and pointed his finger at Carlisle to emphasize his point. After a substantial gulp of scotch, he returned to the point he was making.

"All right Tom, what can you point to as an indication of top command competence in handling the 2nd Corps troops of the Canadian Army? Who emerged as the Canadian equivalent of the audacious commanders of this war: like Rommel, or Guderian, or von Manstein from among the Germans; or Patton or Collins from among the Americans? We never produced any commanders on that level of ability. Ours seemed content to just follow the lead of other generals, without a scrap of inventiveness or imagination."

"That's hogwash, Bill. I think our guys did a good job of developing and carrying out their orders. That's what they're paid to do, even at their high levels. And they had to maintain peace and cooperation between units under their direct command; not always an easy thing between outspoken and impatient commanders."

"That brings up another point of criticism, to my mind," came Shepard's response, and he drained his glass before continuing. "You know as well as I do that there were instances of happy relations between some armored and some infantry units, usually involving tankmen that kept their tanks close to the infantry units they supported, night and day. But some tank outfits pulled back into a laager every bloody night, because that's what they had been taught by a bunch of old cavalry people who never fought a modern tank battle. If you don't think that riled the infantrymen, brother you haven't paid attention. Everyone knows that tanks are more vulnerable after dark, because you can't see out of them. But there were lots of times when it had to be pretty damned comforting for an infantry outfit stuck way out there at the sharp end, to have a tank or two handy that could blast anything big that come in on them. I simply argue that there were cases where the armor should have ignored the old rule to bugger-off at the end of the day. God knows, we lost enough tanks in the daylight; we should have been more willing to risk losing a few more at night, to help our infantry friends sleep better. And top command never did a damned thing about that. That's where they should have stepped in, to greatly improve attitudes between regiments."

"I could sure support that," interjected Lieutenant Brown. "As a Troop officer I felt like I was selling out on the infantry we were supporting, when I got the order to harbor with the rest of the squadron tanks back a comfortable distance from the front. I knew what was in the minds of the infantrymen when we pulled out at the end of the day. If I had been in their shoes, I'd have thought the same thing they did - 'the tanks are just fair weather friends'."

"Touché," grunted Carlisle with a wry smile. Finishing off his brandy he rose to leave. "Our friend and mentor, Major Shepard, wants to get along better with the infantrymen. He's just like Jesus. He loves them all," and he waved amiably in Shepard's direction.

"To change the subject, and it's time we did," said Lieutenant Ellis, "Who saw that popinjay, Captain David Tupper, arrive here last night to visit the Commanding Officer. I never saw so many ribbons and decorations on anyone below a Brigadier in my life. He was the quintessential brigade officer; a nifty new forage cap, beautifully pressed battle dress and all these God-damned decorations. What's he been doing anyway? He wasn't much of a fighter when we had him, as I recall."

Captain Sanderson's face darkened like a black, thundercloud, when Tupper's name was mentioned. "That pompous son-of-a-bitch couldn't fight his way out of a wet paper bag," he snarled. "He's the guy that became completely incoherent in his first action as a Troop Officer at the Albert Canal back in Belgium. Went right out of his head when the German artillery worked us over there. His crew said that when they got into a position to shoot, Tupper began grabbing things in the turret. They finally stopped him when he felt that he had to do something quickly to load the gun, and was trying to load the fire extinguisher into the breech. Right after that, he was transferred to brigade Headquarters. But he's going to be a big hero when he gets home, mark my words."

"Why so?" asked Lieutenant Brown quite innocently.

"Well just look at him," Sanderson continued, as he angrily yanked the cigarette from his mouth. "A 'pretty boy' look to him that appeals to people in brigade Headquarters. And he's so full of his own importance that he believes that he commands the Brigade, rather than just delivers their orders. I've seen enough of his type to last a lifetime or two: dashing good looks, complete with 'hairy martial garbage,' as

Oscar Wilde would describe his moustache; greatly impressed with rank and anyone who has it, whether deserved or not; and a glib tongue that he uses to flatter everyone above him. But as a fighting soldier, a completely inept bastard who would put anybody's life in jeopardy that had to work with him in the presence of the enemy."

'I don't think you like Captain Tupper," commented Major Shepard, with a sly grin.

Captain Collins, the 2 I.C. of No. 1 Squadron, who had just joined the group in the mess, chimed in at that point. "I've run into our Captain Tupper a few times too, and I know the type. Yet he's the guy who will tell them back in Canada about 'his service overseas with the 4th Canadian Armored Brigade:' with full details of the date he sailed away and the many months he served abroad. Without any extensive exaggeration, he can build a picture of himself as a real old sweat, with all kinds of fighting experience behind him. They'll swallow that image completely at home. They'll never know that guys like him, and there are plenty of them, were worse than useless over here."

"But that's the way it works out sometimes," added Major Shepard. "There have always been people like Tupper around military forces and there always will be. The Germans probably have their share of them too. Just be damned thankful you won't have much longer to put up with them."

"Which brings me to a questions I'd really like to hear discussed, Major Shepard," came the voice of Lieutenant Brown again, usually an extremely quiet and inconspicious member of the officers group. Brown had only recently joined the regiment as a replacement troop officer. He had earned a solid reputation for himself in the fighting since the Hochwald Gap as a calm, thoughtful type of leader with an intense interest in the men he commanded.

"I would like to hear why it is that our men do the dangerous things that we ask of them," the young lieutenant began. "Why do they advance, on foot or in a tank, just because their commanders tell them to? They know that they are probably much safer staying where they are, and yet they move out. Can it all be put down to training

236

and discipline in the background? If so, wouldn't every army seek the professional-soldier type to do all of the real fighting? And yet they don't. They get wonderful support from volunteer soldiers, like we have in Canada. I guess my question could be shortened by saying, what induces a soldier, or any military serviceman for that matter, to come half-way around the world to fight in a war that may not even directly menace his own home, and fight to the death in many cases? These men have no intention of ever becoming permanent soldiers. They'll return to civilian life if they are spared to do so, after the war is over. Why?"

"You've asked a very penetrating question, Brown," said Captain Sanderson. "Most of us have wondered about it, without really trying to explain it to anyone many times. For my own part, I remain convinced that the training and the discipline introduced into their lives are the chief motivating factors. Without that, you just have a mob of men that will not respond to a leader."

"Without disagreeing with you, I think that what you have raised is only part of the answer to Brown's question," said Major Carlisle, as he shifted uneasily on his hard wooden chair. "What about the cause they have been fighting for? Don't you feel that the average Canadian soldier really felt sincerely that Nazi Germany had to be destroyed? I don't mean that they were all a bunch of political zealots, who wanted to raise the Canadian flag and trample on the German flag in a clash of political ideologies. Hell, they didn't think about politics for ten minutes. But they knew instinctively, and could see with their own eyes, especially those of them that saw the concentration camps, what Germany was up to, and they knew it had to be stopped. They felt, 'better stop it in Europe or we'll have to stop it in our own country." I think this had a powerful influence on the attitude of men ordered to go forward. They knew that every step forward was a step closer to ending the war and getting home again. That's my thought on it," and he reached for another cigarette.

Major Shepard relit his pipe and returned the stares which seemed to have focused on him. Here was the student, the man with the academic background in history, toward whom everyone in the mess looked expectantly.

"I suppose some comment is anticipated from me," Major Shepard observed dryly. "Okay, here's what I think about your very provocative question, Mr. Brown. And I'm not going to sail off into the wild blue yonder with some high-flown philosophy either. I think that there is real merit in what each of you has been saying about the drive that takes volunteer soldiers forward on command, but I would add one thought that I believe history has proven time and again. Professional soldiers can and will get the job of fighting done for you in a campaign, and to a large extent, that is what we have encountered in the German Army, where the emphasis has been on trained and experienced levies of men whose job it has been to soldier competently. That means looking after your comrades and responding to orders when received and understood, even in the face of danger."

"But there is evidence that soldier's can be brought to fight for a cause which is well above comradeship and preserving one's life, so that conducting a war becomes more than just professional capability. In such instances, I believe that making war takes on itself a moral dimension of its own. I believe that the Allies in this war became convinced that their own very existence was menaced by the Axis countries, and faced with that threat, once the right leaders were identified and put into command, the war made by the allies became more terrible, and more consuming than even the Axis countries could develop or imagine. That's a rather far-out opinion, but it is mine, and I hold it after giving this sort of question a great deal of thought.

"Well, that's something to really think about while we eat," said Major Carlisle, as he beckoned all the officers to follow him downstairs for dinner. Dinner in the mess was important to Carlisle, who felt that it presented a splendid opportunity to build a team spirit, a regimental pride unity among the officers, a difficult objective as long as hostilities continued and officer turnover was a weekly occurrence. Under Major Carlisle as president of the mess, officers' meals became much more of a regimental function. Close friendships developed between men who had been quite distant and detached from one another during the fighting.

CHAPTER XV

DÉNOUMENT

Only shortly after the announcement that the European war had ended, and before any movements of men or vehicles began, word reached everyone in the Canadian Grenadier Guards of a double tragedy that had occurred 12 hours earlier. The Regimental Padre, Captain McCreery, and Lieutenant Goldie, a friendly new troop officer in No. 1 Squadron, had set out on the evening of May 4th, the last day of the war in Europe, on a mercy mission to bring in some wounded German soldiers on a side road. They were both killed in the course of their mission, and only one of their bodies was ever found. Both officers were new recruits to the Grenadiers in the last month of the war.

With the cessation of hostilities in Northwest Europe, the Regiment began its participation in the occupation forces, which took it to a succession of new locations during the ensuing months. For MacLean and about 120 other members of the unit, after taking their tanks back to a disposal centre in Holland, they would follow a different course. They had volunteered to join a new edition of their regiment, which was mobilized on June 1, 1945 for the projected Canadian Army Pacific Force (C.A.P.F.). It was to be commanded by their erstwhile hero and Commanding Officer, Lieutenant Colonel E.A.C. Amy, who relinquished command in Europe on June 10 to take over the new battalion. The preservation of their own regimental name and commander for the tank regiment in the new force was influential in attracting recruits like MacLean to its ranks. All members of the C.A.P.F. were sent home to Canada directly. Then, after some leave, training was resumed at Camp Borden, to bring the Force together and up to fighting standards before departing for more advanced armored training in the U.S.A. The plans called for them to be transferred ultimately to the Far East, where they would become involved with the fighting against the Japanese forces in a formation out there.

The surrender of Japan resulted in the disbandment of this force on November 1, and the return of its members to their respective military district depots across Canada by year-end. After a short sojourn at a holding camp at Newmarket, Ontario, MacLean was sent on to Toronto to await the completion of the necessary documentation that would return him to civilian life. As a sergeant, with a broad experience in tank warfare, he had little indeed to interest the personnel officers combing through the records of thousands of soldiers who had served overseas. They were searching for a small number of men who would be suitable for a peace-time regular force, and the barrack life into which it would move. MacLean wanted nothing to do with that sort of employment, and so informed the personnel officer.

After a brief stint in Chorley Park Hospital in Toronto to have some small pieces of shrapnel removed from an ankle which had bothered him on occasion, he moved from one army camp to another in Ontario for brief periods of time, awaiting action on his application for discharge.

Early in January of 1946, Ken MacLean was called before the very same personnel officer who had signed his enlistment papers years earlier at M.D. 13 Headquarters in Calgary. He was handed an ex-serviceman's lapel badge to go with his honorable discharge certificate, and walked out of Mewata Armory a civilian once again. It was a strange feeling, being finally and completely severed from the army's umbilical cord, though he had looked forward to it for a long time.

He did not have a detailed design plan for his future life, because he had been extremely unsure of the likelihood of a future life, ever since landing in Normandy those many months ago. But the time had arrived to determine what he wanted to do with the rest of his life, and to begin making preparations for it. MacLean had obtained an offer of employment from a company in the north country, where he would be able to earn his living as part of a work crew, while pondering his future possibilities in neutral surroundings.

The first stop for him however, as for any returning soldier, was to visit and spend some time with his aging and mightily relieved parents in Edmonton. In their unswerving belief and their faith, like many other parents, they believed that their prayers had been answered. The proof of it was shown in the return of sons that they had sometimes despaired of ever seeing again. Although he had visited his parents upon his early return from overseas during the previous August, while preparing for a campaign in the Far East, MacLean very much wanted to see and visit them as a civilian once again. He wanted to talk with them of his future, and theirs, in a peaceful atmosphere where he did not have to hurry back to some army camp to prepare for more fighting.

The first step for him was to hustle over to the C.P.R. station in Calgary to catch the afternoon train to Edmonton. The day coach was only half full, and MacLean had no trouble finding an empty seat, away from chattering groups elsewhere in the train. It was pleasant to sit in the warmth of his coach, as the train made its regular stops at all the small towns he had come to know years ago while traveling the same familiar route. Blasts of cold, mid-winter air swept into the coach when its doors were opened to admit new passengers from the snow-covered farmland outside.

The ride past the familiar grain elevators, with large printed town names boldly painted on them; the well remembered bridges over the frozen rivers; and the steaming doors and frost-covered windows of the stations, all silently but powerfully contributed to the feeling of seminal pleasure which slowly spread over him. He was almost home.

Wrapped in his thoughts as he rode onward in the comfortable train, Ken tried to review in his mind what had launched him on the course that he followed. He had never once fancied himself as part of some sacred mission. He suffered no impulse to "get at the throat of the enemy and tear it out," as some returnees had expressed themselves, probably people who had never heard a shot fired in anger, though they passed themselves off as fire-breathing terrors. He had not craved promotions, nor power to order people around in their daily lives.

The animus behind Ken MacLean's entry into the army was not a lot of flag-waving, or violently patriotic speeches he had seen or heard. Just hearing the whistle of the locomotive moan in the frosty prairie air, and seeing once again the wide open land in the gentle country-side through which he was once again passing, brought home to him what it was all worth. While still a boy in high school he had seen pictures of the chaos and destruction that the war was bringing to Europe and elsewhere. He became convinced then, after hearing his parents and others talk about it, that if it was not stopped in Europe, it would spread to other countries in the world, including his own. Canada had gone to war to attempt to defeat the enemy in Europe. His friends were enlisting in various services, to play their parts in their nation's cause, and MacLean wanted to do the same. His motives had been no more noble nor lofty than that, but they had been strong, and rightly directed.

Reading of the legendary army commander of long ago, who had prayed before battle that God would "steel my soldiers' hearts," and hearing it repeated by the Padré just before embarking for Normandy, MacLean felt that in some indeterminate way, his heart had indeed been steeled by what he had seen and done. He was also certain, as he approached his home and his loved ones, that for him at least, it had all been worth it.

ADDENDUM

The names of the characters in this story are their real names, as the author recalls them, but where recollection dims over the years, fictional names have been assigned to men who lived and fought as described. Those still alive who were with the author will recognize themselves under whatever name is given them. The *nom de guerre* of the central character, Kenneth Maclean, was used for a number of personal reasons.

The few discussions described in officers' messes were fabricated *in toto*, since the author was not present when they were supposed to have taken place. However, from extensive studies of World War II as an amateur historian, something like these discussions may have, and the author believes, should have occurred between battle commanders. As the actions developed, often to the advantage of the out-numbered Germans, the records teach us that the Allied soldier, man for man, was as good as his adversaries, but he was surely not as well trained for battle; he fought with inferior tanks and other weapons; and he served under senior commanders usually greatly inferior to those of the enemy.

After the war, the author embarked on a course of studies: Arts at the University of Alberta; Law at the University of British Columbia; and Business Administration at Northwestern University. He practiced law; served as a senior executive with an international oil company; chaired regulatory boards of the Canadian government in Ottawa; organized the Calgary Military Museum; maintained an active interest in the Canadian Reserve Army; and was appointed Honourary Lieutenant Colonel of the King's Own Calgary Regiment. Between semesters at university, he worked as a hard rock miner; a truck driver; a cat-skinner; and a deckhand on a boat, in various locations in the Canadian north.

He has now retired, with his wife of 48 years, to Victoria, British Columbia, where he writes and gardens.

ISBN 1552124398

9 781552 124390